THE OSWALD CHAMBERS DEVOTIONAL READER

THE OSWALD CHAMBERS DEVOTIONAL READER

52 Weekly Themes

CHOSEN AND EDITED BY
HARRY VERPLOEGH

FOREWORD BY
GORDON MacDONALD

OLIVER NELSON

A Division of Thomas Nelson Publishers
Nashville

Published in Nashville, Tennessee, by Oliver-Nelson Books, a division of Thomas Nelson, Inc., Publishers, and distributed in Canada by Lawson Falle, Ltd., Cambridge, Ontario.

Printed in the United States.

Library of Congress Cataloging-in-Publication Data

Chambers, Oswald, 1874–1917.

The Oswald Chambers devotional reader / chosen and edited by Harry Verploegh ; foreword by Gordon MacDonald.

p. cm.

ISBN 0-8407-9107-0

1. Devotional calendars. I. Verploegh, Harry. II. Title.

BV4811.C454 1990

242′.2—dc20 90–33717

CIP

CONTENTS

FOREWORD

I first "met" Oswald Chambers when I was a student in prep school. The campus librarian, a grandmotherly type, knew of my love for books, and for a birthday gift, she gave me a copy of the daily devotional *My Utmost for His Highest,* Chambers' most renown work.

The man, of course, had been dead for forty years at that point, so you must understand that our introduction was a matter of my engaging him through his writings. When my friend the librarian brought us together, I had no clue that he would become someone who would nourish me through the best and worst days of my life. So attached to him would I become that I would later refer to him as simply OC when I reflected on his words in my journal.

I must be candid to say that I was disappointed in the first encounters I had with OC because his words, which often challenged one to wait in silence upon God, were so adverse to my activist, make-it-all-happen-yourself mind-set. I neglected him for many months at a time and got back in touch only when I felt a surge of spiritual hunger or curiosity.

A second copy of Chambers' best-selling book came to me years later as a wedding gift. For the first months of our married life, Gail and I frequently looked into *My Utmost* . . . , and I discovered that my friend was making more and more sense to me. OC tends to make that happen in the life of one who is getting older and feeling more and more beat up by the realities of life.

Since then I have received many more copies of Chambers' *Utmost* as gifts. And I have enjoyed using each one, marking the pages, underlining phrases, and writing blunt little notes to myself such as "he's sure got your number on this one."

Then there came the day when I spent several hours in delightful conversation with an aged woman who had known Oswald Chambers when she was a small girl. "Tell me everything you remember," I asked. And she did.

From her I learned that OC was a highly artistic man who could become consumed with the beauties of creation. Indeed, a reading of his journals (which I pursued much later) reveals this side of him when he goes to great lengths to describe the shadows and colors of a sunset on the Egyptian desert.

I learned that Chambers was a man with a brilliant mind and wit, and that he could seize and mold the minds and spirits of tough men when he gave lectures on the Bible and on the classics. I learned that Chambers was a mentor to young people, a lover of children, and a shepherd to soldiers. Having heard all that, I returned to his writings and began to read far and wide everything that had been put into print under his name.

But this friendship with Oswald Chambers never reached its peak until I went through a deep personal trough in my life and was in great need of God's mercy. My sense of loss was indescribable. Turning to my old friend, I began to realize that he must have known some deep personal losses of his own. No man could ever have written with the sensitivity and understanding of the restorative grace and kindness of Christ as he did unless he had somehow one day drawn upon them. That was a part of Chambers I'd not seen until I was in great need of them.

At that time I heard Chambers say (and I am paraphrasing), "When God permits you to be stripped of everything to do with your exterior life and work, he desires that you enhance the activities of your interior." I heard my friend encouraging me to seek silence, an enhanced intercessory life, and a deeper sense of the majesty of God. In just a sentence or two, OC had revitalized me with a sense of purpose and mission that no one could deny me. There would be others swift to judge, quick to provide answers, and sharp to think that they understood causes and consequences. But Chambers understood that a person's worst moments can be (in some cases) God's greatest opportunity to develop a person after His own heart. Themes of God's redeeming love began to leap out at me from all over Chambers' books, and I came to consider this man—even though he died more than twenty years before I was born—as among my closest friends.

I am delighted therefore to commend my "friend," Oswald Chambers, and this collection of his insights to you. He speaks to you and me out of his years among students and fighting men. He speaks from his days on the North African desert, which he loved, where he clearly derived many of his metaphors and appreciations of God's grandeur. He speaks from pain, from silence, from disciplined thought, and from a highly intimate journey with Jesus. In your desert moments, and in your spiritually curious hours, drink deeply from his well.

GORDON MACDONALD

TO THE READER

If the reader is serious about life and death and all in between, this book can be a source of comfort and joy—but to readers who are not serious, be careful! These are chastening words—real words. "They are like the Bible; they do not thrill, they nourish," for like the biblical writers, Chambers nourishes us—but roughly.

The reader should also know that while Chambers' words do not appear in their original context, a careful effort has been made to present each statement complete in itself. The statements are reprinted exactly as they appear in the first editions, with one exception: To maintain the flow of Chambers' words, his quotations from Scripture appear without citations.

I count it an honor and privilege to have compiled this anthology. I can claim no praise, for none of these words are mine. But as a reader, I have found them full of wonder. To me they seem to echo what God is saying to mankind.

HARRY VERPLOEGH

INTRODUCTION

Oswald Chambers was remembered as a child for his readiness to pray and his confidence that God would answer his prayers, but it was not until his teenage years that prayer became the working of the miracle of Redemption in him. Chambers was born on July 24, 1874, in Aberdeen, the fourth son of Clarence and Hannah Chambers. Hannah had been raised an Irvingite but became a Baptist under Spurgeon. Oswald's father was pastor of the Crown Terrace Baptist Church in Aberdeen, and later ministered in Stoke-on-Trent, Perth, and London.

As a boy Chambers studied drawing at Sharp's Institute in Perth. After hearing Spurgeon preach in Dulwich, the city where his father retired, Chambers asked to be baptised and began visiting men in the YMCA lodging house. He won an arts scholarship to study abroad from the Art School in South Kensington, but instead took the Arts Course at the University of Edinburgh until he decided at twenty-three to follow the counsel of a number of Scottish men of God who were aware of his spiritual gifts and to accept God's call to the ministry.

He attended the Dunoon Training School, founded by Duncan MacGregor, and within a year became a tutor in philosophy and psychology, taught art, and formed a Browning Society. Chambers became known at Dunoon as a man of prayer who relied unequivocally on God to supply his needs. He was admired for his love of art and poetry, his radiant disposition, and his generosity to others. At this time he began to speak in open air meetings. He worked in city missions and taught Sunday school.

After seven years of study and teaching, Chambers left Dunoon in 1905. In that same year he met Bishop Juji Nakada, the Japanese evangelist, at a Pentecostal League meeting in Perth. Together these two men—Chambers, long "like a poker," and Nakada, "short like a shovel"—planned to stir up the Spirit of God among the Holiness people in an evangelistic tour of America and Japan. Of this tour in 1906–1907, Chambers wrote in his diary that he felt a perfect sense of God's call and leading. In America he was one of "the Lord's spoilt bairns" who was being introduced in Brooklyn, Providence, Cincinnati, and Seattle to "choice souls." In considering the evangelist's work he wrote,

> The goodness of God strikes me. People don't know Him, but it is not a wicked ignoring, it is ignorance. The full compassionate love of the Holy Ghost for the crowd is a precious, though intolerable compassion.

During his tour of Japan, Chambers visited the Oriental Mission Bible Society in Tokyo and several interior mission stations. He preached, and he witnessed the mighty preaching of Nakada.

Upon returning to London via Hong Kong, the Suez, Rome, and Paris, Chambers continued evangelistic work with the League of Prayer and made the acquaintance of the family of the Reverend David Lambert, then a junior minister in Sunderland. Lambert became one of the circle around Gertrude Chambers who later helped publish Chambers' messages, lectures, and prayers and who in the 1970s published a valuable account of Chambers' life and works, *Oswald Chambers: An Unbribed Soul*. David Lambert wrote of the Chambers of this period of evangelistic preaching:

> at the big London meetings he would find an odd corner to be alone with God before speaking in public. Now I know how much preparation there had been in years of discipline, and Christ-following, and strenuous thinking. I did not know it then, yet felt that there was insight and authority and spiritual power far above that of the average minister or missioner.

In the years 1911–1915 preceding his principleship of the Bible Training School near Clapham Common, London, Chambers preached and taught many missions for the League of Prayer in England, Scotland, and Ireland. He began to develop some of the characteristic emphases of his ministry. He stressed the artificiality of man-made religion. He insisted on God's high intention of blessing toward the lowliest and most ordinary Christian who abandons himself or herself in faith to Jesus Christ and makes an absolute commitment to the Word of God. He believed in disciplined study of the humanities as well as of the Bible lest the student learn no method to study God's Word and be forced, in Chambers' terms, to wander aimlessly in it as in a cultivated park. He stressed the importance of seeking a means of applying the experience of sanctification in practical Christian service.

Chambers' own characteristic readiness for God's use is demonstrated in a comment he made to H. Stark upon arriving in Plymouth for meetings: "I hope we shall have a very blessed week-end, Mr. Chambers," said Stark. Chambers replied, "If we behave ourselves, the Lord will help Himself to all He wants from us."

In the spring of 1910 Chambers married Gertrude Hobbs ("Biddy"), the woman who would later use her language skills to publish after his death Oswald Chambers' manuscripts and her notes of his lectures, sermons, and talks, including the devotional classic, *My Utmost for His Highest,* which she compiled.

After their marriage, Mrs. Chambers accompanied Chambers on a four-month mission to the United States. On their return, Chambers settled into his work as Principal of the new nondenominational Bible Training College for the education of home and foreign workers founded in Battersea, London, the center of the League of Prayer. After Chambers' death, student after student wrote of the special features of Chambers' leadership of the school in the five years before he went to the Eastern front as a chaplain for the YMCA. As a teacher Chambers knew instinctively which students could not be forced to change their pet theories and required only his listening ear and patience to develop new understanding and which students needed a devastating but salutary blow to their prejudices and pettinesses. Chambers was a beloved example to them of child-like trust in God and self-discipline ("Get out of bed and think about it afterwards" he would advise) and of a rare balance between flexibility and strength in both spiritual and practical matters.

At the outbreak of World War I, Chambers felt a deep and urgent need to exercise his ministry among the British forces but waited patiently for almost nine months for the details to fall into place. Between the fall of 1915 and his death in November 1917,

Chambers established desert mission camps for British troops in Egypt at Zeitoun, nine miles from Cairo and at Ismailia, on the banks of the Suez Canal.

These places of peace in the midst of war preparation were built of native rush mats. The Zeitoun camp included a refreshment marquee for soldiers, a devotional hut for worship services, a smaller hut where Chambers and his assistants conducted Bible classes, a tiny "items" hut where stationery and books were sold, and a dugout. The Chambers family, which now included the tiny Kathleen and their devoted helper, Mary Riley, lived in a bungalow built for them. There they entertained a constant stream of guests. Former students from the Bible Training College assisted Chambers with the administration of the camp activities and the care of souls.

During his two-year ministry in Egypt, Chambers kept a diary where he recorded his early morning thoughts, activities of the day, plans for Bible studies or talks, the responses of his audiences, and encounters with individuals. Sixteen years after his death, extracts from this diary were published with many tributes to his influence on the Mediterranean Expeditionary Forces in *Oswald Chambers: His Life and Work*. With a painter's eye, Chambers repeatedly described the sunrise on the desert, sublime and dazzling with praise to God, a "sealing witness of peace," and at other times a scene of desperate turmoil about which he could be equally delighted:

> This morning is thick with Khamseen wind. As I write, the sky is a most formidable colour, dense lurid copper, and the wind is rampaging with the old antique heat of leagues of desert, not a heat like the sun's heat, but the heat of blinding devastation. . . .

Chambers found his work among the men and the activity of the desert camps constantly invigorating. Of the sunrise near the Suez, he wrote:

> The splendor of these sunrises is unique. . . . All the noises of the camp are stirring and fine, the men are astir at 4 A.M., the stir, the movement of horses, the bugles, the whirr

of aeroplanes, all makes this life a real delight to me somehow.

And of an Egyptian noon in July, Chambers noted:

> Sun! I have been considering it. One cannot conceive of such sun unless one has summered in Egypt. It is the only power that makes this land possibly habitable. It is fierce, appallingly so, but fascinating; my own experience is that desert life is productive of intense vitality and energy, not of languor.

Boundless energy and vitality is precisely what Chambers gave to thousands of soldiers from all parts of the Commonwealth who passed through the YMCA mission camps. Living in the discomfort of military bases, their futures uncertain, many afterwards gave tribute to the eloquence and spiritual influence of this gifted man of God. Douglas Downes described Chambers at work in Egypt:

> One of my early memories of Oswald Chambers is that of a lithe figure in khaki, with the eyes of a prophet and the profile of a Savaronola, seated with a group of younger men at a table in the Central YMCA in Cairo. He is telling them in his delightful, sparkling, humorous way that he cannot see the need of so much entertainment stuff to keep the men together of an evening. Out there in his hut at Zeitoun he can get a crowd of Australians night after night attracted by nothing but the message of Redemption.
>
> I went over to Zeitoun, and found the unheard-of thing had come to pass. Men whom no one could accuse of being religious turned up in large numbers on a week-night to hear a religious talk. But it is no ordinary talk, and the man who gives it is no ordinary man. There is no appeal to the emotions, no cant religious phrases, no anecdotes, just a flow of clear convincing reasoning—stark sincerity, speaking with the authority of deep personal experience; you are brought to the point where the natural man breaks down and where the supernatural must come in to carry you with its confidence right into the presence of God.

Men who visited the mission huts used similar words to describe Chambers' discernment of biblical truth as well as of human need. They mentioned his "penetrating gaze," his keen and alert face, his "canny" understanding of individual men. Many remembered the personal words of comfort Chambers gave them on their departure for front lines in Palestine or France. Others were visited by him while laid aside in hot canvas hospitals. He was for more than one soldier a "detective of the soul, one who has been in intimate fellowship with the unseen." With others who have written of the heightened intensity that war brings to the experience of life, Chambers knew that for many men bound for the front, irresponsible pleasure-seeking would end and stern issues would confront them. He relished the opportunity to speak to them at a time when they would be more open to talk about God and the soul, when the faith of many would be strained. He insisted that in the midst of life-threatening circumstances, a soldier could maintain an unchanging relationship to God through the redemptive work of Christ.

Throughout the period of his chaplaincy Chambers would not allow the disruption, devastation, and death that impinged on his consciousness and crippled many spirits working near the front to undermine his natural buoyancy and confidence in God's sovereignty. He was steadfast in his belief that "the lack of ability and master-mindedness to conduct the war" was an occasion for men to cast themselves on God and find His order in the "haphazard" of ordinary experience or in the midst of an appalling war when hundreds of thousands of men would be battered into eternity.

Chambers was aware, however, that his confidence in God's ends could seem like indifference to the senses of others assaulted by the horror and the contradictions of war. Together with the soldiers who visited the YMCA camps, he probed the meaning of war to men of faith, lecturing boldly on such topics as "Religious Problems Raised by War," "Is Human Sacrifice Redemptive?", "Has History Disproved the Song of the Angels?" (a Christmas talk), and "Does War Create or Reveal Wickedness?" Chambers read other men's attempts to sustain a Christian hope in wartime and was particularly helped by Denny's *War and the Fear of God* and Forsyth's *The Christian Ethics of War.*

At one point in his dairy, Chambers recorded his mistaken intuition that the war would end by late 1916. Chambers found that his miscalculation was an indication that "the Holy Spirit must be recognized as the sagacious Ruler in all affairs, and not our astute common sense." In his own experience and in his detailed study of the Old Testament prophets in the last months of his life, Chambers found God's ways inscrutable, but that in the mystery of Redemption.

> God is prepared to run the risk of evil, so to speak, and the Cross is the proof that He Himself has taken the responsibility of its removal.

With many Christians of the Great War period, Chambers looked with amazement, wonder, and tears at the great bravery of the young men who, made of "grand human stuff," withstood the wrath and chaos of war. He prayed that their sacrifices would be acts of worship mirroring the obedience of Christ's painful sacrifice as the means of God's redeeming work. In the last weeks of his life, Chambers meditated on Israel's history as seen through the eyes of the prophets Hosea, Joel, and Amos and considered the spectacle of human evil in his own time. He noted that Amos ascribes to God the power to effect "blasting and mildew and disease and pestilence and error and wrong." He concluded with Amos that all these occurrences are beyond the control of man, that all the consequences are in the "powerful hand of God, and not of blind cause and effect." Again and again Chambers recorded his "joyful detection of God's ruling in the haphazard" in his diary. A month before his death, on a glorious morning when the East was "like a celestial scheme of shot silk" Chambers' heart sprang up to the call of the prophet Amos:

> Seek him that maketh the Pleiades and Orion, and maketh the day dark with night, and turneth the shadow of death into the morning. (Amos 4:8)

In the entries for October 1917, one senses that Chambers had extended himself to the limit of God's requirement. Twice he had to lump diary entries together for lack of opportunity to write. He persuaded Swan, a colleague in the YMCA mission, to lecture on Islam for him. Then in preparation for a mission to Palestine to minister to the wounded and dying for General Allenby, he asked his wife to conduct services and rejoiced in the "lift" of inspiration he felt at those she led. Soon Mrs. Chambers would be called upon to carry Chambers' work, for by November 15, 1917, Oswald Chambers was at rest from the intense labor of biblical interpretation and spiritual counsel he fulfilled for the church in the period of the Great War.

It is hoped that this new anthology of excerpts from the Chambers publications will introduce a rising generation of Christians to the profound themes this gifted and faithful teacher explored during his vital ministry in God's joy and under His hand in the second decade of this century.

VIRGINIA VERPLOEGH STEINMETZ
Durham, North Carolina

KEY TO SOURCES

Quotations are followed by letter codes with numbers that indicate the title of the work from which the extract is taken and the page number on which it appears. For example,

> The God I infer by my common sense has no power over me at all. DI. 12

The letters DI indicate the quotation is taken from *Disciples Indeed;* the number 12 indicates the quotation is found on page 12 of that work.

Following are the letter codes used in this collection to refer to the works of Oswald Chambers. *My Utmost for His Highest* was published by Dodd, Mead & Company, Inc., in New York, New York. The year of publication follows each title.

AUG	*Approved unto God,* 1973
BE	*Biblical Ethics,* 1964
BFB	*Baffled to Fight Better,* 1973
BP	*Biblical Psychology* 1973
BSG	*Bringing Sons to Glory,* 1973
CD.VOL.1	*Christian Discipline,* Vol. I, 1965
CD.VOL.2	*Christian Discipline,* Vol. II, 1965
CHI	*Conformed to His Image,* 1971
DI	*Disciples Indeed,* 1960
GW	*God's Workmanship,* 1960
HG	*The Highest Good,* 1965
HGM	*He Shall Glorify Me,* 1965
IWP	*If Thou Wilt Be Perfect,* 1962
IYA	*If Ye Shall Ask,* 1965
LG	*The Love of God,* 1965
MFL	*The Moral Foundations of Life,* 1961
MUH	*My Utmost for His Highest,* 1935

Key to Sources

NKW	*Not Knowing Whither,* 1957
OBH	*Our Brilliant Heritage,* 1965
OPG	*Our Portrait in Genesis,* 1973
PH	*The Place of Help,* 1973
PR	*The Psychology of Redemption,* 19??
PS	*The Philosophy of Sin,* 1961
RTR	*Run Today's Race,* 1968
SA	*The Shadow of an Agony,* 1965
SHH	*Shade of His Hand,* 1961
SHL	*The Servant as His Lord,* 1973
SSM	*Studies in the Sermon on the Mount,* 1973
SSY	*So Send I You,* 1973
WG	*Workmen of God,* 1965

LIST OF THEMES

ABANDONMENT

He who finds his life will lose it, and he who loses his life for My sake will find it.

—Matthew 10:39

Beware of any hesitation to abandon to God. It is the meanest characteristics of our personality that are at work whenever we hesitate, there is some element of self-interest that won't submit to God. CHI. 31

The great aim of the Holy Spirit is to get us abandoned to God. HGM. 78

When God's voice will come you do not know, but whenever the realization of God comes again in the faintest way imaginable, recklessly abandon. It is only by abandon that you find Him. GW. 58

Jesus Christ always brings us back to one thing—'Stand in right relationship to Me first,' then the marvellous doing will be performed in you.' It is a question of abandoning all the time, not of doing. IWP. 115

Vacillation in a crisis is the sign of an unabandoned nature. An abandoned nature never can vacillate because there is nothing to weigh; such a nature is completely abandoned to another. KNW. 83

Abandon to God is of more value than personal holiness. MUH. 52

When we are abandoned to God, He works through us all the time. MUH. 52

We are in danger of getting the barter spirit when we come to God, we want the witness before we have done what God tells us to do. "Why does not God reveal Himself to me?" He cannot, it is not that He will not, but He cannot, because you are in the road as long as you won't abandon absolutely to Him. Immediately you do, God witnesses to Himself, He cannot witness to you, but He witnesses instantly to His own nature in you. If you had the witness before the reality, it would end in sentimental emotion. Immediately you transact on the Redemption, and stop the impertinence of debate, God gives on the witness. As soon as you abandon reasoning and argument, God witnesses to what He has done, and we are amazed at our impertinence in having kept Him waiting. MUH. 296

God nowhere tells us to give up things for the sake of giving them up; He tells us to give them up for the sake of the only thing worth having, viz. life with Himself. NKW. 124

If you are abandoned to God and do the duty that lies nearest, God will not abandon you; but if you trust in your wits and bring in the amateur providence idea, He will have to abandon you, and there will be heartbreaks and distresses that He is not in at all. Present the whole thing where it ought to be presented—in abandonment to God, and He will engineer everything in His own way. NKW. 145

The note of the Christian life is abandonment to Jesus Christ. PH. 165

To surrender to God is not to surrender to the fact that we have surrendered. That is not coming at all. To come means that we come to God in complete abandonment and give ourselves right over to Him and leave ourselves in His hands. PR. 23

We must abandon to God at all costs. Abandon is of infinitely more value than self-scrutiny. PR. 94

The weakest saint can experience the power of the Deity of the Son of God if he is willing to 'let go.' PR. 116

. . . what is needed in spiritual matters is reckless abandonment to the Lord Jesus Christ, reckless and uncalculating abandonment, with no reserve anywhere about it; not sad, you cannot be sad if you are abandoned absolutely. PS. 23

The tendency is strong to say—"O God won't be so stern as to expect me to give up that!" *but He will;* "He won't expect me to walk in the light so that I have nothing to hide," *but He will;* "He won't expect me to draw on His grace for everything" *but He will.* RTR. 8

Whenever the call is given for abandon to Jesus Christ, people say it is offensive and out of taste. The counterfeit of abandon is that misleading phrase 'Christian service.' I will spend myself for God, I will do anything and everything but the one thing He asks me to do, viz., give up my right to myself to Him. SHL. 85

God can do what He likes with the man who is abandoned to Him. SSM. 73

Many of us are subtly serving our own ends, and Jesus Christ cannot help Himself to our lives; if I am abandoned to Jesus, I have no ends of my own to serve. SSY. 22

None of us know the absolute 'go' of abandon to Jesus until we are in unconditional identification with Him. SSY. 56

Week 2

ATONEMENT

Christ died for our sins according to the Scripture.

—1 Corinthians 15:3

The marvel of the Atonement is that Jesus Christ can create endlessly in lives the oneness which He had with the Father. BE. 87

The marvel of the Atonement is that any man or woman who will make the moral decision that the 'old man' ought to be crucified, and will accept the gift of the Holy Spirit which was manifested in Jesus Christ, will receive the new disposition which introduces him into the kingdom of God, and raises him to sit in heavenly places in Christ Jesus, which surely means a present experience, not a future one. BE. 110

This is the doctrine of the Atonement: "Him who knew no sin" (not sins)—Him who had not the disposition of sin, who refused steadfastly, and to the death on Calvary, to listen to the temptations of the prince of this world, who would not link Himself on with the ruling disposition of humanity, but came to hew a way single-handed through the hard face of sin back to God—"He made to be sin on our behalf; that we might become the righteousness of God in Him."
BE. 116

The modern view of the Atonement is that it simply reveals the oneness of God and man; immediately we turn to the New Testament we find that the doctrine of the Atonement is that God can readjust man to Himself, indicating that there is something wrong, something out of joint, something that has to be put right. BE. 119

Jesus Christ became identified not only with the disposition of sin, but with the very body of sin. He Who had no sin, no connection in Himself with the body of sin, became identified with sin, 'Him who knew no sin, He made to be sin.' Language can hardly bear the strain put upon it, but it may nevertheless convey the thought that Jesus Christ went straight through identification with sin in order that every man and woman on earth might be freed from sin through the Atonement. He went through the depths of damnation, through the deepest depths of death and hell, and came out more than conqueror; consequently anyone and everyone who is willing to be identified with Him will find that he is freed from the disposition of sin, freed from his connection with the body of sin, and that he too can come out 'more than conqueror' because of what Jesus Christ has done. BP. 35

We have to be solemnly careful that we do not travesty and belittle the work of God and the Atonement of the Lord Jesus Christ. If we belittle it in the tiniest degree, although we may do it in ignorance, we shall surely suffer. The first thing which will make us belittle the Atonement is getting out of sympathy with God into sympathy with human beings, because when we do this we begin to drag down the tremendous revelation that the essential nature of God is Will and Love and Light, and that it is these characteristics which are imparted to us by the Holy Ghost. BP. 218

The meaning of the Atonement is that man's spirit can be restored into harmony with God. BSG. 76

If our best obedience, our most spotless moral walking, our most earnest prayers, are offered to God in the very least measure as the ground of our acceptance by Him, it is a fatal denial of the Atonement. CHI. 80

Until we have become spiritual by new birth the Atonement of Jesus has no meaning for us; it only begins to get meaning when we live "in heavenly places in Christ Jesus." DI. 56

Our Lord came to make atonement for the sin of the world, not by any impulse of a noble nature, but by the perfect conscious Self-sacrifice whereby alone God could redeem man. DI. 56

The Atonement means that in the Cross of Jesus Christ God redeemed the whole human race from the possibility of damnation through the heredity of sin. IWP. 27

Through the Atonement God deals with the wrong disposition in us, then He gives us the glorious privilege of making our bodies "instruments of righteousness unto God." IWP. 53

The Atonement of our Lord never contradicts human reason, it contradicts the logic of human intellect that has never partaken of regeneration. MFL. 24

The salvation of God does not stand on human logic, it stands on the sacrificial Death of Jesus. We can be born again because of the Atonement of Our Lord. Sinful men and women can be changed into new creatures, not by their repentance or their belief, but by the marvelous work of God in Christ Jesus which is prior to all experience. The impregnable safety of justification and sanctification is God Himself. We have not to work out these things ourselves; they have been worked out by the Atonement. The supernatural becomes natural by the miracle of God; there is the realization of what Jesus Christ has already done—*"It is finished."* MUH. 302

The Atonement of the Lord alone touches sin. We must not tamper with it for one second. We can do nothing with sin; we must leave God's Redemption to deal with it. NKW. 149

If we make the Atonement of the Lord Jesus Christ the great exerting influence of our life, every phase of our life will bear fruit for God. Take time and get to know whether the Atonement is the central point of all power for you, and remember that Satan's aim is to keep you away from that point of power. OBH. 123

All the distress and all the sacrifice in the world will never atone for sin. PR. 90

The Atonement means that the whole of the human race has been atoned for, Redemption is complete, and any man can get straight to the throne of God without let or hindrance through the wonder of all that our Lord has done. He is now at the right hand of the Father, not only as Son of God, but as Son of Man. PR. 120

The Bible deals with the worst tragedy that human nature and the devil could concoct. We seem to have forgotten this nowadays. The Atonement has been made a kind of moral "lavatory" wherein a man can wash and go out and get dirty again. SHH. 102

If we have have not caught the meaning of the tremendous moral aspect of the Atonement it is because we have never prayed this prayer, 'Search me, O God.' SHL. 50

Week 3

BIBLE

All Scripture is given by inspiration of God, and is profitable for doctrine, for reproof, for correction, for instruction in righteousness.

—2 Timothy 3:16

Immediately a man becomes spiritual by being born from above, the Bible becomes his authority, because he discerns a law in his conscience that has no objective resting place save in the Bible; and when the Bible is quoted, instantly his intuition says, 'Yes, that must be the truth'; not because the Bible says so, but because he discerns what the Bible says to be the word of God for him. AUG. 16

Never use your text as a title for a speculation of your own, that is being an impertinent exploiter of the word of God. AUG. 21

The Bible is a world of revelation facts, and when you explain the Bible, take into account all the record of it. The Bible nowhere says we have to believe it is the Word of God before we can be Christians. The Bible is not the Word of God to me unless I come at it through what Jesus Christ says, it is of no use to me unless I know Him. AUG. 79

You may believe the Bible is the Word of God from Genesis to Revelation and not be a Christian at all. AUG. 79

We hear much about 'key words' to the Scriptures, but there is only one 'key word' to the Scriptures for a believer, and that is our Lord Jesus Christ Himself. AUG. 104

How one wishes that people who read books about the Bible would read the Bible itself! BE. 116

The only way to understand the Scriptures is not to accept them blindly, but to read them in the light of a personal relationship to Jesus Christ. BFB. 91

If the Bible agreed with modern science, it would soon be out of date, because, in the very nature of things, modern science is bound to change. BP. 5

The Bible is the only Book that throws light on our physical condition, on our soul condition, and on our spiritual condition. In the Bible the sense of smell and sight, etc., are not used as metaphors only; they are identified with the nature of the soul's life. This accounts for what people are apt to call the vulgar teaching of the Bible. BP. 53

The Bible not only explains God, it explains the world in which we live, it explains not only things that are right, but things that are wrong. BP. 235

When a man's heart is right with God the mysterious utterances of the Bible are 'spirit and life' to him. BSG. 42

Beware of the trick of exposition which externalizes Scripture so that we teach but never learn its lessons. CD. VOL. 2, 19

The Epistles are not the cogitations of men of extraordinary spiritual genius, but the posthumous work of the Ascended Christ and they have therefore a peculiar significance in the programme of Redemption. The Holy Ghost used these men, with all their personal idiosyncrasies, to convey God's message of salvation to the world. Our Lord, so to speak, incarnated Himself in them—the message of God must always be incarnated, but it remains the message *of God*. CHI. 34

Bible facts are either revelation facts or nonsense. It depends on me which they are to me. DI. 6

Our attitude to the Bible is a stupid one; we come to the Bible for proof of God's existence, but the Bible has no meaning for us until we know God does exist. DI. 6

If we understood what happens when we use the Word of God, we would use if oftener. The disablement of the devil's power by means of the Word of God conveyed through the lips of a servant of His, is inconceivable. DI. 6

The Bible states and affirms facts for the benefit of those who believe in God; those who don't believe in God can tear it to bits if they choose. DI. 6

It is what the Bible imparts to us that is of value. DI. 8

The Bible does not thrill, the Bible nourishes. Give time to the reading of the Bible and the recreating effect is as real as that of fresh air physically. DI. 8

Beware of reasoning about God's Word, obey it. DI. 9

Don't go to your Bible in a yawning mood. DI. 50

Take stock of your views and compare them with the New Testament, and never get tricked into thinking that the Bible does not mean what it says when it disagrees with you. Disagree with what our Lord says by all means if you like, but never say that the Bible does not mean what it says. HG. 64

To use the New Testament as a book of proof is nonsense. If you do not believe that Jesus Christ is the Son of God, the New Testament will not convince you that He is; if you do not believe in the Resurrection, the New Testament will not convince you of it. The New Testament is written for those who do not need convincing. HGM. 35

In the Bible there is no twilight, but intense light and intense darkness. HGM. 39

The test of regeneration is that the Bible instantly becomes the Book of books to us. HG. 97

The Bible never deals with the domains our human minds delight to deal with. The Bible deals with heaven and hell, good and bad, God and the devil, right and wrong, salvation and damnation; we like to deal with the things in between. HGM. 39

The Context of the Bible is our Lord Jesus Christ, and personal relationship to Him. The *words* of God and The *Word* of God stand together; to separate them is to render both powerless. Any expounder of the words of God is liable to go off at a tangent if he or she does not remember this stern undeviating standard of exposition, viz., that no individual experience is of the remotest value unless it is up to the standard of The Word of God. GW. 70

Have you ever noticed the vague indefiniteness of the Bible? Unless we are spiritual we shall say, 'I do wish the Bible would talk clearly; why does it not talk as clearly as some little books I have?' If it did, the Bible would be interpretable without any knowledge of God at all. The only way we can understand whether Jesus Christ's teaching of God is by the Spirit that is in Jesus. IWP. 77

Learn to get into the quiet place where you can hear God's voice speak through the words of the Bible, and never be afraid that you will run dry, He will simply pour the word until you have no room to contain it. It won't be a question of hunting for messages or texts, but of opening the mouth wide and He fills it. IWP. 93

The Bible does not deal with the domain of common-sense facts, we get at those by our senses; the Bible deals with the world of revelation facts which we only get at by faith in God. LG. 23

The mystery of the Bible is that its inspiration was direct from God. MFL. 26

Most of us leave the sweat of brain outside when we come to deal with the Bible. MFL. 77

The Bible is like life and deals with facts, not with principles, and life is not logical. OBH. 92

Read the Bible, whether you understand it or not, and the Holy Spirit will bring back some word of Jesus to you in a particular set of circumstances and make it living; the point is—will you be loyal to that word? OBH. 121

The Bible is not the word of God to us unless we come to it through what Jesus Christ says. The Scriptures, from Genesis to Revelation, are all revelations of Jesus Christ. The context of the Bible is Our Lord Himself, and until we are rightly related to Him, the Bible is no more to us than an ordinary book. OBH. 127

The New Testament was not written in order to prove that Jesus Christ is the Son of God; but written to confirm the faith of those who believe that Jesus Christ is the Son of God. OBH. 127

There are people who vagabond through the Bible, taking sufficient only out of it for the making of sermons, they never let the word of God walk out of the Bible and talk to them. Beware of living from hand to mouth in spiritual matters; do not be a spiritual mendicant. OBH. 127

The Bible treats us as human life does—roughly. OBH. 128

✓ The Bible does not deal in common-sense facts; the natural universe deals in common-sense facts, and we get at these by our senses. The Bible deals with revelation facts, facts we cannot get at by our common sense, facts we may be pleased to make light of by our common sense. PR. 20

✓ After we are born again, the Bible becomes a new Book to us, and we search the Scriptures, not to get 'life' out of them, but to know more about Jesus Christ. PR. 22

The Bible is the only Book that tells us anything about the originator of sin. PS. 9

To people who are satisfied on too shallow a level the Bible is a book of impertinences, but whenever human nature is driven to the end of things, then the Bible becomes the only Book and God the only Being in the world. PS. 9

✓ As long as we live on the surface of things merely as splendid animals, we shall find the Bible nonsense. PS. 13

Since Adam, men, individually and collectively, present a muddle morally which has puzzled everyone; the Bible is the only Book that tells us how the moral muddle has been produced, viz. by sin. PS. 69

If you want to find an analysis of every kind of moral and immoral character, the Bible is the place to look for it. PS. 78

Do we come to the Bible to be spoken to by God, to be made "wise unto salvation," or simply to hunt for texts on which to build addresses? RTR. 58

We are apt to come to the conclusion that the Bible is tepid. Why, some of the most heroic and drastic thinking is within the covers of the Bible! St. John and St. Paul reconstructed religious thought, quoting from no one; there are no thinkers like them, yet it has been fashionable to belittle them. SHH. 3

The Bible always emphasizes the facts of life as they are. SHH. 48

The Bible attitude to things is absolutely robust, there is not the tiniest whine about it; there is no possibility of lying like a limp jellyfish on God's providence, it is never allowed for a second. There is always a sting and a kick all through the Bible. SHH. 60

As long as you live a logical life without realising the deeper depths of your personality, the Bible does not amount to anything; but strike lower down where mathematics and logic are of no account, and you find that Jesus Christ and the Bible tell every time. SHH. 87

There are bald shocking statements in the Bible, but from cover to cover the Bible will do nothing in the shape of harm to the pure in heart, it is to the impure in heart that these things are corrupting. SSM. 33

God's spiritual open air is the Bible. SSM. 103

The understanding of the Bible only comes from the indwelling of the Holy Spirit making the universe of the Bible real to us. SSM. 107

Jesus says that the way to put foundations under spiritual castles is by hearing and doing "these sayings of Mine." Pay attention to His words, and give time to doing it. Try five minutes a day with your Bible. SSM. 108

A remarkable thing about this Book of God is that for every type of human being we come across there is a distinct, clear line laid down here as to the way to apply God's truth to it. The stupid soul, the stubborn soul, the soul that is mentally diseased, the soul that is convicted of sin, the soul with the twisted mind, the sensual soul—everyone of the facts that you meet in your daily walk and business has its counterpart here, and God has a word and a revelation fact with regard to every life you come across. WG. 13

✓ We must not read the Bible like children. God requires us to read it as men and women, spiritual men and women, I mean. There are things in the Bible that stagger us, things that amaze and terrify; and the worker for God needs to understand not only the terrors of life around, but the terrors of life as God's Book reveals it. WG. 51

Week 4

BODY/SOUL/SPIRIT

You are not in the flesh but in the Spirit, if indeed the Spirit of God dwells in you.

—Romans 8:9

. . . "the time is come that judgment must begin at the house of God." Where is the house of God? My body. AUG. 28

The best I have is my claim to my right to myself, my body. If I am born again of the Spirit of God, I will give up that body to Jesus Christ. AUG. 88

The Bible nowhere says that God has a soul; the only way in which the soul of God is referred to is prophetically in anticipation of the Incarnation. Angels are never spoken of as having souls, because soul has reference to this order of creation and angels belong to another order. Our Lord emphatically had a soul, but of God and of angels the term 'soul' is not used. The term 'soul' is never applied to plants. A plant has life, but the Bible never speaks of it as having soul. BP. 44

Nothing can enter the soul but through the senses, God enters into the soul through the senses. BP. 51

Immediately we receive the Holy Spirit and are energized by God, we shall find our bodies are the first place of attack for the enemy, because the body has been the centre which ruled the soul and divided it from spiritually intelligent standards; consequently the body is the last 'stake' of Satan. The body is the 'margin of the battle' for you and me. BP. 52

We have to treat the body as the servant of Jesus Christ: when the body says 'Sit,' and He says 'Go,' go! When the body says 'Eat,' and He says 'Fast,' fast! When the body says 'Yawn,' and He says 'Pray,' pray! BE. 57

Our present-day 'wise talk' is to push all the teaching of Jesus Christ into a remote domain, but the New Testament drives its teaching straight down to the essential necessity of the physical expression of spiritual life; that just as the bad soul life shows itself in the body, so the good soul life will show itself there too. BP. 71

The body makes itself inward by means of the soul, and the spirit makes itself outward by means of the soul. The soul is the binder of these two together. There is not one part of the human body left out in God's Book; every part is dealt with and made to have a direct connection either with sin or with holiness. It is not accidental but part of the Divine revelation. BP. 72

Jesus Christ had a fleshly body as we have, but He was never tempted by lust, because lust resides in the ruling disposition, not in the body. When God changes the ruling disposition, the same body that was used as the instrument of sin to work all manner of uncleanness and unrighteousness, can now be used as the slave of the new disposition. It is not a different body; it is the same body, with a new disposition. BP. 77

The Bible nowhere says the soul sleeps; it says that the body sleeps but never the personality; the moment after death, unhindered consciousness is the state. BP. 94

. . . our body is the most gracious gift God has given us, and that if we hand over the mainspring of our life to God we can work out in our bodily life all that He works in. It is through our bodily lives that Satan works and, thank God, it is through our bodily lives that God's Spirit works. God gives us His grace and His Spirit; He puts right all that was wrong, He does not suppress it nor counteract it, but readjusts the whole thing; then begins our work. BP. 132

The Bible, instead of ignoring the fact that we have a body, exalts it. BP. 167

The Bible never says any thing so vague as 'present your "all,"' but 'present your "bodies."' There is nothing ambiguous or indefinite about that statement, it is definite and clear. The body means only one thing to us all, viz., this flesh and blood body. BP. 167

Instead of our body being a hindrance to our development, it is only through our body that we are developed. BP. 167

We express our character through our body: you cannot express a character without a body. When we speak of character, we think of a flesh and blood thing; when we speak of disposition, we think of something that is not flesh and blood. Through the Atonement God gives us the right disposition; that disposition is inside our body, and we have to manifest it in character through our body and by means of our body. BP. 167

. . . the chief glory of man is not that he is in the image of God spiritually, but that he is made "of the earth, earthy." This is not man's humiliation but his glory, because through his mortal body is to be manifested the wonderful life and disposition of Jesus Christ. BP. 168

Just think of the time when our thinking will be in language as soon as we think it! If we have the idea that we are to be penned up for ever in a little physical temple, we are twisted away from the Bible revelation. Just now in this order of things we are confined in this bodily temple for a particular reason, but at any second, in the "twinkling of an eye," God can change this body into a glorified body. BP. 256

Soul and body depend upon each other, spirit does not, spirit is immortal. Soul is simply the spirit expressing itself in the body. Immediately the body goes, the soul is gone, but the moment the body is brought back, soul is brought back, and spirit, soul and body will again be together. Spirit has never died, can never die, in the sense in which the body dies; the spirit is immortal, either in immortal life or in immortal death. There is no such thing as annihilation taught in the Bible. The separation of spirit from body and soul is temporary. The resurrection is the resurrection of the body. BP. 259

The human soul is so mysterious that in the moment of a great tragedy men get face to face with things they never gave heed to before, and in the moment of death it is extraordinary what takes place in the human heart towards God. CD. VOL. 1, 110

When I am born again my human nature is not different, it is the same as before, I am related to life in the same way, I have the same bodily organs, but the mainspring is different, and I have to see now that all my members are dominated by the new disposition. CHI. 21

Never run away with the idea that you are a person who has a spirit, has a soul, and has a body; you are a person that *is* spirit, soul and body. Man is one; body, soul and spirit are terms of definition. My body is the manifest "me." CHI. 38

It is not what man puts into his body or on his body, but what he brings out of his body, and what he brings out of what he puts on his body, viz. his money, that reveals what he considers his chief end. HG. 50

God is the Architect of the human body and He is also the Architect of the Body of Christ. There are two Bodies of Christ: the Historic Body and the Mystical Body. The historic Jesus was the habitation of the Holy Ghost, and the Mystic Christ, i.e., the Body of Christ composed of those who have experienced regeneration and sanctification, is likewise the habitation of the Holy Ghost. HGM. 25

'Soul' refers to the way a personal spirit reasons and thinks in a human body. We talk about a man exhibiting 'soul' in singing or in painting, that is, he is expressing his personal spirit. HGM. 74

By the Fall man not only died from God, but he fell into disunion with himself; that means it became possible for him to live in one of the three parts of his nature. We want to live a spiritual life, but we forget that that life has to work out in rational expression in our souls; or we want to live a clear life in the soul and forget altogether that we have a body and spirit; or else we want to live the life of a splendid animal and forget altogether the life of the soul and spirit. IWP. 32

God never allows a Christian to carry on his life in sections—so much time for study and meditation and so much for actual work; the whole life, spirit, soul and body must progress together. IWP. 36

Immediately we try to live a spiritual life with God and forget our soul and body, the devil pays attention to our body, and when we pay attention to our body he begins to get at our spirit, until we learn there is only one way to keep right—to live the life hid with Christ in God, then the very life and power of God garrisons all three domains, spirit, soul and body, but it depends on us whether we allow God to do it. IWP. 37

The body we have is not sinful in itself; if it were, it would be untrue to say that Jesus Christ was sinless. IWP. 55

Our spiritual life does not grow *in spite of* the body, but *because* of the body. "Of the earth, earthy," is man's glory, not his shame; and it is in the "earth, earthy" that the full regenerating work of Jesus Christ has its ultimate reach. MFL. 39

Have I ever realised that the most wonderful thing in the world is the thing that is nearest to me, viz., my body? Who made it? Almighty God. Do I pay the remotest attention to my body as being the temple of the Holy Ghost? Remember our Lord lived in a body like ours. The next reality that I come in contact with by my body is other people's bodies. All our relationships in life, all the joys and all the miseries, all the hells and all the heavens, are based on bodies; and the reality of Jesus Christ's salvation brings us down to the Mother Earth we live on, and makes us see by the regenerating power of God's grace how amazingly precious are the ordinary things that are always with us. Master that, and you have mastered everything. We imagine that our bodies are a hindrance to our development, whereas it is only through our bodies that we develop. We cannot express a character without a body. MFL. 62

As we walk in this body according to the new life that has been imparted to us by the Holy Spirit, we shall find it is no longer mounting up in ecstasy, running and not being weary, but walking with an infinite, steady, uncrushable, indescribable patience until men take knowledge that the Son of God is walking through us again. OBH. 84

"Present your bodies a living sacrifice, holy, acceptable unto God," not 'Present your *all,*' but present your *'body.'* If you obey in this matter of dedication, you can keep your bodily life free from vice and sin. OBH. 110

Soul is the expression of my personal spirit in my body, the way I reason and think and act, and Jesus taught that a man must lose his soul in order to gain it; he must lose absolutely his own way of reasoning and looking at things, and begin to estimate from an entirely different standpoint. PH. 64

"Present your bodies . . ." Do not ask God to take your body, but give your body to God. PH. 133

Beware of dividing man up into body, soul and spirit. Man *is* body, soul and spirit. Soul is the expression of man's personal spirit in his body. Spirit means I, myself, the incalculable being that is 'me,' the essence that expresses itself in the soul. The immortal part of a man is not his soul, but his spirit. Man's spirit is as indestructible as Almighty God; the expression of his spirit in the soul depends on the body. In the Bible the soul is always referred to in connection with the body. The soul is the holder of the body and spirit together, and when the body disappears, the soul disappears, but the essential personality of the man remains. PR. 10

The life of nature is neither moral nor immoral; our bodies are neither moral nor immoral, we make them moral or immoral. PS. 12

It is not a sin to have a body, to have natural appetites, but it is a sin to refuse to sacrifice them at the word of God. PS. 12

'Soul' in the Bible nearly always refers to the fleshly nature, it is the only power a man has for expressing his true spirit. PS. 15

When I become a Christian I have exactly the same body as before, but I have to see that my members which were used as 'servants of sin' are now used as 'servants of righteousness.' SHL. 77

Week 5

CHRIST

I am the way, the truth, and the life. No one comes to the Father except through Me.

—John 14:6

In presenting Jesus Christ never present Him as a miraculous Being Who came down from heaven and worked miracles and Who was not related to life as we are; that is not the Gospel Christ. The Gospel Christ is the Being Who came down to earth and lived our life and was possessed of a frame like ours. He became Man in order to show the relationship man was to hold to God, and by His death and resurrection He can put any man into that relationship. Jesus Christ is the last word in human nature. AUG. 44

Jesus Christ is not an individual iota of a man; He is the whole of the human race centered before God in one Person, He is God and Man in one. Man is lifted up to God in Christ, and God is brought down to man in Christ. Jesus Christ nowhere said, 'He that hath seen *man* hath seen the Father'; but He did say that God was manifest in human flesh in His own Person that He might become the generation centre for the same manifestation in every human being, and the place of His travail pangs is the incarnation, Calvary, and the Resurrection. AUG. 70

The character of Jesus Christ is exhibited in the New Testament, and it appeals to us all. He lived His life straight down in the ordinary amalgam of human life, and He claims that the character He manifested is possible for any man if he will come in by the door He provides. AUG. 81

Jesus Christ is a Fact; He is the most honourable and the holiest Man, and two things necessarily follow—first, He is the least likely to be deceived about Himself, second, He is least likely to deceive anyone else. AUG. 82

Jesus Christ never asks anyone to define his position or to understand a creed, but—'Who am I to you?' . . . Jesus Christ makes the whole of human destiny depend on a man's relationship to Himself. AUG. 82

The Great Life is to believe that Jesus Christ is not a fraud. AUG. 114

The expression 'the blood of Christ' means not only that Christ shed His blood, but that He poured out His very life before God. In the Old Testament the idea of sacrifice is that the blood, which is the life, is poured out to God, its Giver. BE. 60

When Jesus Christ shed His blood on the Cross it was not the blood of a martyr, or the blood of one man for another; it was the life of God poured out to redeem the world. BE. 60

Jesus Christ claims that He can do in human nature what human nature cannot do for itself, viz., "Destroy the works of the devil," remove the wrong heredity and put in the right one. He can satisfy the last aching abyss of the human heart, He can put the key into our hands which will give the solution to every problem that ever stretched before our minds. He can soothe by His pierced hands the wildest sorrow with which Satan or sin or death ever racked humanity. There is nothing for which Jesus Christ is not amply sufficient and over which He cannot make us more than conquerors. BE. 111

On the ground of His absolute, not coercive, authority, every man recognizes sooner or later that Jesus Christ stands easily first. BFB. 90

The only way we can explain Jesus Christ is the way He explains Himself—and He never explains Himself away. Why did Jesus Christ live and die? The Scriptures reveal that He lived and died and rose again that He might be readjusted to the Godhead, i.e., that we might be delivered from sin and be brought back into the relationship of favour with God. If we teach that Jesus Christ cannot deliver from sin we shall end in nothing short of blasphemy. BP. 36

The law of gravitation is the explanation given by scientific men of certain observed facts, and to say that Jesus Christ "broke the law of gravitation" when He walked on the sea, and when He ascended, is a misstatement. He brought in a new series of facts for which the law of gravitation, so-called, could not account. BP. 55

Science

Jesus Christ insists on the fact that if we are His disciples it will be revealed in the blood, i.e., the physical life. The old soul tyranny and disposition, the old selfish determination to seek our own ends, manifests itself in our body, through our blood; and when that disposition of soul is altered, the alteration shows itself at once in the blood also. Instead of the old tempers and the old passions being manifested in our physical blood, the good temper reveals itself. It never does to remove Jesus Christ's spiritual teaching into the domain of the inane and vague, it must come right down where the devil works; and just as the devil works not in vague ways but through flesh and blood, so does the Lord, and the characteristics of the soul for better or worse are shown in the blood. BP. 70

We are apt to look upon the blood of Christ as a kind of magic-working thing, instead of an impartation of His very life. BP. 71

The writers try to prove that Jesus is not mad according to the standards of this world; but He is mad, absolutely mad, and there is no apology needed for saying it. Either the modern attitude to things must alter, or it must pronounce Jesus Christ mad. BP. 160

In the silent years Our Lord learned how to *be;* at His Baptism He had revealed to Him what He had to *do;* in the Temptation what to *avoid.* BSG. 29

Jesus Christ is not a Being with a dual personality, He is a unique Personality with two manifestations: Son of God and Son of Man. He gives clear indication of how He lived a holy life, of how He thought and spoke, and He also gives clear expositions of God. Those expositions were given in a human body like ours, and the New Testament reveals how it is possible for us to live the same kind of life that Jesus lived through the marvel of the Atonement because the disposition which ruled Him is ruling us. BSG. 60

The Jesus who saves our souls and identifies us with Himself is 'this same Jesus' who went to sleep as a Babe on His mother's bosom; and it is 'this same Jesus,' the almighty, powerful Christ, with all power in heaven and on earth, who is at work in the world to-day by His Spirit. BSG. 72

Jesus Christ had a two-fold personality: He was Son of God revealing what God is like, and Son of Man revealing what man is to be like. BSG. 77

When the flatteries, the eulogies, the enthusiasms and the extravagances regarding Jesus Christ have become enshrined sentiments in poetry and music and eloquence, they pass, like fleeting things of mist, coloured but for a moment by reflected splendours from the Son of God, and our Lord's own words come with the sublime staying of the simple gentleness of God: "I AM THE WAY, AND THE TRUTH, AND THE LIFE." CD. VOL. 1, 11

Every man who comes to Jesus Christ has to go through the ordeal of condemnation, he has to have his beauty "consume away like a moth," and his righteousness drop from him "as filthy rags" when he stands face to face with God. CD. VOL. 1, 158

Jesus Christ always speaks from the source of things, consequently those who deal only with the surface find Him an offence. CD. VOL. 2, 74

What weakness! Our Lord lived thirty years in Nazareth with His brethren who did not believe on Him; He lived three years of popularity, scandal and hatred; fascinated a dozen illiterate men who at the end of three years all forsook Him and fled; and finally He was taken by the powers that be and crucified outside the city wall. Judged from every standpoint save the standpoint of the Spirit of God, His life was a most manifest expression of weakness, and the idea would be strong to those in the pagan world who thought anything about Him that surely now He and His crazy tale were stamped out. CD. VOL. 2, 144

The task which confronted Jesus Christ was that He had to bring man, who is a sinner, back to God, forgive him his sin, and make him as holy as He is Himself; and He did it single-handed. The revelation is that Jesus Christ, the last Adam, was "made to be sin," the thing which severed man from God, and that He put away sin by the sacrifice of Himself—"that we might become the righteousness of God in Him." He lifted the human race back, not to where it was in the first Adam, He lifted it back to where it never was, viz.: to where He is Himself. CHI. 15

Get into the habit of recalling to your mind what Jesus was like when He was here, picture what He did and what He said, recall His gentleness and tenderness as well as His strength and sternness, and then say, "That is what God is like." CHI. 77

Imputed righteousness must never be made to mean that God puts the robe of His righteousness over our moral wrong, like a snowdrift over a rubbish heap; that He pretends we are all right when we are not. The revelation is that "Christ Jesus is made unto us, righteousness"; it is the distinct impartation of the very life of Jesus on the ground of the Atonement, enabling me to walk in the light as God is in the light, and as long as I remain in the light God sees only the perfections of His Son. We are "accepted in the Beloved." CHI. 81

Jesus Christ's thought about man is that he is lost, and that He is the only One who can find him. "For the Son of Man came to seek and to save that which was lost." CHI. 97

There have been great military geniuses, intellectual giants, geniuses of statesmen, but these only exercise influence over a limited number of men; Jesus Christ exercises unlimited sway over all men because He is the altogether Worthy One. CHI. 120

In the days of His flesh Jesus Christ exhibited this Divine paradox of the Lion and the Lamb. He was the Lion in majesty, rebuking the winds and demons: He was the Lamb in meekness, "who when He was reviled, reviled not again." He was the Lion in power, raising the dead: He was the Lamb in patience—who was "brought as a lamb to the slaughter, and as a sheep before her shearers is dumb, so He openeth not His mouth." He was the Lion in authority, "Ye have heard that it hath been said . . . *but I say unto you* . . .": He was the Lamb in gentleness, "Suffer the little children to come unto Me . . . and He took them up in His arms, put His hand upon them and blessed them."

In our personal lives Jesus Christ proves Himself to be all this—He is the Lamb to expiate our sins, to lift us out of condemnation and plant within us His own heredity of holiness: He is the Lion to rule over us, so that we gladly say, "the government of this life shall be upon His shoulders." And what is true in individual life is to be true also in the universe at large. The time is coming when the Lion of the Tribe of Judah shall reign, and when "the kingdoms of this world shall become the kingdoms of our Lord, and of His Christ."
CHI. 121

If I try to be right, it is a sure sign I am wrong; the only way to be right is by stopping the humbug of trying to be and remaining steadfast in faith in Jesus Christ. 'He that *doeth* righteousness is righteous, even as He is righteous.' GW. 46

Jesus Christ is not a mere sympathizer, He is a Saviour, and the only One, 'for neither is there any other name under heaven, that is given among men wherein we must be saved.' GW. 72

Our Lord never worried, nor was He ever anxious, because He was not 'out' to realize His own ideas, He was 'out' to realize God's ideas.
GW. 81

The enemies of Christ are triumphant, Christianity is a failure, they say; and the Church of God herself looks on in pain at the shortcomings in her midst. But lo, at length from the very heart of the shadows appears the majestic Figure of Jesus; His countenance is as the sun shineth in His strength, around those wounds in Brow and Side and Hands and Feet—those wounds which shelter countless thousands of broken hearts—are healing rays; in that glorious Figure meets every beauty inconceivable to the imagination of man.
GW. 146

A healthy-hided moral man does not want Jesus Christ; a ritualist does not want Jesus Christ; a rationalist does not want Jesus Christ. It is along this line we begin to understand why Jesus said, "I am not come to call the righteous," i.e. the whole and the healthy, "but sinners to repentance." 'I am come to those who mourn, to those who are afflicted, to those who are in a condition of insatiable thirst.' HG. 54

We can never take any one virtue and say Jesus Christ was the representative of that virtue; we cannot speak of Jesus Christ being a holy Man or a great Man or a good Man; Jesus Christ cannot be summed up in terms of natural virtues, but only in terms of the supernatural. HG. 85

Never take Jesus Christ as the Representative of God: He *is* God or there is none. If Jesus Christ is not God manifest in the flesh, we know nothing whatever about God; we are not only agnostic, but hopeless. But if Jesus Christ is what He says He is, then He is God to me. HGM. 38

". . . and thou shalt call His name JESUS: for it is He that shall save His people from their sins." The character of the Name is that Jesus Christ is Saviour, and the evidence that I belong to Him is that I am delivered from sin; if I am not, I have a name to live, but am dead. HGM. 97

Jesus Christ is not only Saviour, He is King, and He has the right to exact anything and everything from us at His own discretion. HGM. 129

There is an amazing sanity in Jesus Christ that shakes the foundations of death and hell, no panic, absolute dominant mastery over everything—such a stupendous mastery that He let men take His strength from Him: "He was crucified through weakness," that was the acme of Godlike strength. IWP. 98

The most staggering thing about Jesus Christ is that He makes human destiny depend not on goodness or badness, not on things done or not done, but on Who we say He is. IWP. 116

The Holy Spirit will glorify Jesus only, consequently the interpretation of the Bible and of human life depends entirely on how we understand the character of Jesus Christ. IWP. 122

Jesus Christ is the last word on God, on sin and death, on heaven and hell; the last word on every problem that human life has to face. IWP. 125

Jesus Christ is not a social reformer; He came to alter us first, and if there is any social reform to be done on earth, we must do it. IYA. 14

Many who knew Our Lord while He was on earth saw nothing in Him; only after their disposition had been altered did they realize Who He was. Our Lord lived so ordinary a life that no one noticed Him. LG. 43

Jesus Christ is the love of God incarnated. LG. 68

"Let this mind be in you, which was also in Christ Jesus . . ." That is a command. God does not give us the mind of Christ, He gives us the Spirit of Christ, and we have to see that the Spirit of Christ in us works through our brains in contact with actual life and that we form His mind. Jesus Christ did not become humbled—"He humbled Himself." LG. 71

When once the Spirit of God energises our spirit, we are responsible for forming the mind of Christ. God gives us the disposition of Jesus Christ, but He does not give us His mind, we have to form that, and we form it by the way we react on external things. MFL. 48

Jesus Christ—He is the Truth; He is the Honourable One; He is the Just One; He is the Pure One; He is the altogether Lovely One; He is the only One of Good Report. No matter where we start from, we will always come back to Jesus Christ. MFL. 91

Our Lord is the time-representation of a Self-disglorified God. MFL. 104

No one is ever united with Jesus Christ until he is willing to relinquish not sin only, but his whole way of looking at things. To be born from above of the Spirit of God means that we must let go before we lay hold, and in the first stages it is the relinquishing of all pretence. What our Lord wants us to present to Him is not goodness, nor honesty, nor endeavour, but real solid sin; that is all He can take from us. And what does He give in exchange for our sin?

Real solid righteousness. But we must relinquish all pretence of being anything, all claim of being worthy of God's consideration. MUH. 68

We are acceptable with God not because we have obeyed, or because we have promised to give up things, but because of the death of Christ, and in no other way. MUH. 303

The modern view of the death of Jesus is that He died for our sins out of sympathy. The New Testament view is that He bore our sin not by sympathy, but by identification. He was *made to be sin*. Our sins are removed because of the death of Jesus, and the explanation of His death is His obedience to His Father, not His sympathy with us. MUH. 303

Never allow the thought that Jesus Christ stands with us against God out of pity and compassion; that He became a curse for us out of sympathy with us. Jesus Christ became a curse for us by the Divine decree. MUH. 326

Our Lord was not a recluse nor an ascetic, He did not cut Himself off from society, but He was inwardly disconnected all the time. He was not aloof, but He lived in another world. He was so much in the ordinary world that the religious people of His day called Him a glutton and a wine-bibber. MUH. 332

Thousands of people are happy without God in this world. If I was happy and moral till Jesus came, why did He come? Because that kind of happiness and peace is on a wrong level; Jesus Christ came to send a sword through every peace that is not based on a personal relationship to Himself. MUH. 354

If you are outside the crucible you will say that Jesus Christ is cruel, but when you are in the crucible you see that it is a personal relationship with Himself that He is after all the time. He is after the true gold, and the devil is after it too. NKW. 115

We are invited, we are commanded and pleaded with, to believe the gospel of the grace of God, which is, "Christ in you, the hope of glory." OBH. 19

Jesus Christ does not make us original characters, He makes our characters replicas of His own; consequently, argues the Spirit of God, when men see us, they will not say, 'What wonderful, original, extraordinary characters.' No, none of that rubbish! They will say, 'How marvellous God must be to take poor pieces of human stuff like those men, and turn them into the image of Jesus Christ!'" ". . . which things the angels desire to look into." OBH. 28

Jesus Christ is *Saviour* and *Lord* in experience, and *Lord* and *Saviour* in discernment. OBH. 88

The coming of Jesus Christ is not a peaceful thing, it is a disturbing thing, because it means the destruction of every peace that is not based on a personal relationship to Himself. PH. 61

We are apt to look upon the blood of Jesus Christ as a magic-working power instead of its being the very life of the Son of God poured forth for men. PH. 162

Identification with the death of Jesus Christ means identification with Him to the death of everything that never was in Him, and it is the blood of Christ, in the sense of the whole personal life of the Son of God, that comes into us and "cleanseth us from all sin." PH. 162

Jesus Christ is not a Being with two personalities; He is Son of God (the exact expression of Almighty God), and Son of Man (the presentation of God's normal man). As Son of God, He reveals what God is like; as Son of Man, He mirrors what the human race will be like on the basis of Redemption—a perfect oneness between God and man. PR. 13

Jesus Christ was born *into* this world, not *from* it. He came into history from the outside of history; He did not evolve out of history. Our Lord's birth was an advent; He did not come from the human race, He came into it from above. Jesus Christ is not the best human being, He is a Being Who cannot be accounted for by the human race at all. He is God Incarnate, not man becoming God, but God coming into human flesh, coming into it from the outside. His Life is the Highest and the Holiest entering in at the lowliest door. Our Lord entered history by the Virgin Mary. PR. 29

Jesus Christ did not come to do anything less than to bear away the sin of the world, that is His vocation as Son of Man. PR. 48

As Son of Man Jesus Christ deliberately limited omnipotence, omnipresence, and omniscience in Himself; now they are His in absolute full power. As Deity, they were always His; now as Son of Man they are His in absolute full power. PR. 124

Jesus Christ is not the way to God, not a road we leave behind us, a fingerpost that points in the right direction; He is the way itself. PR. 137

Jesus Christ is to us the faithful Face of God. PR. 138

It was not the blood of a martyr, not the blood of goats and calves, that was shed, but "the blood of Christ." The very life of God was shed for the world—"the church of God which He purchased with His own blood." . . . All the perfections of the essential nature of God were in that blood; all the holiest attainments of man were in that blood. PS. 18

The offering of Jesus is not pathetic in the tiniest degree; it is beyond all pathos. PS. 19

If men and Satan could only get rid of Jesus Christ, they would never be involved in perplexity, never be upset. Jesus put it very clearly: "If I had not come and spoken unto them, they had not had sin: but now they have no cloke for their sin." The greatest annoyance to Satan and to humanity is Jesus Christ. PS. 72

You can never measure what God will do through you if you are rightly related to Jesus Christ. RTR. 36

There is only one God for the Christian, and He is Jesus Christ. SA. 15

Let Plato or Socrates, for instance, say, "I am the Way, the Truth, and the Life," and we see what it involves. Jesus Christ is either mad or what He claims to be, viz.: the only revelation of God Almighty that there is. SA. 36

There are two views of Jesus Christ's death. One is that He was a martyr—that is not the New Testament view; the other is that the

Cross of Jesus Christ was the Cross of God, not of a man at all—not a man doing his level best for God, but "God doing the very best for man." SA. 38

Jesus Christ effaced the God-head in Himself so effectually that men without the Spirit of God despised Him. SA. 50

To-day we have all kinds of Christs in our midst, the Christ of Labour and of Socialism; the Mind-cure Christ and the Christ of Christian Science and of Theosophy; but they are all abstract Christs. The one great sign of Christ is not with them—there are no marks of the Atonement about these Christs. Jesus Christ is the only One with the marks of atonement on Him, the wounded hands and feet, a symbol of the Redeemer Who is to come again. There will be signs and wonders wrought by these other Christs, and great problems may be solved, but the greatest problem of all, the problem of sin, will not be touched. SA. 57

If Jesus Christ is only a Teacher, then all He can do is to tantalize us, to erect a standard we cannot attain to; but when we are born again of the Spirit of God, we know that He did not come only to teach us, *He came to make us what He teaches we should be.* SA. 85

Our Lord's whole life was rooted and grounded in God, consequently He was never wearied or cynical. SHH. 16

The coming of Jesus Christ is not a peaceful thing, it is a disturbing, an overwhelming thing. SHL. 43

If all Jesus Christ came to do was to upset me, make me unfit for my work, upset my friendships and my life, produce disturbance and misery and distress, then I wish He had never come. But that is not all He came to do. He came to lift us up to 'the heavenly places' where He is Himself. The whole claim of the Redemption of Jesus is that He can satisfy the last aching abyss of the human soul, not hereafter only, but here and now. SHL. 45

The great characteristic of our Lord's life was that of 'golden ignorance'; there were things He did not know and that He refused to know. SHL. 66

'It is enough for the disciple that he be as his Master.' At first sight this looks like an enormous honor: to be 'as his Master' is marvellous glory—is it? Look at Jesus as He was when He was here, it was anything but glory. He was easily ignorable, saving to those who knew Him intimately; to the majority of men He was 'as a root out of a dry ground.' For thirty years He was obscure, then for three years He went through popularity, scandal, and hatred; He succeeded in gathering a handful of fishermen as disciples, one of whom betrayed Him, one denied Him, and all forsook Him; and He says, 'It is enough for you to be like that.' The idea of evangelical success, Church prosperity, civilized manfestation, does not come into it at all. When we fulfil the conditions of spiritual life we become unobtrusively real. SHL. 105

If Jesus Christ has done no mighty works for me it is either because I don't believe He can, or I don't want Him to. I may say—"Oh yes, I believe Jesus Christ will give me the Holy Spirit"; but I am not prepared for Him to do it, I don't want Him to. Will you launch out on what Jesus says? If you will, you will find that God is as good as His word. SSH. 92

Jesus Christ is the expression of the wisdom of God. SSM. 48

Jesus Christ did not come to found religion, nor did He come to found civilisation, they were both here before He came; He came to make us spiritually real in every domain. In Jesus Christ there was nothing secular and sacred, it was all real, and He makes His disciples like Himself. SSM. 49

. . . the teaching of Jesus Christ does not appear at first to be what it is. At first it appears to be beautiful and pious and lukewarm; but before long it becomes a ripping and tearing torpedo which splits to atoms every preconceived notion a man ever had. SSM. 51

Unless Jesus Christ can remake us within, His teaching is the biggest mockery human ears ever listened to. SSM. 52

All our righteousness is "as filthy rags" unless it is the blazing holiness of Jesus in us uniting us with Him until we see nothing but Jesus first, Jesus second, and Jesus third. SSM. 54

Notice the essential simplicity of our Lord's teaching all through—right towards God, right towards God. SSM. 60

. . . our Lord told the disciples not to rejoice because the devils were subject to them, but to rejoice because they were rightly related to Himself. We are brought back to the one point all the time—an unsullied relationship to Jesus Christ in every detail, private and public. SSM. 106

We must get to the place of real solitude with Christ. He is our mountain-height and our sea-calm; He is the recreating power; He is the universal Sovereign. He tells us to consider the lilies; we say—'No, we must consider life.' We mistake the mechanism of life for life itself, and that idea has become incorporated into Christian work. SSY. 134

Jesus Christ came to do what no human being can do, He came to redeem men, to alter their disposition, to plant in them the Holy Spirit, to make them new creatures. Christianity is not the obliteration of the old, but the transfiguration of the old. Jesus Christ did not come to teach men to be holy: He came to make men holy. His teaching has no meaning for us unless we enter into His life by means of His death. The Cross is the great central point. SSY. 154

Jesus Christ was not a recluse. He did not cut Himself off from society, He was amazingly in and out among the ordinary things of life; but He was disconnected fundamentally from it all. He was not aloof, but He lived in another world. His life was so social that men called Him a glutton and a wine-bibber, a friend of publicans and sinners. His detachments were inside towards God. SSY. 164

Men's minds will always assent that Jesus Christ is right,—why? Because Jesus Christ is Incarnate Reason. There is something in Jesus Christ that appeals to every man, no matter what condition he is in. If once Jesus Christ is brought into contact with a man, let that man seem to us dead and indifferent, destitute of anything like goodness—let him come in contact with Jesus Christ by the Holy Spirit, and you will instantly see that he can grasp something about Him in a way we cannot understand unless we know the Holy Spirit. WG. 24

So many people try to explain things about Jesus Christ, but no worker need ever try to do that. You cannot explain things about Jesus Christ, rely on the Holy Spirit and He will explain Jesus to the soul. WG. 25

. . . from Jesus Christ's point of view all men are lost, but we have so narrowed and so specialised the term 'lost' that we have missed its evangelical meaning; we have made it mean that only the people who are down and out in sin are lost. WG. 30

People say that it is so hard to bring Jesus Christ and present Him before the lives of men to-day. Of course it is, it is so hard that it is impossible except by the power of the indwelling Holy Ghost. WG. 38

If all Jesus Christ can do is to tell a man he has to cheer up when he is miserable; if all the worker for God can do is to tell a man he has no business to have the 'blues'—I say if that is all Jesus Christ's religion can do, then it is a failure. But the wonder of our Lord Jesus Christ is just this, that you can face Him with any kind of men or women you like, and He can cure them and put them into a right relationship with God. WG. 60

Week 6

CHRISTIAN

For us there is one God, the Father, of whom are all things, and we for Him; and one Lord Jesus Christ, through whom are all things, and through whom we live.

—1 Corinthians 8:6

We are ambassadors for Christ, as though God were pleading through us: we implore you on Christ's behalf, be reconciled to God.

—2 Corinthians 5:20

Human strength and earnestness cannot make a man a Christian any more than they can make him an angel; he must receive something from God, and that is what Jesus Christ calls 'being born from above.' AUG. 78

You can always tell whether Christians are spiritually minded by their attitude to the supernatural. BP. 91

Righteousness—conformity to a right standard, where no one but God sees us. That is where very few of us are Christians. BE. 21

Manners refer to Christian character, and we are responsible for our manners. BP. 42

As long as a Christian complies with the standards of this world, the world recognizes him; but when he works from the real standard, which is God, the world cannot understand him, and consequently it either ignores or ridicules him. BP. 187

I am not here to be a specimen of what God can do; I am here to live the life so hid with Christ in God that what Jesus said will be true, 'Men will see your good works, and glorify your Father which is in heaven.' BSG. 45

A Christian is a sanctified man in his business, or legal or civic affairs, or artistic and literary affairs. CD. VOL. 2, 86

In every age it has always been the despised crowd that have been called Christians. CD. VOL. 2, 146

We should make less excuses for the weaknesses of a Christian than for any other man. A Christian has God's honour at stake. DI. 72

No Christian has any right to be un-enthusiastic. 'And be not drunk with wine, wherein is excess; but be filled with the Spirit.' It is easy for many men to obey the first part of this injunction while they disobey the latter. GW. 68

Our conception of things has to be torn to shreds until we realize that what makes a man a Christian is a simple heart-relationship to Jesus Christ, not intellectual conceptions. HG. 53

A Christian is an impossible being unless a man can be made all over again. HGM. 14

If you are trying to be a Christian it is a sure sign you are not one. IWP. 63

It is a great boon to know there are deep things to know. The curse of the majority of spiritual Christians is that they are too cocksure and certain there is nothing more to know than they know. That is spiritual insanity. IWP. 76

The New Testament view of a Christian is that he is one in whom the Son of God has been revealed, and prayer deals with the nourishment of that life. One way it is nourished is by refusing to worry over anything, for worry means there is something over which we cannot have our own way, and is in reality personal irritation with God. Jesus Christ says, 'Don't worry about your life, don't fear them which kill the body; be afraid only of not doing what the Spirit of God indicates to you.' IYA. 13

A Christian's duty is not to himself or to others, but to Christ. IYA. 83

We are apt to have a disproportionate view of a Christian because we look only at the exceptions. The exceptions stand out *as* exceptions. The extraordinary conversions and phenomenal experiences are magnificent specimen studies of what happens in the life of everyone, but not one in a million has an experience such as the Apostle Paul had. The majority of us are unnoticed and unnoticeable people. LG. 35

The secret of the Christian is that he knows the absolute Deity of Jesus Christ. LG. 118

If I find it hard to be a Christian it is a sign that I need the awakening of a new birth. Only a spiritually ignorant person tries to be a Christian. MFL. 21

. . . you cannot be a Christian by trying; you must be born into the life before you can live it. MFL. 21

The outstanding characteristic of a Christian is this unveiled frankness before God so that the life becomes a mirror for other lives. By being filled with the Spirit we are transformed, and by beholding we become mirrors. You always know when a man has been beholding the glory of the Lord, you feel in your inner spirit that he is the mirror of the Lord's own character. MUH. 23

A Christian is one who trusts the wits and the wisdom of God, and not his own wits. MUH. 218

It is a shameful thing for a Christian to talk about getting the victory. The Victor ought to have got us so completely that it is His victory all the time, and we are more than conquerors through Him. MUH. 298

The one essential thing which makes a man a Christian is not what he believes in his head but what he is in disposition. PH. 61

. . . there is one definite aim in every Christian life, and that aim is not ours, it is God's. PH. 177

The Christian is neither Adam nor Jesus Christ, the Christian is a new man in Christ Jesus. PR. 10

The characteristics that Jesus Christ exhibited in His human life are to be exhibited in the Christian. PR. 18

If we have been trying to be holy, it is a sure sign we are not. Christians are born, not made. They are not produced by imitation, nor by praying and vowing; they are produced by new birth. PR. 35

Until a man is born again, he cannot think as a Christian. PR. 98

"For we are unto God a sweet savour of Christ." We are enwheeled with the odour of Jesus, and wherever we go we are a wonderful refreshment to God. RTR. 46

That a Christian can smilingly do a smart trick is a staggering thing. Destruction of conscientiousness means we have lost the fierce purity of the Holy Ghost and taken on the pattern and print of the age. RTR. 71

We are not Christians at heart, we don't believe in the wisdom of God, but only in our own. We go in for insurance and economy and speculation, everything that makes us secure in our own wisdom. SHH. 143

A Christian is to be consistent only to the life of the Son of God in him, not consistent to hard and fast creeds. Men pour themselves into creeds, and God Almighty has to blast them out of their prejudices before they become devoted to Jesus Christ. SSM. 44

Week 7

CHRISTIANITY

The life was manifested, and we have seen, and bear witness, and declare to you that eternal life which was with the Father and was manifested to us.

—1 John 1:2

Christianity is in its essence social. When once we begin to live from the otherworldly standpoint, as Jesus Christ wants us to live, we shall need all the fellowship with other Christians we can get. Some of us can do without Church fellowship because we are not Christians of the otherworldly order. Immediately a man dares to live on Jesus Christ's line, the world, the flesh and the devil are dead against him in every particular. 'The only virtue you will have in the eyes of the world as My disciples,' says Jesus, 'is that you will be hated.' That is why we need to be knit together with those of like faith; and that is the meaning of the Christian Church. AUG. 17

If . . . Jesus Christ is not a humbug, and not a dreamer, but what He claims to be, then Christianity is the grandest fact that ever was introduced to any man. AUG. 84

Christianity is personal, passionate devotion to Jesus Christ as God manifest in the flesh. AUG. 115

Always now is the secret of the Christian life. AUG. 128

There is a presentation of Christianity which is sentimental and weak and unworthy of God; the Christianity of the New Testament is something "angels desire to look into." BE. 65

Christianity is not consistency to conscience or to convictions; Christianity is being true to Jesus Christ. BE. 66

It is absurd to call Christianity a system of non-resistance; the great doctrine of Christianity is resistance 'unto blood' against sin. BE. 67

The Christian life does not take its pattern from good men, but from God Himself, that is why it is an absolutely supernormal life all through. BE. 80

The Christian faith affirms the existence of a personal God Who reveals Himself. Pseudo-Christianity departs from this, we are told we cannot know anything at all about God, we do not know whether He is a personal Being, we cannot know whether He is good. The Christian revelation is that God is a personal Being and He is good. By 'good,' I mean morally good. BE. 102

The central citadel of Christianity is the Person of our Lord Jesus Christ. The final standard for the Christian is given at the outset—"to be conformed to the image of His Son." BE. 108

Men have tried to get at the truth of Christianity head-first, which is like saying you must think how you will live before you are born. We instantly see the absurdity of that, and yet we expect to reason out the Christian life before we have been born into the realm of Jesus Christ. "Except a man be born again, he cannot see the kingdom of God." BFB. 102

The test of Christianity is that a man lives better than he preaches. BFB. 104

Christianity does not consist in telling the truth, or walking in a conscientious way, or adhering to principles; Christianity is something other than all that, it is adhering in absolute surrender to a Person, the Lord Jesus Christ. BFB. 106

God has loved me to the end of all my sinfulness, the end of all my self-will, all my selfishness, all my stiff-neckedness, all my pride, all my self-interest; now He says—"love one another; as I have loved you." I am to show to my fellow-men the same love that God showed to me. That is Christianity in practical working order. BP. 192

The greatest test of Christianity is the wear and tear of daily life, it is like the shining of silver, the more it is rubbed the brighter it grows. DI. 30

Christianity is not service for Jesus Christ, not winning souls, it is nothing less than the life of Jesus being manifested more and more in my mortal flesh. DI. 37

In our modern conception of Christianity there is no miracle, the emphasis is put not on the regenerating power of the Cross, but on individual consecrations, individual fasting and prayer, individual devotion. It is simply individualism veneered over with religious phraseology. There is no need for the Cross of Christ for all that kind of thing. GW. 55

People have the idea that Christianity and Stoicism are alike; the writings of the stoics sound so like the teaching of Jesus Christ, but just at the point where they seem most alike, they are most divergent. A stoic overcomes the world by making himself indifferent, by passionlessness; the saint overcomes the world by passionateness, by the passion of his love for Jesus Christ. HG. 34

If Jesus Christ cannot produce a meekness and lowliness of heart like His own, Christianity is nonsense from beginning to end, and His teaching had better be blotted out. HG. 60

Christianity is a complete sham or a supernatural miracle from beginning to end; immediately we admit it is a miracle we are responsible for walking in the light of what we know Jesus Christ to be. HG. 74

As long as we pretend to be believers in Jesus Christ and are not, we produce humbugs, and people say, 'Do you call that Christianity?' 'There is nothing in it!'; or what is worse, we produce frauds, and the worst type of fraud is the religious fraud. HG. 104

The bedrock of Christianity is not decision for Christ, for a man who decides banks on his decision, not on God. It is the inability to decide—'I have no power to get hold of God, no power to be what I know He wants me to be.' Then, says Jesus, "Blessed are you." "Blessed are the poor in spirit: for theirs is the kingdom of heaven." HGM. 28

Once let that man realize that Christianity is not a decision for Christ, but a complete surrender to let Him take the lordship, and Jesus will appear to him. He will do more, He will put into him a totally new heredity, the heredity that was in Himself. That is the amazement of regeneration. HGM. 37

Christianity is a personal history with Jesus. "And ye shall be My witnesses." HGM. 38

Christianity is not devotion to work, or to a cause, or a doctrine, but devotion to a Person, the Lord Jesus Christ. HGM. 113

The passion of Christianity is that I deliberately sign away my own rights and become a bondslave of Jesus Christ. HGM. 130

Christianity is not a thing of times and seasons, but of God and faith. LG. 15

Both nations and individuals have tried Christianity and abandoned it, because it has been found too difficult; but no man has ever gone through the crisis of deliberately making Jesus Lord and found Him to be a failure. LG. 127

The main thing about Christianity is not the work we do, but the relationship we maintain and the atmosphere produced by that relationship. That is all God asks us to look after, and it is the one thing that is being continually assailed. MUH. 217

The Christian religion bases everything on the positive, radical nature of sin. Other religions deal with sins; the Bible alone deals with sin. MUH. 281

Many of us think that God wants us to give up things; we make Christianity the great apotheosis of giving up! NKW. 124

The Christian life is not a bandbox life. We must live where we can be tested by the whole of life. OBH. 107

Jesus Christ comes to the central part of a man's life, and the bedrock of Christianity is that Jesus Christ has done something for me I could not do for myself. PH. 61

Christianity is not adherence to a set of principles or to a plan of salvation, but a personal relationship to Jesus Christ. PH. 62

If Christianity does not affect my money and my marriage relationships, it is not worth anything. PH. 62

Christianity is not my consciousness of God, but God's consciousness of me. We must build our faith on the reality that we are taken up into God's consciousness in Christ, not that we take God into our consciousness. PH. 111

Christianity is not devotion to a cause or to a set of principles, but devotion to a Person, and the great watchword of a Christian is not a passion for souls, but a passion for Christ. PH. 166

The main thing about Christianity is not the work we do, but the relationship we maintain. The only things God asks us to look after are the atmosphere of our life and our relationships, these are the only things that preserve us from priggishness, from impertinence and from worry, and it is these things that are assailed all through. PH. 178

Christianity is the vital realisation of the unsearchable riches of Christ. PH. 223

We have made Christianity to mean the saving of our skins. PH. 226

Christianity means staking ourselves on the honour of Jesus; His honour means that He will see us through time, death and eternity. PH. 226

Christianity has always been a forlorn hope because the saints are in alien territory; but it is all right, God is working out His tremendous purpose for the overthrow of everything Satan and sin can do. PS. 75

The Christian life is the simplest, the gayest, the most regardless-of-consequences life, lived as it is taught by Jesus. The plan of our life comes through the haphazard moments, but behind it is the order of God. RTR. 9

Christianity makes no allowance for heroic moods. It is easy to feel heroic in an armchair, when everything goes well, but Christianity deals with God's standard in the common days when you are out of your arm-chair, and when things are not going well. RTR. 14

The essence of Christianity is that we give the Son of God a chance to live and move and have His being in us. RTR. 70

Jesus Christ's view is that the Christian religion has been tried and abandoned, but never been tried and failed. SA. 27

Christian evidences don't amount to anything; you can't convince a man against his will. SA. 32

There is much teaching abroad to-day that is veneered over as Christianity. Men preach, and undermine the very ground they stand on while they preach. SA. 39

The revelation of Christianity is that God, in order to be of use in human affairs, had to become a typical Man. That is the great revelation of Christianity, that God Himself became human; became incarnate in the weakest side of His own creation. SA. 59

Christianity is not adherence to a set of principles—righteousness, goodness, uprightness—all these things are secondary. The first great fundamental thing about Christianity is a personal relationship to Jesus Christ which enables a man to work out the ideal and actual as one in his own personal life. SA. 82

Our Christianity has been as powerless as dish-water with regard to things as they are; consequently the net result of Christianity is judged to be a failure. But Christianity, according to Jesus Christ, has never been tried and failed; it has been tried and abandoned in individual cases because it has been found a bit too hard, too definite and emphatic, and for the same reason it has been abandoned in nations and in Churches; but Christianity has never been tried and gone through with honourably and found to fail. SA. 88

The Christian religion founds everything on the radical, positive nature of sin. Sin is self-realization, self-sufficiency, entire and complete mastership of myself—gain that, and you lose control of everything over which God intended you to have dominion. SA. 116

The essence of Christianity is not adherence to principles; but a personal relationship to God through Jesus Christ at work in the whole of my life. SHH. 39

The Christian faith is exhibited by the man who has the spiritual courage to say that that is the God he trusts in, and it takes some moral backbone to do it. SHH. 44

The basis of Christianity is not primarily virtue and honesty and goodness, not even holiness, but a personal relationship to God in Jesus Christ which works out all the time by "spontaneous moral originality." SHH. 124

. . . there is nothing more heroic or more grand than the Christian life. SSM. 36

The Christian life is a holy life; never substitute the word 'happy' for 'holy.' We certainly will have happiness, but as a consequence of holiness. SSM. 97

Christianity is not a 'sanctified' anything; it is the life of Jesus manifested in our mortal flesh by the miracle of His Redemption, and that will mean that whenever a crisis comes, Jesus is instantly seen to be Master without a moment's hesitation; there is no debate. SSY. 87

Week 8

CHURCH

Christ also loved the church and gave Himself for her.
—Ephesians 5:25

The Church confronts the world with a message the world craves for but resents because it comes through the Cross of Christ. AUG. 39

The Church does not lead the world nor echo it; she confronts it. Her note is the supernatural note. AUG. 39

The institutions of Churchianity are not Christianity. AUG. 83

Our Lord said that His Church would be so completely taken up with its precedents and preconceptions that when He came it would be "as a thief in the night"; they would not see Him because they were taken up with another point of view. BFB. 22

The Church of Jesus Christ . . . seeking favour in the eyes of the world, seeking signs and wonders, and Christ stands without the door knocking. BSG. 41

The Church is a separated band of people who are united to God by the regenerating power of the Spirit, and the bedrock of membership in the Church is that we know who Jesus is by a personal revelation of Him. The indwelling Spirit is the supreme Guide, and He keeps us absorbed with our Lord. The emphasis to-day is placed on the furtherance of an organisation; the note is, "We must keep this thing going." If we are in God's order the thing will go; if we are not in His order, it won't. CHI. 50

The most fundamental heresies which split the Christian Church are those built on what Jesus Christ can do instead of on Himself. Wreckage in spiritual experience always follows. DI. 3

The Church is called to deliver God's message and to be for the praise of His glory, not to be a socialistic institution under the patronage of God. GW. 73

The gifts of the Spirit are not for individual exaltation, but for the good of the whole Body of Christ. The Body of Christ is an organism, not an organization. How patient God is in forming the Body of Christ. HGM. 11

According to our Lord, the bedrock of membership in the Christian Church is a personal revelation from God as to Who Jesus is, and a public declaration of it. LG. 127

The Church ceases to be a spiritual society when it is on the lookout for the development of its own organization. MUH. 194

All our Lord succeeded in doing during His life on earth was to gather together a group of fishermen—the whole Church of God and the enterprise of our Lord on earth in a fishing boat! PH. 180

The Church of Jesus Christ is built on these two things: the Divine revelation of Who Jesus Christ is, and the public confession of it. PR. 76

The Church is the new Spirit-baptized Humanity based on the Redemption of Jesus Christ. SA. 18

The divisions of the churches are to be deplored, and denominationalism is to be deplored, but we must not forget that denominations have reared up the best men we know. SA. 76

The Church of Jesus Christ is an organism; we are built up into Him, baptized by one Spirit into one body. Churchianity is an organization; Christianity is an organism. Organization is an enormous benefit until it is mistaken for the life. God has no concern about our organizations. When their purpose is finished He allows them to be swept aside, and if we are attached to the organization, we shall go with it. Organization is a great necessity, but not an end in itself, and to live for any organization is a spiritual disaster. SA. 118

The personal Holy Spirit builds us up into the body of Christ. All that Jesus Christ came to do is made ours experimentally by the Holy Spirit, and all His gifts are for the good of the whole body, not for individual exaltation. LG. 131

Our word "Church" is connected with civilized organizations of religious people; Our Lord's attitude to the Church is different. He says it is composed of those who have had a personal revelation from God as to Who Jesus Christ is, and have made a public declaration of the same. SA. 119

According to Our Lord, there is not a home church and a foreign church, it is all one great work, beginning at home and then going elsewhere, 'beginning from Jerusalem.' SSY. 79

Week 9

CIRCUMSTANCES

My grace is sufficient for you, for My strength is made perfect in weakness.

—2 Corinthians 12:9

Never allow that your circumstances exonerate you from obeying any of the commands of Jesus. BE. 59

God brings us into circumstances where we have to 'prove all things,' where we form the mind of Christ and make our thinking like His—robust, vigorous and strong, right towards God, not because we are in earnest, but because we have received the earnest Holy Ghost. BE. 98

We are not responsible for the circumstances we are in, but we are responsible for the way we allow those circumstances to affect us; we can either allow them to get on top of us, or we can allow them to transform us into what God wants us to be. CHI. 40

There are circumstances in life which make us know that Satan's sneer is pretty near the mark. I love God as long as He blesses me, saves my soul and puts me right for heaven; but supposing He should see fit to let the worst things happen to me, would I say, "Go on, do it" and love Him still? CHI. 111

Recognize Jesus as Lord, obey Him, and let the next thing happen as He wills. GW. 58

God seems to have a delightful way of upsetting things which we have calculated on without Him. We get into places and circumstances He never chose, and suddenly they are shaken and we find we have been calculating on them without God; He has not entered in as a living factor. GW. 80

"In my distress . . ." There are elements in our circumstances if we are children of God that can only be described by the word *'distress'*; it would be untruthful to say it was otherwise. HG. 9

God engineers circumstances to see what we will do. HG. 16

"Consider the lilies of the field," said Jesus; we consider motor-cars and aeroplanes, things full of energy. Jesus never drew His illustrations from these things, but always from His Father's handiwork. A lily grows where it is put and does not fuss; we are always inclined to say 'I would be all right if only I were somewhere else.' HGM. 32

It is only the loyal saint who believes that God engineers circumstances. HGM. 131

We take such liberties with our circumstances, we treat the things that happen as if they were engineered by men, although we say that we believe God engineers them. HGM. 131

A man is never what he is *in spite of* his circumstances, but *because* of them. IYA. 15

Jesus Christ, by the Spirit of God, always keeps us on top of our circumstances. IYA. 15

If you are a child of God and there is some part of your circumstances which is tearing you, if you are living in the heavenly places you will thank God for the tearing things; if you are not in the heavenly places you cry to God over and over again—'O Lord, remove this thing from me. If only I could live in golden streets and be surrounded with angels, and have the Spirit of God consciously indwelling me all the time and have everything wonderfully sweet, then I think I might be a Christian.' That is not being a Christian! LG. 88

A Christian is one who can live in the midst of the trouble and turmoil with the glory of God indwelling him, while he stedfastly looks not at the things which are seen, but at the things which are not seen. We have to learn to think only of things which are seen as a glorious chance of enabling us to concentrate on the things which are not seen. LG. 89

God engineers external things for the purpose of revealing to us whether we are living in this imperturbable place of unutterable strength and glory, viz., the life hid with Christ in God. If we are, then let the troubles and difficulties work as they may on the outside, we are confident that they are working out a grander weight of glory in the heavenlies. LG. 89

We have an idea that we have to alter things, we have not; we have to remain true to God in the midst of things as they are, to allow things as they are to transmute us. 'Things as they are' are the very means God uses to make us into the praise of His glory. LG. 90

No matter what your circumstances may be, don't try to shield yourself from things God is bringing into your life. We have the idea sometimes that we ought to shield ourselves from some of the circumstances God brings round us. Never! God engineers circumstances; we have to see that we face them abiding continually with Him in His temptations. They are *His* temptations, they are not temptations to us, but to the Son of God in us. LG. 156

We talk about 'circumstances over which we have no control.' None of us have control over our circumstances, but we are responsible for the way we pilot ourselves in the midst of things as they are. MFL. 95

Never allow to yourself that you could not help this or that; and never say you reach anywhere *in spite of* circumstances; we all attain *because* of circumstances and no other way. MFL. 95

It is impossible for Christ to be where you are, that is why He has put you there. You have to put on the new man in the actual circumstances you are in and manifest Him. NKW. 41

Don't loaf along like a strayed poet on the fringes of God's providence; the Almighty has got you in hand, leave yourself alone and trust in Him. Half the sentimental pious folks that strew the coasts of emotional religious life are there because we will engineer our own circumstances. NKW. 133

Remember, we go through nothing that God does not know about. OBH. 82

. . . all the grace of God is ours without let or hindrance through the Lord Jesus, and He is ready to tax the last grain of sand and the remotest star to bless us. What does it matter if circumstances are hard? Why shouldn't they be! We are the ones who ought to be able to stand them. OBH. 86

When once the saint begins to realize that God engineers circumstances, there will be no more whine, but only a reckless abandon to Jesus. OBH. 104

We are not to be changing and arranging our circumstances ourselves. Our Lord and Master never chose His own circumstances, He was meek towards His Father's dispensation for Him; He was at home with His Father wherever His body was placed. OBH. 107

. . . if you have seen God face to face your circumstances will never arouse any panic in you. OPG. 64

The circumstances of our Lord were anything but ideal, they were full of difficulties. Perhaps ours are the same, and we have to watch that we remain true to the life of the Son of God in us, not true to our own aims and ends. There is always a danger of mistaking our own aim and end for the aim of the life God in us. PR. 43

If God has made your cup sweet, drink it with grace; if He has made it bitter, drink it in communion with Him. RTR. 49

It is one thing to go through a crisis grandly, and another thing to go through every day glorifying God when nobody is paying any attention to you. RTR. 51

Circumstances make a man reveal what spirit he is of. Crises reveal character more quickly than anything else. SA. 101

. . . you cannot locate yourself, you are placed in circumstances over which you have no control. You do not choose your own heredity or your own disposition, these things are beyond your control, and yet these are the things which influence you. You may rake the bottom of the universe, but you cannot explain things; they are wild, there is nothing rational about them. We cannot get to the bottom of things; we cannot get behind the before of birth or the after of death; therefore the wise man is the one who trusts the wisdom of God, not his own wits. SHH. 121

The proof that God has altered our disposition is not that we persuade ourselves He has, but that we prove He has when circumstances put us to the test. SSM. 30

Week 10

COMMON SENSE

Blessed are those who have not seen and yet have believed.

—John 20:29

For we walk by faith, not by sight.

—2 Corinthians 5:7

The God I infer by my common sense has no power over me at all. DI. 12

The majority of us do not enthrone God, we enthrone commonsense. We make our decisions and then ask the real God to bless our god's decision. HG. 29

If I enthrone common sense as God, there are great regions of my life in which I do not countenance God. HG. 37

The Bible speaks about the Redemption, viz., what God has done for the human race, not about what we can get at by our common sense. HGM. 63

We never turn to God unless we are desperate, we turn to common sense, to one another, to helps and means and assistances, but when we do turn to the Lord it is always in desperation. The desperation of consecration is reached when we realize our indolence and our reluctance in coming to God. HGM. 71

The danger with us is that we want to water down the things that Jesus says and make them mean something in accordance with common sense; if it were only common sense, it was not worth while for Him to say it. MUH. 147

Common sense is not faith, and faith is not common sense; they stand in the relation of the natural and the spiritual; of impulse and inspiration. Nothing Jesus Christ ever said is common sense, it is revelation sense, and it reaches the shores where common sense fails. MUH. 304

To debate with God and trust common sense is moral blasphemy against God. NKW. 11

How many amateur providences there are!—'I must do this and that, and this one must not do this and that,' and God retires and lets us go our own way. When we say—'But it is common sense to do this and that,' we make our common sense almighty God, and God has to retire right out, then after a while He comes back and asks us if we are satisfied. There must not be a bit of that order left. God totally re-creates us on the inside until "all things are of God." OBH. 100

The reason we know so little about God's wisdom is that we will only trust Him as far as we can work things out according to our own reasonable common sense. OPG. 35

The Lord Jesus Christ is not a commonsense fact, that is, we do not understand Him by means of our common sense. PR. 19

In order to get scientific knowledge we must use our common sense; but if we are going to know the facts with which Jesus Christ deals, the facts which He says belong to the Kingdom of God, we must have them revealed to us. 'Marvel not that I say unto you, You must be born again before you can come into contact with the domain in which I live.' PR. 20

Never let common sense obtrude and push the Son of God on one side. Common sense is a gift which God gave to human nature; but it is not the gift of His Son; never enthrone common sense. The Son detects the Father; common sense never yet detected the Father and never will. RTR. 18

Every time you venture out in the life of faith you will find something in your common sense cares that flatly contradicts your faith. RTR. 68

It is appalling to find spiritual people when they come into a crisis taking an ordinary common-sense standpoint as if Jesus Christ had never lived or died. SHH. 65

We hear it said that Jesus Christ taught nothing contrary to common sense: everything Jesus Christ taught was contrary to common sense. Not one thing in the Sermon on the Mount is common sense. The basis of Christianity is neither common sense nor rationalism, it springs from another centre, viz. a personal relationship to God in Christ Jesus in which everything is ventured on from a basis that is not seen. We are told that God expects us to use our "sanctified common sense"; but if we mean that that is Christianity, we will have to come to the conclusion that Jesus Christ was mad. SHH. 141

If you listen to the talk of the day in which we live you find it is sagacious common sense that rules, the spiritual standpoint is taboo, like a fairy-story. SHL. 94

We live in two universes: the universe of common-sense in which we come in contact with things by our senses, and the universe of revelation with which we come in contact by faith. The wisdom of God fits the two universes exactly, the one interprets the other. SSM. 48

. . . when we come to the domain which Jesus Christ reveals, no amount of studying or curiosity will avail an atom, our ordinary common-sense faculties are of no use, we cannot see God or taste God, we can dispute with Him, but we cannot get at Him by our senses at all, and common-sense is apt to say there is nothing other than this universe. SSM. 49

Faith is our personal confidence in a Being Whose character we know, but Whose ways we cannot trace by common-sense. SSM. 66

If a man is going to do anything worth while, there are times when he has to risk everything on a leap, and in the spiritual world Jesus Christ demands that we risk everything we hold by our common-sense and leap into what He says. Immediately we do, we find that what He says fits on as solidly as our common-sense. SSM. 71

Jesus sums up common-sense carefulness in a man indwelt by the Spirit of God as infidelity. SSM. 72

At the bar of common-sense Jesus Christ's statements are those of a fool; but bring them to the bar of faith and the Word of God, and you begin to find with awestruck spirit that they are the words of God. SSM. 74

CONSCIENCE

The purpose of the commandment is love from a pure heart, from a good conscience, and from sincere faith.

—1 Timothy 1:5

◆

The most universal thing among men is conscience, and the Cross is God's conscience in supreme energy. AUG. 59

Another standard of authority is that of conscience, or 'the inner light'—what Socrates called 'the presiding daemon,' an un-get-at-able, indefinable spirit which gives liberty or check to whatever a man feels impelled to do. BE. 13

Conscience is a constituent in a natural man, but a Christian is judged by his personal relationship to God, not by his conscience. BFB. 27

Conscience is the 'eye of the soul,' and the orbit of conscience, that marvellous recorder, is the heart. BP. 143

Probably the best illustration of conscience is the human eye. The eye records what it looks at, and conscience may be pictured as the eye of the soul recording what it looks at, and, like the eye, it will always record exactly what it is turned towards. BP. 194

Conscience is the innate law in human nature whereby man knows he is known. BP. 194

The phrase, 'Conscience can be educated,' is a truth that is half error. Strictly speaking, conscience cannot be educated. What is altered and educated is a man's reasoning. A man reasons not only on what his senses bring him, but on what the record of his conscience brings him. Immediately you face a man with the 'white light' of Jesus Christ (white is pure, true light, and embraces all shades of colour), his conscience records exactly what he sees, his reason is startled and amazed, and his conscience condemns him from every standpoint. BP. 196

Conscience is the standard by which men and women are to be judged until they are brought into contact with the Lord Jesus Christ. BP. 202

It is not sufficient for a Christian to live up to the light of his conscience; he must live in a sterner light, the light of the Lord Jesus Christ. BP. 202

My conscience makes me know what I ought to do, but it does not empower me to do it. DI. 26

We are never told to walk in the light of conscience, but to walk in the light of the Lord. HG. 16

Conscience is not peculiarly a Christian thing, it is a natural asset, it is the faculty in a man that fits on to the highest he knows. HGM. 76

Never go contrary to your conscience, no matter how absurd it may be in the eyes of others. MFL. 37

Conscience is that faculty in a man that attaches itself to the highest he knows and tells him what the highest he knows demands that he does. MFL. 45

If the voice of God does not correspond with what conscience says, I need pay no attention to it; but when it says the same thing as conscience, I must either obey or be damned in that particular. NKW. 53

Conscience is the faculty of the spirit that fits itself on to the highest a man knows, whether he be an agnostic or a Christian; every man has a conscience, although every man does not know God. OBH. 67

When conscience has been enlightened by the Son of God being formed in me, I have to make an effort to keep my conscience so sensitive that I obey that which I perceive to be God's will. I have to be so keen in the scent of the Lord, so sensitive to the tiniest touch of His Spirit, that I know what I should do. If I keep my soul inwardly open to God, then when I come in contact with the affairs of life outside, I know immediately what I should do; if I do not, I am to blame. OBH. 68

We avoid forming a sensitive conscience when we say—'Oh well, God cannot expect me to do this thing, He has not told me to do it.' How do we expect God to tell us? The word is "not in heaven . . . neither is it beyond the sea . . . but the word is very nigh unto thee, in thy mouth, and in thy heart, that thou mayest do it." OBH. 68

The sensitiveness of conscience is maintained by the habit of always being open towards God. At the peril of your soul you allow one thing to obscure your inner communion with God. Drop it whatever it is and see that you keep your inner vision clear. OBH. 69

Conscience is the eye of the soul recording what it looks at, but if what Ruskin calls "the innocence of the eye" is lost, then the recording of conscience may be distorted. If I continually twist the organ of my soul's recording, it will become perverted. If I do a wrong thing often enough, I cease to realise the wrong in it. A bad man can be perfectly happy in his badness. That is what a seared conscience means. OBH. 69

When Our Lord is presented to the conscience, the first thing conscience does is to rouse the will, and the will agrees with God always. You say—'I do not know whether my will is in agreement with God'—look to Jesus, and you will find that your will and your conscience are in agreement with God every time. OBH. 129

Before a man is rightly related to God, his conscience may be a source of torture and distress to him, but when he is born again it becomes a source of joy and delight because he realizes that not only are his will and his conscience in agreement with God, but that God's will *is* his will, and the life is as natural as breathing, it is a life of proving, or making out, what is "the good, and acceptable, and perfect will of God." OBH. 130

'If only God would not be so holy as my conscience tells me He is.' It is a mixed-up certainty, I know I am not right with God and I don't want to be—and yet I do. OPG. 8

The man who has done wrong has such a guilty conscience that he imagines everything is against him: everything *is* against him—God is against him, every bit of earth is against him; he stands absolutely alone. OPG. 11

Some of us have a social conscience, we are shocked at moral crime; some of us have a religious conscience, we are shocked at the things that go against our creeds. The conscience formed in us by the Holy Spirit makes us amazingly sensitive to the things that tell against the honour of God. PS. 23

The eye in the body records exactly what it looks at. The eye simply records, and the record is according to the light thrown on what it looks at. Conscience in the eye of the soul which looks out on what it is taught is God, and how conscience records depends entirely upon what light is thrown upon God. Our Lord Jesus Christ is the only true light on God. When a man sees Jesus Christ he does not get a new conscience, but a totally new light is thrown upon God, and conscience records accordingly, with the result that he is absolutely upset by conviction of sin. PS. 61

One effect of the disturbance caused by the light of conscience is to drive us into the outside hubbub of things. In the early days of Christianity men brooded on their sins, nowadays psychologists tell us the more wholesome way is to forget all about sin—fling yourself into the work of the world. Rushing into work in order to deaden conscience is characteristic of the life we live to-day. 'Live the simple life; keep a healthy body; never let your conscience be disturbed; for any sake keep away from religious meetings; don't bring before us the morbid tendency of things.' We shall find that the morbid tendency of things is the conviction of the Holy Ghost. PS. 63

When conscience begins to be awakened by God, we either become subtle hypocrites or saints, that is, either we let God's law working through conscience bring us to the place where we can be put right, or we begin to hoodwink ourselves, to affect a religious pose, not before other people, but before ourselves, in order to appease conscience—anything to be kept out of the real presence of God because wherever He comes, He disturbs. PS. 63

. . . when conscience is illuminated by the Holy Ghost, these three amazing articles—God is Love, God is Holy, God is Near—are brought straight down to our inner life and we can neither look up nor down for terror. PS. 66

"Conscience is the innate law in human nature whereby man knows he is known." SA. 44

Conscience is best thought of as the eye of the soul recording what it looks at; it will always record exactly what it is turned towards. SA. 44

If we keep our individual consciences open towards God as He is revealed in Jesus Christ, God will bring hundreds of other souls into oneness with Himself through us. SA. 53

Week 12

CROSS

For the message of the cross is foolishness to those who are perishing, but to us who are being saved it is the power of God.

—1 Corinthians 1:18

The central keystone for all Time and Eternity on which the whole purpose of God depends is the Cross. AUG. 39

The aspect of the cross in discipleship is lost altogether in the present-day view of following Jesus. The cross is looked upon as something beautiful and simple instead of a stern heroism. Our Lord never said it was easy to be a Christian; He warned men that they would have to face a variety of hardships, which He termed 'bearing the cross.' AUG. 49

What the Cross was to our Lord such also in measure was it to be to those who followed Him. The cross is the pain involved in doing the will of God. AUG. 51

Most of our emphasis to-day is on what Our Lord's death means to us: the thing that is of importance is that we understand what God means in the Cross. AUG. 56

The Cross of Christ is the Self-revelation of God, the way God has given Himself. AUG. 59

Our cross is something that comes only with the peculiar relationship of a disciple to Jesus. It is the sign that we have denied our right to ourselves and are determined to manifest that we are no longer our own, we have given away for ever our right to ourselves to Jesus Christ. AUG. 97

Either the Cross is the only way there is of explaining God, the only way of explaining Jesus Christ, and of explaining the human race, or there is nothing in it at all. BE. 61

There is nothing more certain in Time or Eternity than what Jesus Christ did on the Cross: He switched the whole human race back into right relationship to God and made the basis of human life Redemptive, consequently any member of the human race can get into touch with God *now.* BE. 61

If the human race apart from the Cross is all right, then the Redemption was a useless waste. BE. 61

All heaven is interested in the Cross of Christ, all hell terribly afraid of it, while men are the only beings who more or less ignore its meaning. BE. 119

The Cross did not *happen* to Jesus: He came on purpose for it. BSG. 40

The death of Jesus Christ holds the secret of the mind of God. BSG. 49

The Cross is a tragedy to man, but a tremendous triumph to God, an absolute triumph. BSG. 52

To ignore the Cross in either living or thinking is to become a traitor to Jesus Christ. BSG. 67

The Cross of Jesus Christ stands unique and alone. His Cross is not our cross. Our cross is that we manifest before the world the fact that we are sanctified to do nothing but the will of God. By means of His Cross, our cross becomes our divinely appointed privilege. CD. VOL. 1, 90

The Bible says that God Himself accepted the responsibility for sin; the Cross is the proof that He did. It cost Jesus Christ to the last drop of blood to deal with "the vast evil of the world." CHI. 45

The true portrayal is that the Cross is not the cross of a man, but the Cross of God. The tragedy of the Cross is the hurt to God. In the Cross God and sinful man merge; consequently the Cross is of more importance than all the world's civilisations. CHI. 45

The Cross of Christ is God's last and endless Word. There the prince of this world is judged, there sin is killed, and pride is done to death, there lust is frozen, and self-interest slaughtered, not one can get through. DI. 66

The Cross of Christ alone makes me holy, and it does so the second I am willing to let it. GW. 54

On the Cross men crucified the Son of God—and God forgave them while they did it. GW. 85

The Cross of Christ pronounced final and irrevocable judgement against the prince of this world. GW. 129

. . . our human life viewed from a moral standpoint is a tragedy, and that preaching precepts while we ignore the Cross of Jesus Christ is like giving "a pill to cure an earthquake," or a poultice for a cancer. HG. 56

The Cross is the crystallized point in history where Eternity merges with Time. HG. 98

The cross is the gift of Jesus to His disciples and it can only bear one aspect: 'I am not my own.' HG. 99

We talk about the joys and comforts of salvation; Jesus Christ talks about taking up the cross and following Him. HGM. 129

Re-state to yourself what you believe, then do away with as much of it as possible, and get back to the bedrock of the Cross of Christ. In external history the Cross is an infinitesimal thing; from the Bible point of view it is of more importance than all the empires of the world. MUH. 330

Very few of us have any understanding of the reason why Jesus Christ died. If sympathy is all that human beings need, then the Cross of Christ is a farce, there was no need for it. What the world needs is not "a little bit of love," but a surgical operation. MUH. 355

The Cross of Christ reveals that the blazing centre of the love of God is the holiness of God, not His kindness and compassion. If the Divine love pretends I am all right when I am all wrong, then I have a keener sense of justice than the Almighty. PH. 65

In the Cross we may see the dimensions of Divine love. The Cross is not the cross of a man, but the exhibition of the heart of God. At the back of the wall of the world stands God with His arms outstretched, and every man driven there is driven into the arms of God. The Cross of Jesus is the supreme evidence of the love of God. PH. 65

The New Testament emphasises the death of Christ because the Cross is the Centre that reveals the very heart of God. PH. 136

In the Cross God is revealed not as One reigning in calm disdain above all the squalors of earth, but as One Who suffers more keenly than the keenest sufferer—"a man of sorrows, and acquainted with grief." PH. 137

The Cross of Jesus Christ is not the cross of a martyr, but the door whereby God keeps open house for the universe. Anyone can go in through that door. PR. 25

Through His Cross He prepared a place for us to "sit with Him in the heavenly places, in Christ Jesus" *now,* not by and bye. PR. 82

The cross we have to carry is that we have deliberately given up our right to ourselves to Jesus Christ. PR. 92

Our cross is what we hold before the world, viz., the fact that we are sanctified to do nothing but God's will. We have given away our right to ourselves for ever, and the cross we take up is a sign in heaven, on earth and to hell, that we are His and our own no longer. PR. 102

We cannot be saved by consecration, or by praying, or by giving ourselves up to God. We can only be saved by the Cross of Jesus Christ. PR. 107

The Cross is the point where God and sinful man merge with a crash, and the way to life is opened, but the crash is on the heart of God. God is always the sufferer. PR. 107

Our cross is the steady exhibition of the fact that we are not our own but Christ's, and we know it, and are determined to be unenticed from living a life of dedication to Him. This is the beginning of the emergence of the real life of faith. PS. 38

When a so-called rationalist points out sin and iniquity and disease and death, and he says "How does God answer that?" you have always a fathomless answer—the Cross of Christ. RTR. 87

To ten men who talk about the character of Jesus there is only one who will talk about His Cross. SA. 35

The Cross is the presentation of God having done His "bit," that which man could never do. SA. 38

The cross is the deliberate recognition of what my personal life is for, viz., to be given to Jesus Christ; I have to take up that cross daily and prove that I am no longer my own. Individual independence has gone, and all that is left is personal passionate devotion to Jesus Christ through identification with His Cross. SHL. 79

Week 13

DISCIPLESHIP

Go therefore and make disciples of all the nations.
—Matthew 28:19

Whenever Our Lord talked about discipleship He prefaced it with an 'IF,' never with an emphatic assertion, 'You must.' Discipleship carries an option with it. AUG. 49

There is a method of making disciples which is not sanctioned by Our Lord. It is an excessive pressing of people to be reconciled to God in a way that is unworthy of the dignity of the Gospel. The pleading is on the line of: Jesus has done so much for us, cannot we do something out of gratitude to Him? This method of getting people into relationship to God out of pity for Jesus is never recognized by Our Lord. It does not put sin in its right place, nor does it put the more serious aspect of the Gospel in its right place. Our Lord never pressed anyone to follow Him unconditionally; nor did He wish to be followed merely out of an impulse of enthusiasm. He never pleaded, He never entrapped; He made discipleship intensely narrow, and pointed out certain things which could never be in those who followed Him. Today there is a tendency to take the harshness out of Our Lord's statements. What Jesus says *is* hard; it is only easy when it comes to those who are His disciples. AUG. 49

When we are young a hurricane or thunderstorm impresses us as being very powerful, yet the strength of a rock is infinitely greater than that of a hurricane. The same is true with regard to discipleship. The strength there is not the strength of activity but the strength of *being*. AUG. 123

'If you are My disciple, you will insist only on your right to give up your rights.' BP. 205

The distinction between a saved soul and a disciple is fundamental. The stern conditions laid down by Our Lord for discipleship are not the conditions of salvation; discipleship is a much closer and more conscious relationship. BSG. 23

God Almighty regenerates men's souls; we make disciples. CD. VOL. 2, 110

God is apparently not very careful whom He uses or what He uses for the work of regeneration; but none but the master workmen, that is, the saints, can make disciples. CD. VOL. 2, 110

There is no royal road to sainthood and discipleship. The way of the Cross is the only way. We see God only from a pure heart, never from an able intellect. CD. VOL. 2, 113

To make disciples, then, we must have been made disciples ourselves. There is no royal road to sainthood and discipleship. The way of the Cross is the only way. We see God only from a pure heart, never from an able intellect. CD. VOL. 2, 113

One life straight through to God on the ground of discipleship is more satisfactory in His sight than numbers who are saved but go no further. CHI. 18

The one mark of discipleship is the mastership of Jesus—His right to me from the crown of my head to the sole of my foot. DI. 34

Discipleship and salvation are two different things: a disciple is one who, realizing the meaning of the Atonement, deliberately gives himself up to Jesus Christ in unspeakable gratitude. DI. 34

A disciple is one who not only proclaims God's truth, but one who manifests that he is no longer his own, he has been "bought with a price." DI. 35

'I will make the place of My feet glorious'—among the poor, the devil-possessed, the mean, the decrepit, the selfish, the sinful, the misunderstanding—that is where Jesus went, and that is exactly where He will take you if you are His disciple. GW. 97

. . . a disciple is committed to much more than belief in Jesus; he is committed to his Lord's view of the world, of men, of God and of sin. HG. 64

If we were to estimate ourselves from our Lord's standpoint, very few of us would be considered disciples. HG. 71

Men do not care a bit for Jesus Christ's notion of their lives, and Jesus does not care for our notions. There is the antagonism. If we were to estimate ourselves from our Lord's standpoint, very few of us would be considered disciples. HG. 71

Jesus Christ always talked about discipleship with an 'If.' We are at perfect liberty to toss our spiritual head and say, 'No, thank you, that is a bit too stern for me,' and the Lord will never say a word, we can do exactly what we like. He will never plead, but the opportunity is there, 'If . . .' IWP. 61

Discipleship must always be a personal matter; we can never become disciples in crowds, or even in twos. It is so easy to talk about what 'we' mean to do—'we' are going to do marvellous things, and it ends in none of us doing anything. The great element of discipleship is the personal one. IWP. 104

The following in the steps of Jesus in discipleship is so great a mystery that few enter into it. IWP. 106

Those of us who have entered into a conscious experience of the salvation of Jesus by the grace of God, whose whole inner life is drawn towards God, have the privilege of being disciples, if we will. IWP. 110

The great stumbling-block in the way of some people being simple disciples is that they are gifted, so gifted that they won't trust God. So clear away all those things from the thought of discipleship; we all have absolutely equal privileges, and there is no limit to what God can do in and through us. IWP. 111

. . . the conditions of discipleship are not the conditions for salvation. We are perfectly at liberty to say, 'No, thank you, I am much obliged for being delivered from hell, very thankful to escape the abominations of sin, but when it comes to these conditions it is rather too much; I have my own interests in life, my own possessions.' IWP. 118

Discipling is our work. When God's great redemptive work has issued in lives in salvation and sanctification, then the work of the worker begins. It is then that we find the meaning of being 'workers together with Him.' LG. 91

Discipleship is based on devotion to Jesus Christ, not on adherence to a belief or a creed. MUH. 171

If we are going to live as disciples of Jesus, we have to remember that all noble things are difficult. The Christian life is gloriously difficult, but the difficulty of it does not make us faint and cave in, it rouses us up to overcome. MUH. 189

The great privilege of discipleship is that I can sign on under His Cross, and that means death to sin. Get alone with Jesus and either tell Him that you do not want sin to die out in you; or else tell Him that at all costs you want to be identified with His death. Immediately you transact in confident faith in what Our Lord did on the Cross, a supernatural identification with His death takes place, and you will know with a knowledge that passeth knowledge that your "old man" is crucified with Christ. MUH. 358

We shall not always be respected if we are disciples of Jesus. OBH. 60

If you want a good time in this world, do not become a disciple of Jesus. OBH. 61

Jesus Christ's last command to His disciples was not to go and save the world, the saving is done; He told them to go and make disciples. OBH. 61

Not what the disciple says in public prayer, not what he preaches from pulpit or platform, not what he writes on paper or in letters, but what he is in his heart which God alone knows, determines

God's revelation of Himself to him. Character determines revelation. PH. 11

The first step to sacramental discipleship is the crowning of Jesus as Lord. PH. 137

The secret of sacramental discipleship is to be so abandoned to the disposition of God in us that He can use us as broken bread and poured out wine for His purpose in the world, even as He broke the life of His own Son to redeem us. PH. 139

The secret of a disciple's life is devotion to Jesus Christ, and the very nature of the life is that it is unobstrusive; it falls into the ground and dies: but presently it springs up and alters the whole landscape. PH. 145

A man may be saved without being a disciple, and it is the point of discipleship that is always kicked against. Our Lord is not talking of eternal salvation, but of the possibility of our being of temporal worth to Himself. PR. 103

Jesus Christ always said, "*If* any man will be My disciple"—He did not clamour for him, or button-hole him. He never took a man off his guard, or used a revivalistic meeting to get a man out of his wits and then say, "Believe in Me," but, "Take time and consider what you are doing; if you would be My disciple, you must lose your 'soul,' i.e., your way of reasoning about things." SA. 87

The romance of the life of a disciple is not an external fascination but an inner martyrdom. SHH. 43

If we are to be disciples of Jesus Christ, our independent right to our individual self must go, and go altogether. SHL. 84

It never cost a disciple anything to follow Jesus; to talk about cost when you are in love with anyone is an insult. SHL. 109

The motive of a disciple is to be well-pleasing to God. SSM. 16

If I let God alter my heredity, I will become devoted to Him, and Jesus Christ will have gained a disciple. SSM. 29

The Example of a disciple is God Almighty and no one less; not the best man you know, nor the finest saint you ever read about, but God Himself. SSM. 51

Following Jesus Christ is a risk absolutely; we must yield right over to Him, and that is where our infidelity comes in, we will not trust what we cannot see, we will not believe what we cannot trace, then it is all up with our discipleship. SSM. 71

There is a difference between salvation and discipleship. A man can be saved by God's grace without becoming a disciple of Jesus Christ. Discipleship means a personal dedication of the life to Jesus Christ. Men are 'saved so as by fire' who have not been worth anything to God in their actual lives. SSM. 93

"If ye love Me, ye will keep My commandments." Jesus makes this the test of discipleship. The motto over our side of the gate of life is—'All God's commands I can obey.' SSM. 96

We have to do our utmost as disciples to prove that we appreciate God's utmost for us, and to learn never to allow 'I can't' to creep in. 'Oh, I am not a saint, I can't do that.' If that thought comes in, we are a disgrace to Jesus Christ. God's salvation is a glad thing, but it is a holy, difficult thing that tests us for all we are worth. SSM. 96

The walk of a disciple is gloriously difficult, but gloriously certain. SSM. 104

In our Lord's calling of a disciple He never puts personal holiness in the front, He puts in the front absolute annihilation of my right to myself and unconditional identification with Himself—such a relationship with Him that there is no other relationship on earth in comparison. SSY. 56

As long as we have the endeavour and the strain and the dead-set purpose of being disciples, it is almost certain we are not. Our Lord's making of a disciple is supernatural; He does not build on any natural capacity. SSY. 64

Discipleship is built not on natural affinities but entirely on the supernatural grace of God. The one characteristic of discipleship is likeness to Jesus Christ. SSY. 66

We are called to be unobtrusive disciples, not heroes. When we are right with God, the tiniest thing done out of love to Him is more precious to Him than any eloquent preaching of a sermon. We have introduced into our conception of Christianity heroic notions that come from paganism and not from the teaching of Our Lord. SSY. 68

Many of us want to be disciples, but we do not want to come by way of His atoning Death; we do not want to be compelled to be orthodox to the Cross of Christ, to drink the cup that He drank. But there is no other way. We must be regenerated, supernaturally made all over again, before we can be His disciples. SSY. 71

We have become so taken up with the idea of being prepared for something in the future that that is the conception we have of discipleship. It is true, but it is also untrue. The attitude of the Christian life is that we must be prepared *now,* this second; this is the time. SSY. 72

It is easy to talk, easy to have fine thoughts; but none of that means being a disciple. Being a disciple is to be something that is an infinite satisfaction to Jesus every minute, whether in secret or in public. SSY. 72

Jesus Christ is the only One Who has the right to tell us what it means to be His, and in Luke 14:26–33 He is laying down the conditions of discipleship. These conditions are summed up in one astounding word—'*hate.*' 'If any man cometh unto me, and hateth not . . .' (i.e., a hatred of every good thing that divides the heart from loyalty to Jesus) 'he cannot be my disciple.' SSY. 167

Week 14

FAITH

Without faith it is impossible to please Him, for he who comes to God must believe that He is, and that He is a rewarder of those who diligently seek Him.

—Hebrews 11:6

We begin our religious life by believing our beliefs, we accept what we are taught without questioning; but when we come up against things we begin to be critical, and find out that the beliefs, however right, are not right for us because we have not bought them by suffering. What we take for granted is never ours until we have bought it by pain. A thing is worth just what it costs. AUG. 78

It is absurd to tell a man he must believe this and that; in the meantime he can't! Scepticism is produced by telling men what to believe. We are in danger of putting the cart before the horse and saying a man must believe certain things before he can be a Christian; his beliefs are the effect of his being a Christian, not the cause of it. Our Lord's word 'believe' does not refer to an intellectual act, but to a moral act. With Him 'to believe' means 'to commit.' AUG. 78

Faith is deliberate confidence in the character of God Whose ways you cannot understand at the time. 'I don't know why God allows what He does, but I will stick to my faith in His character no matter how contradictory things look.' AUG. 84

Faith is not a conscious thing, it springs from a personal relationship and is the unconscious result of believing someone. AUG. 84

We sentimentally believe, and believe, and believe, and nothing happens. We pray "Lord, increase our faith," and we try to pump up the faith, but it does not come. What is wrong? The moral surrender has not taken place. AUG. 112

The Great Life is begun when we believe, belief cannot be pumped up. If we in our hearts believe in Jesus Christ, not *about* Him, but *in* Him, "*He* is all right anyway," it is an evidence that God is at work in our souls. AUG. 115

The one thing that tells is the great fundamental rock: "Believe also in Me." Many know a good deal about salvation, but not much about this intense patience of 'hanging in' in perfect certainty to the fact that what Jesus Christ says is true. AUG. 117

All our efforts to pump up faith in the word of God is without quickening, without illumination. You reason to yourself and say, 'Now God says this and I am going to believe it,' and you believe it, and re-believe it, and re-re-believe it, and nothing happens, simply because the vital power that makes the words living is not there. BE. 72

Traditional belief has the root of the matter in it, but its form is often archaic. We begin our religious life by believing our beliefs, we accept what we are taught without questioning; then when we come up against things we begin to be critical and we find that however right those beliefs are, they are not right for us because we have not bought them by suffering. BFB. 55

Faith in God is a terrific venture in the dark; I have to believe that God is good in spite of all that contradicts it in my experience. BFB. 100

The reason people disbelieve God is not because they do not understand with their heads—we understand very few things with our heads, but because they have turned their hearts in another direction. BP. 144

Faith is built on heroism. CD. VOL. 2, 87

The life of faith is the life of a soul who has given over every other life but the life of faith. Faith is not an action of the mind, nor of the heart, nor of the will, nor of the sentiment, it is the centering of the entire man in God. CD. VOL. 2, 149

Belief must be the will to believe, and I can never will to believe without a violent effort on my part to dissociate myself from all my old ways of looking at things and putting myself right over on to God. CHI. 28

The proof that we have a healthy vigorous faith is that we are expressing it in our lives, and bearing testimony with our lips as to how it came about. CHI. 55

The business of faith is to convert Truth into reality. CHI. 58

Faith means that I commit myself to Jesus, project myself absolutely on to Him, sink or swim—and you do both, you sink out of yourself and swim into Him. CHI. 60

You can't pump up faith out of your own heart. Whenever faith is starved in your soul it is because you are not in contact with Jesus; get in contact with Him and lack of faith will go in two seconds. CHI. 60

We begin our Christian life by believing what we are told to believe, then we have to go on to so assimilate our beliefs that they work out in a way that redounds to the glory of God. The danger is in multiplying the acceptation of beliefs we do not make our own. CHI. 125

I have no right to say I believe in God unless I order my life as under His all-seeing Eye. DI. 1

Belief is the abandonment of all claim to merit. That is why it is so difficult to believe. DI. 1

Watch the things you say you can't believe, and then recall the things you accept without thinking, e.g., your own existence. DI. 3

When once you come in contact with Jesus you are not conscious of any effort to believe in Him. DI. 4

When a man says he can't believe, don't argue with him on what he doesn't believe but ask him what he does believe, and proceed from that point; disbelief as often arises from temperament as from sin.

Every man believes in a good character, then refer to Jesus Christ as the best character in history, and ask him to believe that what He says is likely to be true, and get him to transact business on that. DI. 4

Beware of worshipping Jesus as the Son of God, and professing your faith in Him as the Saviour of the world, while you blaspheme Him by the complete evidence in your daily life that He is powerless to do anything in and through you. DI. 5

The great paralysis of our heart is unbelief. Immediately I view anything as inevitable about any human being, I am an unbeliever. DI. 5

Believe what you do believe and stick to it, but don't profess to believe more than you intend to stick to. If you say you believe God is love, stick to it, though all Providence becomes a pandemonium shouting that God is cruel to allow what He does. DI. 12

In the face of problems as they are, we see in Jesus Christ an exhibition of where our faith is to be placed, viz., in a God whose ways we do not understand. DI. 12

It is easy to say we believe in God as long as we remain in the little world we choose to live in; but get out into the great world of facts, the noisy world where people are absolutely indifferent to you, where your message is nothing more than a crazy tale belonging to a bygone age, can you believe God there? GW. 92

To be able to state explicitly in words what you know by faith is an impossibility; if you can state it in words, it is not faith. GW. 108

It is the trial of our faith that is precious. If we go through the trial, there is so much wealth laid up in our heavenly banking account to draw upon when the next test comes. HG. 18

We all have faith in good principles, in good management, in good common sense, but who amongst us has faith in Jesus Christ? Physical courage is grand, moral courage is grander, but the man who trusts Jesus Christ in the face of the terrific problems of life is worth a whole crowd of heroes. HG. 61

If you deal with people without any faith in Jesus Christ it will crush the very life out of you. If we believe in Jesus Christ, we can face every problem the world holds. HG. 66

Our practical life is to be moulded by our belief in the Redemption, and our declared message will be in accordance with our belief. If we say we believe "It is finished" we must not blaspheme God by unbelief in any domain of our practical life. HG. 95

To believe that the Lord God omnipotent reigneth and redeemeth is the end of all possible panic, moral, intellectual or spiritual. HG. 104

Nowadays the tendency is to switch away from "the righteousness which is of God by faith," and to put the emphasis on doing things. You cannot do anything at all that does not become, in the rugged language of Isaiah, "as filthy rags," if it is divorced from living faith in Jesus Christ. If we have the tiniest hankering after believing we can be justified by what we have done, we are on the wrong side of the Cross. HG. 108

A man's beliefs are the effect of his being a Christian, not the cause of it. HGM. 28

It is not faith to believe that God is making things work together for good unless we are up against things that are ostensibly working for bad. HGM. 32

Unless I receive a totally new Spirit, all the believing and correct doctrine in the world will never alter me; it is not a question of believing, but of *receiving*. HGM. 34

We have no faith at all until it is proved, proved through conflict and in no other way. HGM. 58

Faith is confidence in God before you see God emerging, therefore the nature of faith is that it must be tried. HGM. 70

Belief is not that God can do the thing, but belief *in God*. HGM. 71

Faith cannot be intellectually defined; faith is the inborn capacity to see God behind everything, the wonder that keeps you an eternal child. HGM. 143

Faith means keeping absolutely specklessly right with God, He does all the rest. LG. 73

No one is surprised over what God does when once he has faith in Him. LG. 149

We have to learn how to 'go out' of everything, out of convictions, out of creeds, out of experiences, out of everything, until so far as our faith is concerned, there is nothing between us and God. LG. 151

Faith gets us into the middle, which is God and God's purpose. MFL. 64

Never run away with the idea that it does not matter much what we believe or think; it does. What we think and believe, we *are;* not what we say we think and believe, but what we really do think and believe, we are; there is no divorce at all. To believe, in the sense our Lord used the word, is never an intellectual act but a moral act. MFL. 84

A spiritually minded man will never come to you with the demand—"Believe this and that;" but with the demand that you square your life with the standards of Jesus. We are not asked to believe the Bible, but to believe the One Whom the Bible reveals. MUH. 127

Believe steadfastly on Him and all you come up against will develop your faith. MUH. 242

Faith is unutterable trust in God, trust which never dreams that he will not stand by us. MUH. 242

Every time you venture out in the life of faith, you will find something in your common-sense circumstances that flatly contradicts your faith. Common sense is not faith, and faith is not common sense, they stand in the relation of the natural and the spiritual. MUH. 242

I am not saved by believing; I realize I am saved by believing. MUH. 302

Faith in the Bible is faith in God against everything that contradicts Him—I will remain true to God's character whatever He may do.

"Though He slay me, yet will I trust Him"—this is the most sublime utterance of faith in the whole of the Bible. MUH. 305

Faith that is sure of itself is not faith; faith that is sure of God is the only faith there is. MUH. 356

We must remember that faith in God always demands a concession from us personally. NKW. 17

Faith must be tried, and it is the trial of faith that is precious. If you are faint-hearted, it is a sign you won't play the game, you are fit for neither God nor man because you will face nothing. NKW. 36

There is nothing more heroic than to have faith in God when you can see so many better things in which to have faith. NKW. 45

The whole discipline of the life of faith is to mix together the light of heaven and the sordid actuality of earth. NKW. 45

Faith is not that I see God, but that I know God sees me; that is good enough for me, I will run out and play—a life of absolute freedom. NKW. 60

It is the height of madness from common-sense standpoints to have faith in God. Faith is not a bargain with God—I will trust You if You give me money, but not if You don't. We have to trust in God whether He sends us money or not, whether He gives us health or not. We must have faith in God, not in His gifts. NKW. 61

Beware of the thing that makes you go down before God and sway from side to side spiritually—'I don't know what to do;' then don't do anything. 'I don't see anything;' well, don't look for anything. 'I thought by this time I should see something;' if you don't, be foolish enough to trust in God. NKW. 61

The sure sign that we have no faith in God is that we have no faith in the supernatural. NKW. 66

No man can believe God unless God is in him. NKW. 66

There is only one way to live the life of faith and that is to *live it*. NKW. 70

It is never our merit God looks at but our faith. If there is only one strand of faith amongst all the corruption within us, God will take hold of that one strand. NKW. 80

Weak faith chooses the visible things instead of enduring as seeing Him Who is invisible, and slowly and surely such faith settles down between mammon and righteousness. NKW. 82

Beware of pronouncing any verdict on the life of faith if you are not living it. NKW. 116

Faith is not logical, it works on the line of life and by its very nature must be tried. Never confound the trial of faith with the ordinary discipline of life. Much that we call the trial of our faith is the inevitable result of being alive. NKW. 117

Faith according to the Bible is confidence in God when He is inscrutable and apparently contradictory in His providences. NKW. 117

As long as the soul realises in the simplicity of faith that all that Jesus was and is, is his, then the very life, the very faith, the very holiness of Jesus is imparted to him. OBH. 15

We must never put character in the place of faith, there is a great danger of doing so. Our character can never be meritorious before God: we stand before God on the basis of His grace. Character is the evidence that we are built on the right foundation. OBH. 120

There is no such thing as a *venture* of faith, only a determined *walk with God* by faith. OPG. 19

When we have become rightly related to God, it is the trial of our faith that is precious. OBH. 21

Just as we take food into our bodies and assimilate it, so, Jesus says, we must take Him into our souls. Faith is not seeing food and drink on the table; faith is taking it. OBH. 22

Spiritual character is only made by standing loyal to God's character no matter what distress the trial of faith brings. OPG. 18

It is always easier not to trust; if I can work the thing out for myself then I am not going to trust in God. OPG. 34

When we go through the trial of faith we gain so much wealth in our heavenly banking account, and the more we go through the trial of faith the wealthier we become in the heavenly regions. OBH. 103

If we have faith at all it must be faith in Almighty God; when He has said a thing, He will perform it; we have to remain steadfastly obedient to Him. PH. 41

It is heroism to believe in God. PH. 44

It is easy to *say* God reigns, and then to see Satan, suffering and sin reigning, and God apparently powerless. Belief in God must be tried before it is of value to God or to a child of His. PH. 73

It is a great thing to see physical pluck, and greater still to see moral pluck, but the greatest to see of all is spiritual pluck, to see a man who will stand true to the integrity of Jesus Christ no matter what he is going through. PH. 205

Many of us use religious jargon, we talk about believing in God, but our actual life proves that we do not really believe one tithe of what we profess. PH. 222

When we are standing face to face with Jesus, and He says "Believest thou this?" our faith is as natural as breathing, and we say—'Yes, Lord,' and are staggered and amazed that we are so stupid as not to trust Him before. PH. 226

Faith is not credulity; faith is my personal spirit obeying God. PR. 20

Our beliefs will mock us unless something comes into us from God, because nothing has any power to alter us save the incoming of the life of God. PR. 112

To believe in Jesus means much more than the experience of salvation in any form, it entails a mental and moral commitment to our Lord's view of the world, of the flesh, of the devil, of God, of man, and of the Scriptures. To "believe also in Me" means that we submit our intelligence to Jesus Christ our Lord as He submitted His intelligence to His Father. This does not mean that we do not exercise our reason, but it does mean that we exercise it in submission to Reason Incarnate. PR. 131

Faith is more than an attitude of mind, faith is the complete, passionate, earnest trust of our whole nature in the Gospel of God's grace as it is presented in the Life and Death and Resurrection of our Lord Jesus Christ. RTR. 35

Faith is not intelligent understanding; faith is deliberate commitment to a Person where I see no way. RTR. 36

Unbelief is the most active thing on earth; it is a fretful, worrying, questioning, annoying, self-centred spirit. To believe is to stop all this and let God work. RTR. 44

The New Testament does not say of Jesus Christ, "This man was God Incarnate, and if you don't believe it you will be damned." The New Testament was written for the confirmation of those who believed He was God Incarnate. SA. 32

One of the dangers of denominational teaching is that we are told that before we can be Christians we must believe that Jesus Christ is the son of God, and that the Bible is the Word of God from Genesis to Revelation. Creeds are the effect of our belief, not the cause of it. I do not have to believe all that before I can be a Christian. SA. 35

Bank your faith in God, do the duty that lies nearest and "damn the consequences." SHH. 74

. . . the devil likes to deceive us and limit us in our practical belief as to what Jesus Christ can do. There is no limit to what He can do, absolutely none. *'All things are possible to him that believeth.'* Jesus says that faith in Him is omnipotent. God grant we may get hold of this truth. SHL. 31

You can shut the mouth of the man who has faith in God, but you cannot get away from the fact that he is being kept by God. SHL. 104

Week 15

FORGIVENESS

In Him we have redemption through His blood, the forgiveness of sins, according to the riches of His grace.

—Ephesians 1:7

Forgiveness is the Divine miracle of grace. AUG. 47

If I am forgiven without being altered, forgiveness is not only damaging to me, but a sign of unmitigated weakness in God. BFB. 42

The marvel of conviction of sin, of forgiveness, and of the holiness of God are so interwoven that the only forgiven man is the holy man. If God in forgiving me does not turn me into the standard of the Forgiver, to talk about being saved from hell and made right for heaven is a juggling trick to get rid of the responsibility of seeing that my life justifies God in forgiving me. CHI. 26

The forgiveness of God penetrates to the very heart of His nature and to the very heart of man's nature. That is why God cannot forgive until a man realizes what sin is. DI. 65

Think what God's forgiveness means: it means that He forgets away every sin. GW. 11

Forgiveness is a miracle, because in forgiving a man God imparts to him the power to be exactly the opposite of what he has been: God transmutes the sinner who sinned into the saint who does not sin, consequently the only true repentant man is the holy man. GW. 53

The word 'blood,' which offends so many, speaks of forgiveness of sins. GW. 119

We reason in this way: 'God is so loving that I know He will forgive me.' God is so holy that it is much more likely He will say I must be damned. HG. 105

When we have experienced the unfathomable forgiveness of God for all our wrong, we must exhibit that same forgiveness to others. HGM. 47

God can forgive a man anything but despair that He can forgive him. HGM. 65

Forgiveness is the great message of the Gospel, and it satisfies a man's sense of justice completely. The fundamental factor of Christianity is "the forgiveness of sins." HGM. 100

We may talk as much as we like about forgiveness, but it will never make any difference to us unless we realize that we need it. HGM. 101

God can never forgive the man who does not want to be forgiven. HGM. 101

There is no such thing as God overlooking sin. That is where people make a great mistake with regard to God's love; they say 'God is love and of course He will forgive sin': God is *holy* love and of course He *cannot* forgive sin. Therefore if God does forgive, there must be a reason that justifies Him in doing it. HGM. 102

When we turn to God and say we are sorry, Jesus Christ has pledged His word that we will be forgiven, but the forgiveness is not operative unless we turn, because our turning is the proof that we know we need forgiveness. HGM. 104

The great characteristic of God is not that He says He will pay no more attention to what we have done, but that He forgives us, and in forgiving He is able to deal with our past, with our present and our future. HGM. 105

The distinctive thing about Christianity is forgiveness, not sanctification or my holiness, but forgiveness—the greatest miracle God ever performs through the Redemption. HGM. 105

When God says 'Don't do that any more,' He instils into me the power that enables me not to do it any more, and the power comes by right of what Jesus Christ did on the Cross. That is the unspeakable wonder of the forgiveness of God, and when we become rightly related to God, we are to have the same relationship to our fellow men that God has to us. "And be ye kind one to another, tenderhearted, forgiving one another, even as God for Christ's sake hath forgiven you." HGM. 105

The only ground on which God can forgive us is the tremendous tragedy of the Cross of Christ; to put forgiveness on any other ground is unconscious blasphemy. The only ground on which God can forgive sin and reinstate us in His favour is through the Cross of Christ, and in no other way. MUH. 325

When once you realize all that *it cost God to forgive you,* you will be held as in a vice, constrained by the love of God. MUH. 325

If God were to forgive me my sin without its being atoned for, I should have a greater sense of justice than God. PH. 183

Forgiveness, which is so easy for us to accept, cost God the agony of Calvary. PH. 184

When God forgives, He never casts up at us the mean, miserable things we have done. "I have blotted out, as a thick cloud, thy transgressions, and, as a cloud, thy sins." A cloud cannot be seen when it is gone. PH. 224

The forgiveness of God means that we are forgiven into a new relationship, viz., into identification with God in Christ, so that the forgiven man is the holy man. The only explanation of the forgiveness of God and of the unfathomable depth of His forgetting is the blood of Jesus. We trample the blood of the Son of God under foot if we think we are forgiven in any other way. Forgiveness is the Divine miracle of grace. PH. 224

There is a lot of sentimental talk about God forgiving because He is love: God is so holy that He cannot forgive. God can only destroy for ever the thing that is unlike Himself. The Atonement does not mean that God forgives a sinner and allows him to go on sinning and receiving forgiveness; it means that God saves the sinner and turns him into a saint, i.e. destroys the sinner out of him, and through his conscience he realizes that by the Atonement God has done what He never could have done apart from it. PS. 65

Immediately a man turns to God, Redemption is such that his forgiveness is complete. SA. 18

The background of God's forgiveness is holiness. If God were not holy there would be nothing in His forgiveness. There is no such thing as God overlooking sin; therefore if God does forgive there must be a reason that justifies His doing so. SA. 18

If I am forgiven without being altered by the forgiveness, forgiveness is a damage to me and a sign of the unmitigated weakness of God. SA. 19

God, in forgiving a man, gives him the heredity of His own Son, i.e., He turns him into the standard of the Forgiver. Forgiveness is a revelation—hope for the hopeless; that is the message of the Gospel. SA. 19

The point about Christian forgiveness is not that God puts snow over a dung-heap, but that He turns a man into the standard of the Forgiver. SA. 28

There is a difference between sin and sins; sin is a disposition and is never spoken of as being forgiven; sins are acts for which we are responsible. SA. 105

A man cannot be forgiven for what he is not to blame, but God holds a man responsible for refusing to receive a new heredity when he sees that Jesus Christ can give it to him. SA. 105

The only ground on which God can forgive sin and reinstate us in His favour, is through the Cross of Christ, and in no other way. SSY. 144

Week 16

GIFTS/GIVING

Freely you have received, freely give.

—Matthew 10:8

The Holy Spirit is a gift, remission of sins is a gift, eternal life is a gift, on the ground of the Cross of our Lord and Saviour Jesus Christ. Ignore that, and life is a wayless wilderness, where all our ideals fade and falter, leaving us only a grey, uncertain outlook, gathering to an eternal night. AUG. 93

We must not dictate to Jesus as to where we are going to serve Him. There is a theory abroad to-day that we have to consecrate our gifts to God. We cannot, they are not ours to consecrate; every gift we have has been given to us. Jesus Christ does not take my gifts and use them; He takes me and turns me right about face, and realizes Himself in me for His glory. AUG. 99

It requires the greatest effort, and produces the greatest humility, to receive anything from God, we would much sooner earn it. CHI. 30

As Christians our giving is to be proportionate to all we have received of the infinite giving of God. "Freely ye have received, freely give." Not how much we give, but what we do not give, is the test of our Christianity. When we speak of giving we nearly always think only of money. Money is the life-blood of most of us. We have a remarkable trick—when we give money we don't give sympathy; and when we give sympathy we don't give money. CHI. 77

We have to distinguish between acquiring and receiving. We *acquire* habits of prayer and Bible reading, and we *receive* our salvation, we *receive* the Holy Spirit, we *receive* the grace of God. We give more attention to the things we acquire; all God pays attention to is what we receive. Those things we receive can never be taken from us because God holds those who receive His gifts. DI. 25

We cannot earn things from God, we can only take what is given us. Salvation, sanctification, eternal life, are all gifts wrought out in us through the Atonement. DI. 58

The idea of receiving anything as a gift from God is staggeringly original; we imagine we have to earn things by prayer and obedience. HGM. 14

The Gift of God is the Son of God; the gift from the Gift of God is the Holy Spirit. HGM. 15

The majority of us are not in the place where God can give us 'the hundredfold more.' We say, "A bird in the hand is worth two in the bush," while God is wanting to give us the bush with all the birds in it! HGM. 111

We are never told to consecrate our gifts to God, but we are told to dedicate ourselves. LG. 63

We have the notion that we can consecrate our gifts to God. You cannot consecrate what is not yours; there is only one thing you can consecrate to God, and that is your right to yourself. If you will give God your right to yourself, He will make a holy experiment out of you. God's experiments always succeed. MUH. 165

We have to realize that we cannot earn or win anything from God; we must either receive it as a gift or do without it. The greatest blessing spiritually is the knowledge that we are destitute; until we get there Our Lord is powerless. He can do nothing for us if we think we are sufficient of ourselves, we have to enter into His Kingdom through the door of destitution. As long as we are rich, possessed of anything in the way of pride or independence, God cannot do anything for us. It is only when we get hungry spiritually that we receive the Holy Spirit. MUH. 333

What do we do to earn a gift? Nothing; we take it. If we have the slightest remnant of thinking we can earn it, we will never take it; if we are quite certain we do not deserve it, we will take it. OBH. 22

The nature of love is to give, not to receive. Talk to a lover about giving up anything, and he doesn't begin to understand you! OPG. 45

God and His promises are eternal. "The gift *of God* is eternal life." PH. 76

Salvation is an absolutely free, unmerited gift of God. We would a hundred times rather that God told us to do something than we would accept His salvation as a gift. PR. 107

Much of our modern philanthropy is based on the motive of giving to the poor man because he deserves it, or because we are distressed at seeing him poor. Jesus never taught charity from those motives: He said, 'Give to him that asketh thee, not because he deserves it, but because I tell you to.' The great motive in all giving is Jesus Christ's command. SSM. 46

We enthrone common-sense as God and say, 'It is absurd; if I give to everyone that asks, every beggar in the place will be at my door.' Try it. I have yet to find the man who obeyed Jesus Christ's command and did not realise that God restrains those who beg. SSM. 47

Have no other motive in giving than to please God. In modern philanthropy we are 'egged on' with other motives—It will do them good; they need the help; they deserve it. Jesus Christ never brings out that aspect in His teaching; He allows no other motive in giving than to please God. SSM. 56

GOD

Holy, holy, holy, Lord God Almighty, who was and is and is to come!

—Revelation 4:8

It is God who works in you both to will and to do for His good pleasure.

—Philippians 2:13

Is the essential nature of Deity omniscience, omnipotence and omnipresence? The essential nature of Deity is holiness, and the power of God is proved in His becoming a Baby. That is the staggering proposition the Bible gives—God became the weakest thing we know. AUG. 81

It is a great thing to have a God big enough to believe in. AUG. 118

God's purpose is to bring 'many *sons* to glory.' BFB. 14

We have the idea that prosperity, or happiness, or morality, is the end of a man's existence; according to the Bible it is something other, viz., 'to glorify God and enjoy Him for ever.' When a man is right with God, God puts His honour in that man's keeping. BFB. 29

Trouble always arises when men will not revise their views of God. BFB. 39

It takes the whole man—conscience, intellect, will and emotions, to discover God as Reality. BFB. 97

God Himself is the key to the riddle of the universe, and the basis of things is to be found only in Him. BFB. 100

God is not an abstract truth; He is the Eternal Reality, and is discerned only by means of a personal relationship. BFB. 106

I have never seen God; to call Him omnipotent and omnipresent and omniscient means nothing to me; I do not care one bit for an Almighty Incomprehensible First Cause. To speak the thing which is right about God, I must be in living personal relationship with Him. BFB. 107

God is not satisfying us and glorifying us; He wants to manifest in us what His Son can do. BP. 42

If ever we are going to understand God, we must receive His Spirit, then He will begin to expound to us the things of God. We understand the things of the world by our natural intelligence, and we understand the things of God by "the spirit which is of God." BP. 212

The characteristics of God Almighty are mirrored for us in Jesus Christ; therefore if we want to know what God is like, we must study Jesus Christ. BP. 216

God is not a supernatural interferer; God is the everlasting portion of His people. When a man "born from above" begins his new life he meets God at every turn, hears Him in every sound, sleeps at His feet, and wakes to find Him there. CD. VOL. 1, 5

When all religions and philosophies and philologies have tried to define God, one and all sink inane and pass, while the Bible statements stand like eternal monuments, shrouded in ineffable glory: "GOD IS LIGHT"; "GOD IS LOVE"; "GOD IS HOLY." Every attempted definition of God other than these sublime inspirations negates God, and we find ourselves possessed of our own ideas with never a glimpse of the living God. CD. VOL. 1, 11

God alters our disposition, but He does not make our character. When God alters my disposition the first thing the new disposition will do is to stir up my brain to think along God's line. As I begin to think, begin to work out what God has worked in, it will become character. Character is consolidated thought. God makes me pure in heart; I must make myself pure in conduct. CHI. 58

If you take all the manifestations of God in the Old Testament you find them a mass of contradictions: now God is pictured as a Man, now as a Woman, now as a lonely Hero, now as a suffering Servant, and until we come to the revelation in the New Testament these conflicting characteristics but add confusion to our conception of God. But immediately we see Jesus Christ, we find all the apparent contradictions blended in one unique Person. CHI. 117

I know no other God in Time or Eternity than Jesus Christ; I have accepted all I know of God on the authority of the revelation He gave of Him. CHI. 46

Jesus Christ reveals, not an embarrassed God, not a confused God, not a God who stands apart from the problems, but One who stands in the thick of the whole thing with man. DI. 12

Beware lest your attitude to God's truth reminds Him that He is very unwise. Everything worth while in life is dangerous, and yet we would have God such a tepid Being that He runs no risks! DI. 13

God is true to the laws of His own nature, not to my way of expounding how He works. DI. 14

God cannot come to me in any way but His own way, and His way is often insignificant and unobstrusive. DI. 15

God does not act according to His own precedents, therefore logic or a vivid past experience can never take the place of a personal faith in a personal God. DI. 16

We say that God foresaw sin, and made provision for it: the Bible revelation is that "the Lamb that hath been slain from the foundation of the world" is the exact expression of the nature of God. DI. 16

The greatest demand God makes of us is to believe that He is righteous when everything that happens goes against that faith. GW. 44

There is no element of the vindictive in our great and good God. GW. 50

There is no other time than *now* with God, no past and no future. GW. 105

The one thing God is after is character. HG. 71

Any interest that would induce me away from the shadow of the Almighty is to be treated as a snare. Resolutely treat no one seriously but God. "The Lord is *my* rock, and *my* fortress, and *my* deliverer, *my* God, *my* strong rock . . . *my* shield, and the horn of *my* salvation, *my* high tower." Note the 'my's' here, and laugh at everything in the nature of misgiving for ever after! HG. 114

God never reveals Himself in the same way to everyone, and yet the testimony of each one who has had a revelation of God is the same, viz., that God is love. GW. 145

God is amazingly patient. HGM. 30

We only know God's thought and the expression of it in Jesus Christ, and we only know the meaning of 'God and man one' in Jesus Christ. HGM. 96

My conception of God must embrace the whole of my life. HGM. 108

If we are in Christ the whole basis of our goings is God, not conceptions of God, not ideas of God, but God Himself. We do not need any more ideas about God, the world is full of ideas about God, they are all worthless, because the ideas of God in anyone's head are of no more use than our own ideas. What we need is a real God, not more ideas about Him. IWP. 68

God is never in a panic, nothing can be done that He is not absolute Master of, and no one in earth or heaven can shut a door He has opened, nor open a door He has shut. God alters the inevitable when we get in touch with Him. IWP. 127

We are not built for ourselves, but for God, not for service for God, but for God; that explains the submission of life. IYA. 54

We may say what we like, but God does allow the devil, He does allow sin, He does allow bad men to triumph and tyrants to rule, and these things either make us fiends or they make us saints, it depends entirely on the relationship we are in towards God. IYA. 55

Thou art the God of the early mornings, the God of the late-at-nights, the God of the mountain peaks, the God of the sea; but, my God, my soul has further horizons than the early mornings, deeper darkness than the nights of earth, higher peaks than any mountain, greater depths than any sea can know. My God, Thou art the God of these, be my God! I cannot reach to the heights or depths, there are motives I cannot touch, dreams I cannot fathom, God search me, winnow out my way. IYA. 72

God is the only Being Who can afford to be misunderstood; He deliberately stands aside and lets Himself be slandered and misrepresented; He never vindicates Himself. LG. 24

God does not tell us what He is going to do, He reveals to you who He is. LG. 149

God will do the absolutely impossible. MUH. 60

God has to hide from us what He does until by personal character we get to the place where He can reveal it. MUH. 87

We look for God to manifest Himself to His children: God only manifests Himself *in* His children. MUH. 112

Are you seeking great things for yourself? Not seeking to be a great one, but seeking great things from God for yourself. God wants you in a closer relationship to Himself than receiving His gifts, He wants you to get to know Him. A great thing is accidental, it comes and goes. God never gives us anything accidental. There is nothing easier than getting into a right relationship with God except when it is not God Whom you want but only what He gives. MUH. 118

God's ultimate purpose is that His Son might be manifested in my mortal flesh. MUH. 152

We have the idea that God is going to do some exceptional thing, that He is preparing and fitting us for some extraordinary thing by and bye, but as we go on in grace we find that God is glorifying Himself here and now, in the present minute. If we have God's say-so behind us, the most amazing strength comes, and we learn to sing in the ordinary days and ways. MUH. 156

When it begins to dawn in my conscious life what God's purpose is, there is the laughter of the possibility of the impossible. The impossible is exactly what God does. NKW. 65

How haphazard God seems, not sometimes but always. God's ways turn man's thinking upside down. NKW. 100

The revelation of God in the Old Testament is that of a working God. No other religion presents God either as diligent or as suffering, but as an all-in-all principle, ruling in lofty disdain. NKW. 118

God is never in a hurry. NKW. 119

The revelation of God to me is determined by my character, not by God's. If I am mean, that is how God will appear to me. 'Tis because I am mean, Thy ways so oft Look mean to me.' NKW. 127

God is not an almighty sultan reigning aloof, He is right in the throes of life, and it is there that emotion shows itself. OPG. 16

Beware of egging God on; possess your soul in patience. OPG. 34

It is one thing to deceive other people, but you have to get up very early if you want to take in God! OPG. 48

It is the presence of God that is the secret of victory always. OPG. 71

Love, joy, peace, these things are not seen, yet they are eternal, and God's nature is made up of these things. PH. 155

If I maintain communion with God and recognise that He is taking me up into His purposes, I will no longer try to find out what those purposes are. PH. 182

The symbol of God's nature is the Cross, whose arms stretch out to limitless reaches. PR. 100

God will consume and shake, and shake and consume, till there is nothing more to be consumed, but only Himself—incandescent with the presence of God. PS. 67

God narrows our "shant's" to one explosive point. I don't need to go that way, but God will have to bring me there if I persist in the little disobediences which no one knows but myself, because it is engendering in me a spirit God cannot allow. RTR. 9

A God who did not know the last depth of sorrow and suffering, would be a God "whom to be God is not fit." RTR. 23

God holds us responsible for what we won't look at. We are nowhere judged by the light we have, but by the light we have refused. RTR. 49

God is never away off somewhere else; He is always *there.* RTR. 58

There is only one God for the Christian, and He is Jesus Christ. SA. 15

The majority of us make the character of God out of our own heads; therefore He does not amount to anything at all. That God is called an omnipresent, omniscient, omnipotent Being who rules the universe does not matter one iota to me. But the New Testament reveals the essential nature of God to be not omnipotence, omnipresence, and omniscience, but holiness. God became the weakest thing in His own creation, viz., a Baby; He entered human history on that line. He was so ordinary that the folks of His day paid no attention to Him, and the religious people said He was making a farce of religion. SA. 34

If I . . . say that the essential nature of God can be defined as omnipotence, omniscience, and omnipresence, I shall end by proving that Jesus Christ is a liar, for He was not omnipotent and omniscient and omnipresent when He was on earth; yet He claimed to be the complete revelation of God. SA. 68

The world of wisdom is to bank all on God and disregard the consequences. SHH. 91

A single eye is essential to correct understanding. One idea runs all through our Lord's teaching—Right with God, first, second and third. SSM. 63

To be brought within the zone of God's voice is to be profoundly altered. SSY. 10

Is it not illuminating how God knows where we are, and the kennels we crawl into, no matter how much straw we hide under! He will hunt us up like a lightning flash. No human being knows human beings as God does. SSY. 30

'Lo, I am with you all the days.' He is the one Who is surrounding us, listening and sympathising and encouraging. Our audience is God, not God's people, but God Himself. The saint who realizes that can never be discouraged, no matter where he goes. SSY. 38

Week 18

GOSPEL

This gospel of the kingdom will be preached in all the world as a witness to all the nations, and then the end will come.

—Matthew 24:14

We have no right to preach unless we present the Gospel; we have not to advocate a cause or a creed or an experience, but to present the Gospel, and we cannot do that unless we have a personal testimony based on the Gospel. That is why so many preach what is merely the outcome of a higher form of culture. Until men get into a right relationship with God the Gospel is always in bad taste. There is a feeling of silent resentment, 'Don't talk about being born again and being sanctified; be vague.' 'Do remember the people you are talking to.' 'Preach the simple Gospel, the thing that keeps us sound asleep.' If you take the people as a standard, you will never preach the Gospel, it is too positive. Our obligation to the Gospel is to preach it. AUG. 39

God or sin must die in me. The one elementary Bible truth we are in danger of forgetting is that the Gospel of God is addressed to men as sinners, and nothing else. AUG. 100

Until we realize that God cannot make allowances, the Gospel has no meaning for us; if God made allowances He would cease to be God. BE. 15

The aspect of the Gospel that awakens desire in a man is the message of peace and goodwill—but I must give up my right to myself to get there. BE. 53

There is nothing attractive about the Gospel to the natural man; the only man who finds the Gospel attractive is the man who is convicted of sin. BE. 76

The gospel of Jesus Christ does not present what men want, it presents exactly what they need. As long as you talk about being happy and peaceful, men like to listen to you; but talk about having the disposition of the soul altered, and that the garden of the soul has first of all to be turned into a wilderness and afterwards into a garden of the Lord, and you will find opposition right away. BP. 80

When the Gospel is presented to an unsaved, healthy, happy, hilarious person, there is violent opposition straight away. BP. 80

Numbers of people to-day preach the gospel of temperament, the gospel of 'cheer up.' BP. 116

That the natural heart of man does not want the Gospel of God is proved by the resentment of the heart against the working of the Spirit of God, 'No, I don't object to be forgiven, I don't mind being guided and blessed, but it is too much of a radical surrender to ask me to give up my right to myself and allow the Spirit of God to have absolute control of my heart.' BP. 135

Sermons may weary, the Gospel never does. DI. 49

Jesus Christ can make my disposition as pure as His own. That is the claim of the Gospel. DI. 59

We are apt to put the superb blessings of the Gospel as something for a special few, they are for sinners saved by grace. DI. 63

The Gospel of God awakens an intense craving in men and an equally intense resentment, and the tendency is to do away with the resentment. Jesus Christ claims that He can remove the disposition of sin from every man; the only testimony worthy of the Name of Jesus is that He can make a sinner a saint. The most marvellous testimony to the Gospel is a holy man, one whose living experience reveals what God can do. GW. 61

The Bible never gives definitions, the Bible states facts, and the Gospel that Jesus brought of good news about God is the most astounding thing the world ever heard, but it must be the Gospel that Jesus brought. HG. 51

Whenever the Gospel of Jesus loses the note of unutterable gladness, it is like salt that has lost its savour. HG. 51

Try and imagine what Jesus meant when He said, "Preach the gospel to every creature"; He keeps 'an open house' for the whole universe. It is a conception impossible of human comprehension. HG. 85

We are not here to woo and win men to God; we are here to present the Gospel which in individual cases will mean condemnation or salvation. HG. 102

The message of the Gospel is not that God gives a man a clean heart, but that He gives him a pure heart. HGM. 34

When once a man's conscience is roused he knows God dare not forgive him and it awakens a sense of hopelessness. Forgiveness is a revelation—hope for the hopeless; that is the message of the Gospel. HGM. 101

The Gospel of Jesus Christ always forces an issue of will. MUH. 358

The Gospel of the grace of God awakens an intense longing in human souls and an equally intense resentment, because the revelation which it brings is not palatable. There is a certain pride in man that will give and give, but to come and accept is another thing. I will give my life to martyrdom, I will give myself in consecration, I will do anything, but do not humiliate me to the level of the most hell-deserving sinner and tell me that all I have to do is to accept the gift of salvation through Jesus Christ. MUH. 333

We say that Jesus preached the Gospel, but He did more: He came that there might be a Gospel to preach. PH. 70

The gospel is not so much good news to man as good news about God. PH. 135

. . . the Gospel message is that we can be born from above the second we want to. PR. 122

The first thing Jesus Christ faced in men was this heredity of sin, and it is because we have ignored it in our presentation of the Gospel that the message of the Gospel has lost its sting, its blasting power; we have drivelled it into insurance tickets for heaven, and made it deal only with the wastrel element of mankind. SA. 116

Let Jesus Christ proclaim His Gospel: we can have the very disposition of Jesus imparted to us, and if we have not got it we will have to tell God the reason why. We have to tell God we don't believe He can do it—there are details of our lives He cannot put right, back tracks He cannot clear up, ramifications of evil He cannot touch. Thank God that is a lie! He can. If God cannot do that we have 'followed cunningly devised fables.' That is where the fight has to be fought—along the line of what Jesus Christ can do in the human soul. Unless God has searched us and cleansed us and filled us with the Holy Spirit so that we are undeserving of censure in His sight, the Atonement has not been applied to our personal experience. SHL. 51

The words of our Lord, 'Think not that I came to cast peace on the earth: I came not to cast peace, but a sword,' are a description of what happens when the Gospel is preached—upset, conviction, concern and confusion. SHL. 112

The Gospel of God is not that Jesus died for my sins only, but that He gave Himself for me that I might give myself to Him. SSM. 28

This is the age of the gospel of cheerfulness. We are told to ignore sin, ignore the gloomy people, and yet more than half the human race is gloomy. WG. 64

Week 19

GRACE

Grow in the grace and knowledge of our Lord and Savior Jesus Christ. To Him be the glory both now and forever. Amen.

—2 Peter 3:18

The grace we had yesterday won't do for to-day. "The grace of God"—the overflowing favour of God; we can always reckon it is there to draw on if we don't trust our own merits. AUG. 124

One of the greatest proofs that we are drawing on the grace of God is that we can be humiliated without the slightest trace of anything but the grace of God in us. Draw on the grace of God *now,* not presently. The one word in the spiritual vocabulary is 'NOW'. AUG. 128

The surest sign that God has done a work of grace in my heart is that I love Jesus Christ best, not weakly and faintly, not intellectually, but passionately, personally and devotedly, overwhelming every other love of my life. BP. 134

The essence of the Gospel of God working through conscience and conduct is that it shows itself at once in action. God can make simple, guileless people out of cunning, crafty people; that is the marvel of the grace of God. It can take the strands of evil and twistedness out of a man's mind and imagination and make him simple towards God, so that his life becomes radiantly beautiful by the miracle of God's grace. BP. 206

'Grace' is a theological word and is unfortunately used, because we usually mean by theology something remote that has to do with controversy, something whereby our mind is tied up in knots and our practical life left alone. In the Bible theology is immensely practical. 'Grace' means the overflowing nature of God; we see it in Nature, we have no words to describe the lavishness of God. "The grace of our Lord Jesus Christ" is the overflowing of God's nature in entire and absolute forgiveness through His own sacrifice. BSG. 47

. . . purity in God's children is not the outcome of obedience to His law, but the result of the supernatural work of His grace. "*I* will cleanse you'; '*I* will give you a new heart'; *I* will put My Spirit within you, and cause you to walk in My statutes'; '*I* will do it all.' GW. 75

You cannot argue men into coming to Jesus, or socialize them into coming; only one thing will do it, and that is the power of the Gospel drawing men by the constraint of God's grace. GW. 109

If we know that we have received the unmerited favour of God and we do not give unmerited favour to other people, we are damned in that degree. HG. 82

To be saved by God's grace is not a beautifully pathetic thing; it is a desperately tragic thing. HG. 99

There is no condescension in grace, a sinner is never afraid of Jesus . . . HGM. 14

The grace of God makes us honest with ourselves. We must be humorous enough to see the shallow tricks we all have, no matter what our profession of Christianity. We are so altogether perverse that God Almighty had to come and save us! NKW. 89

The grace of God is absolute, but your obedience must prove that you do not receive it in vain. OBH. 111

Grace is the overflowing immeasurable favour of God; God cannot withhold, the only thing that keeps back His grace and favour is our sin and perversity. OPG. 18

The phrase 'a sinner saved by grace' means that a man is no longer a sinner; if he is, he is not saved. PS. 25

We have the notion at first that when we are saved and sanctified by God's supernatural grace, He does not require us to do anything, but it is only then that He begins to require anything of us. PR. 75

The grace of God which comes through Jesus Christ is revealed in that God laid down His life for His enemies. SA. 16

The miracle of the grace of God is that He can make the past as though it had never been. RTR. 33

It requires the Almighty grace of God to take the next step when there is no vision and no spectator. RTR. 48

Week 20

HEART

Keep your heart with all diligence, for out of it spring the issues of life.

—Proverbs 4:23

Jesus Christ does not simply say, 'Thou shalt not do certain things'; He demands that we have such a condition of heart that we never even think of doing them, every thought and imagination of heart and mind is to be unblameable in the sight of God. BE. 9

The Bible places in the heart everything that the modern psychologist places in the head. BP. 72

Materialistic scientists say that 'the brain secretes thinking as the liver does bile,' they make the brain the centre of thinking. The Bible makes the heart the centre of thinking, and the brain merely the machinery the heart uses to express itself. This point is very vital in our judgment of men. BP. 98

God never judges men by their brains; He judges them by their hearts. BP. 99

The Bible always means more than we are apt to mean. The term 'heart' in the Bible means the centre of everything. The human soul has the spirit in and above it and the body by and about it; but the vital centre of all is the heart. When we speak of the heart, figuratively or actually, we mean the midmost part of a person. The Bible teaching differs from that of science in that makes the heart the soul centre and the spirit centre as well. BP. 99

The use of the Bible term 'heart' is best understood by simply saying 'me.' The heart is not merely the seat of the affections, it is the centre of everything. The heart is the central altar, and the body is the outer court. What we offer on the altar of the heart will tell ultimately through the extremities of the body. BP. 99

If we try, as has been tried by psychologists, to take out of the Bible something that agrees with modern science, we shall have to omit many things the Bible says about the heart. According to the Bible the heart is the centre: the centre of physical life, the centre of memory, the centre of damnation and of salvation, the centre of God's working and the centre of the devil's working, the centre from which everything works which moulds the human mechanism. BP. 100

The heart is the exchange and mart; our words and expressions are simply the coins we use, but the 'shop' resides in the heart, the emporium where all the goods are, and that is what God sees but no man can see. BP. 102

The heart physically is the centre of the body; the heart sentimentally is the centre of the soul; and the heart spiritually is the centre of the spirit. BP. 107

The real spiritual powers of a man reside in the heart, which is the centre of the physical life, of the soul life, and of the spiritual life. BP. 125

The heart is the first thing to live in physical birth and in spiritual birth. It is a wonderful thing that God can cleanse and purify the thinking of our hearts. BP. 125

According to the Bible, thinking exists in the heart, and that is the region with which the Spirit of God deals. We may take it as a general rule that Jesus Christ never answers any questions that spring from a man's head, because the questions which spring from our brains are always borrowed from some book we have read, or from someone we have heard speak; but the questions that spring from our hearts, the real problems that vex us, Jesus Christ answers those. The questions He came to deal with are those that spring from the implicit centre. These problems may be difficult to state in words, but they are the problems Jesus Christ will solve. BP. 125

The heart never dies: it is as immortal as God's Spirit because it is the centre of man's spirit. Memory never dies, mind never dies; our bodily machine dies, and the manifestation of our heart and life in the body dies, but the heart never dies. BP. 140

The only way to alter the hardened heart is to melt it, and the only power that can melt it is the fire of the Holy Ghost. BP. 140

The tiniest bit of sin is an indication of the vast corruption that is in the human heart. CHI. 71

'Heart' is simply another term for 'personality.' MFL. 47

The Bible term "heart" is best understood if we simply say 'me,' it is the central citadel of a man's personality. MFL. 113

The heart is the altar of which the physical body is the outer court, and whatever is offered on the altar of the heart will tell ultimately through the extremities of the body. "Keep thy heart with all diligence; for out of it are the issues of life." MFL. 113

The discovery of the desperate recesses in the human heart is the greatest evidence of the need for the Redemption. OPG. 72

Jesus Christ is the Master of the human soul, He knows what is in the human heart, and He has no illusions about any man. PH. 51

The human heart must have satisfaction, but there is only one Being Who can satisfy the last aching abyss of the human heart, and that is our Lord Jesus Christ. PH. 52

We have not the remotest conception that what Jesus says about the human heart is true until we come up against something further on in our lives. We are apt to be indignant and say—"I don't believe those things are in my heart," and we refuse the diagnosis of the only Master there is of the human heart. We need never know the plague of our own heart and the terrible possibilities in human life if we will hand ourselves over to Jesus Christ; but if we stand on our own right and wisdom at any second an eruption may occur in our personal lives, and we may discover to our unutterable horror that we can be murderers, etc. SHH. 104

Jesus Christ has undertaken through His Redemption to put into us a heart so pure that God Almighty can see nothing to censure in it, and the Holy Spirit searches us not only to make us know the possibilities of iniquity in our heart, but to make us 'unblameable in holiness in His sight.' SHL. 48

Either Jesus Christ must be the supreme Authority on the human heart, or He is not worth listening to. SSM. 27

Week 21

HOLINESS

As He who called you is holy, you also be holy in all your conduct, because it is written, Be holy, for I am holy.

—1 Peter 1:15, 16

To the majority of men, holiness is all in the clouds, but take this message, "Holiness, without which no man shall see the Lord," and drive it home on every line until there is no refuge from the terrific application. Holy not only in my religious aspirations, but holy in my soul life, in my imagination and thinking; holy in every detail of my bodily life. AUG. 21

Never say God's holiness does not mean what it does mean. It means every part of the life under the scrutiny of God, knowing that the grace of God is sufficient for every detail. The temptation comes along the line of compromise, 'Don't be so unbendingly holy; so fiercely pure and uprightly chaste.' Never tolerate by sympathy with yourself or with others any practice that is not in keeping with a holy God. AUG. 60

Holiness is the characteristic of the man after God's own heart. BE. 16

Holiness is militant, Satan is continually pressing and ardent, but holiness maintains itself. It is morality on fire and transfigured into the likeness of God. Holiness is not only what God gives me, but what I manifest that God has given me. I manifest this coruscating holiness by my reaction against sin, the world, and the devil. Wherever God's saints are in the world they are protected by a wall of fire which they do not see, but Satan does. "That wicked one toucheth him not." Satan has to ask and plead for permission; as to whether God grants him permission is to do with the sovereignty of God and is not in our domain to understand. BP. 27

There is only one kind of holiness, and that is the holiness of the Lord Jesus. BP. 40

The holiness of God is absolute, not progressive; that is, it knows no development by antagonism. BSG. 10

Man's holiness must be progressive. The holiness of Jesus developed through antagonism because He revealed what a holy man should be. BSG. 11

There is only one type of humanity, and only one type of holiness, the holiness that was manifested in the life of the Lord Jesus, and it is that holiness which He gives to us. It is not that we are put in a place where we can begin to be like Him: we are put in a place where we *are* like Him. BSG. 58

What Jesus Christ does in new birth is to put in a disposition that transforms morality into holiness. He came to put into the man who knows he needs it His own heredity of holiness; to bring him into a oneness with God which he never had through natural birth. CHI. 22

Holiness is based on repentance, and the holy man is the most humble man you can meet. My realization of God can be measured by my humility. CHI. 70

The only holiness there is is the holiness derived through faith, and faith is the instrument the Holy Spirit uses to organize us into Christ. But do not let us be vague here. Holiness, like sin, is a disposition, not a series of acts. A man can *act* holily, but he has not a holy *disposition.* CHI. 81

Practical holiness is the only holiness of any value in this world, and the only kind the Spirit of God will endorse. CHI. 82

Holiness is the only sign that a man is repentant in the New Testament sense, and a holy man is not one who has his eyes set on his own whiteness, but one who is personally and passionately devoted to the Lord who saved him—one whom the Holy Ghost takes care shall never forget that God has made him what he is by sheer sovereign grace. CHI. 123

God's final purpose is holiness, holy men and women, and He restrains none of the forces which go against that purpose. DI. 13

Watch the margins of your mind when you begin to take the view that it doesn't matter whether God is holy or not; it is the beginning of being a traitor to Jesus Christ. DI. 14

It is quite true to say 'I can't live a holy life'; but you can decide to let Jesus make you holy. 'I can't do away with my past'; but you can decide to let Jesus do away with it. DI. 58

The idea that I grow holy as I go on is foreign to the New Testament. There must have been a place where I was identified with the death of Jesus: "I have been crucified with Christ . . . ;" That is the meaning of sanctification. Then I grow *in* holiness. DI. 59

The ultimate display of Deity is omnipotence, but the essential nature of Deity is holiness. GW. 30

Jesus Christ came *to make us holy,* not to tell us to be holy: He came to do for us what we could not do for ourselves. HG. 57

The only test of spirituality is holiness, practical, living holiness, and that holiness is impossible unless the Holy Ghost has brought you to your 'last day,' and you can look back and say—'That was the day when I died right out to my right to myself, crucified with Christ.' HG. 109

Holiness can only be worked out in and through the din of things as they are. God does not slide holiness into our hearts like a treasure box from heaven and we open the lid and out it comes, holiness works out in us as it worked out in our Lord. LG. 95

Never look for other people to be holy; it is a cruel thing to do, it distorts your view of yourself and of others. MFL. 90

Continually restate to yourself what the purpose of your life is. The destined end of man is not happiness, nor health, but holiness. Nowadays we have far too many affinities, we are dissipated with them; right, good, noble affinities which will yet have their fulfilment, but in the meantime God has to atrophy them. The one thing that matters is whether a man will accept the God Who will make him holy. At all costs a man must be rightly related to God. MUH. 245

Holiness means unsullied walking with the feet, unsullied talking with the tongue, unsullied thinking with the mind—every detail of the life under the scrutiny of God. Holiness is not only what God gives me, but what I manifest that God has given me. MUH. 245

Personal holiness is never the ground of my acceptance with God; the only ground of acceptance is the Death of the Lord Jesus Christ. NKW. 123

The Spirit of God Who wrought out that marvellous Life in the Incarnation will baptize us into the very same life, not into a life like it, but into His life until the very holiness of Jesus is gifted to us. It is not something we work out in Him, it is *in Him,* and He manifests it through us while we abide in Him. OBH. 17

The one marvellous secret of a holy life is not in imitating Jesus, but in letting the perfections of Jesus manifest themselves in our mortal flesh. OBH. 19

If we are born again of the Spirit of God, our one desire is a hunger and thirst after nothing less than holiness, the holiness of Jesus, and He will satisfy it. OBH. 22

No individual can develop a holy life with God without benefiting all other saints. OBH. 42

Abandon in the profound sense is of infinitely more value than personal holiness. Personal holiness brings the attention to bear on my own whiteness, I dare not be indiscreet, or unreserved, I dare not do anything in case I incur a speck. God can't bless that sort of thing, it is as unlike His own character as could be. The holiness produced through the indwelling of His Son in me is a holiness which is never conscious of itself. There are some people in whom you cannot find a speck and yet they are not abundantly blessed of God, while others make grave indiscretions and get marvellously blessed; the reason being that the former have become devotees of personal holiness conscientious to a degree; the latter are marked by abandonment to God. Whatever centres attention on anything other than our Lord Himself will always lead astray. The only way to be kept cleansed is by walking in the light, as God is in the light. Only as we walk in that light is the holiness of Jesus Christ not only imputed, but imparted, to us. OPG. 27

If I am set on my own holiness, I become a traitor to Jesus. PH. 165

What is holiness? Transfigured morality blazing with indwelling God. Any other kind of holiness is fictitious and dangerous. One of the dangers of dealing too much with the Higher Christian Life is that it is apt to fizzle off into abstractions. But when we see holiness in the Lord Jesus, we do know what it means, it means an unsullied walk with the feet, unsullied talk with the tongue, unsullied thinking of the mind, unsullied transactions of the bodily organs, unsullied life of the heart, unsullied dreams of the imagination—that is the actual holiness Jesus says He has given them. This is the meaning of sanctification. PR. 135

When the holiness of God is preached, men are convicted of sin; it is not the love of God that first appeals but His holiness. PS. 20

Wherever Jesus comes He reveals that man is away from God by reason of sin, and he is terrified at His presence. That is why men will put anything in the place of Jesus Christ, anything rather than let God come near in His startling purity, because immediately God comes near, conscience records that God is holy and nothing unholy can live with Him, consequently His presence hurts the sinner. "If I had not come and spoken unto them, they had not had sin: but now they have no cloke for their sin." PS. 62

God's Book reveals all through that holiness will bring persecution from those who are not holy. PS. 80

Holiness is untouched by panic. PS. 80

Personal experience bears out the truth that a testimony to holiness produces either rage or ridicule on the part of those who are not holy. PS. 80

You can never make yourself holy by external acts, but, if you are holy, your external acts will be the natural expression of holiness. RTR. 23

"The Son of Man came eating and drinking." One of the most staggering things in the New Testament is just this commonplace aspect. The curious difference between Jesus Christ's idea of holiness and that of other religions lies here. The one says holiness is not compatible with ordinary food and married life, but Jesus Christ represents a character lived straight down in the ordinary amalgam of human life, and His claim is that the character He manifested is possible for any man, if he will come in by the door provided for him. SA. 33

Jesus Christ's holiness has to do with human life as it is. It is not a mystical, aesthetic thing that cannot work in the ordinary things of life, it is a holiness which "can be achieved with an ordinary diet and a wife and five children." SA. 74

Holiness is the balance between our disposition and the law of God as expressed in Jesus Christ, and it is such a stern thing that the majority of us have either not begun it, or we have begun it and left it alone. SA. 99

Jesus Christ stands for holiness. SA. 100

If once we have allowed Jesus Christ to upset the equilibrium, holiness is the inevitable result, or no peace for ever. SHL. 43

The only safeguard for the Christian worker is, 'Holiness unto the Lord.' If we are living rightly with God, living holy lives in secret and in public, God puts a wall of fire round about us. Beware of calling anything holiness that is only winsome and sweet to the world. God grant we may never lose the touch of God that produces the holy dread. WG. 105

Week 22

HOLY SPIRIT

The Spirit searches all things, yes, the deep things of God.

—1 Corinthians 2:10

You can't indulge in pious pretence when you come to the atmosphere of the Bible. If there is one thing the Spirit of God does it is to purge us from all sanctimonious humbug, there is no room for it. BE. 22

The Holy Ghost makes Jesus Christ both present and real. He is the most real Being on earth, "closer is He than breathing, and nearer than hands and feet." BE. 98

The Holy Ghost is seeking to awaken men out of lethargy; He is pleading, yearning, blessing, pouring benedictions on men, convicting and drawing them nearer, for one purpose only, that they may receive Him so that He may make them holy men and women exhibiting the life of Jesus Christ. BE. 99

The Holy Spirit is not a substitute for Jesus, the Holy Spirit is all that Jesus was, and all that Jesus did, made real in personal experience now. BE. 99

The Holy Spirit alone makes Jesus real, the Holy Spirit alone expounds His Cross, the Holy Spirit alone convicts of sin; the Holy Spirit alone does *in* us what Jesus *did* for us. BE. 99

Immediately the Holy Spirit comes in as life and as light, He will chase through every avenue of our minds; His light will penetrate every recess of our hearts; He will chase His light through every affection of our souls, and make us know what sin is. The Holy Spirit convicts of sin, man does not. BP. 37

Mind the Holy Spirit, mind His light, mind His convictions, mind His guidance, and slowly and surely the sensual personality will be turned into a spiritual personality. BP. 50

The thought is unspeakably full of glory, that God the Holy Ghost can come into my heart and fill it so full that the life of God will manifest itself all through this body which used to manifest exactly the opposite. If I am willing and determined to keep in the light and obey the Spirit, then the characteristics of the indwelling Christ will manifest themselves. BP. 146

We can only discern the spiritual world by the Spirit of God, not by our own spirit; and if we have not received the Spirit of God we shall never discern spiritual things or understand them; we shall move continually in a dark world, and come slowly to the conclusion that the New Testament language is very exaggerated. But when we have received the Spirit of God, we begin to "know the things that are freely given to us of God," and to compare "spiritual things with spiritual," "not in the words which man's wisdom teacheth, but which the Holy Ghost teacheth." BP. 210

"God is a Spirit," therefore if we are going to understand God, we must have the Spirit of God. BP. 215

We cannot give ourselves the Holy Spirit; the Holy Spirit is God Almighty's gift if we will simply become poor enough to ask for Him. BP. 220

. . . when the Holy Spirit has come in, there is something we can do and God cannot do, we can obey Him. If we do not obey Him, we shall grieve Him. BP. 220

When the Holy Spirit comes in, unbelief is turned out and the energy of God is put into us, and we are enabled to will and to do of His good pleasure. When the Holy Spirit comes in He sheds abroad the love of God in our hearts, so that we are able to show our fellows the same love that God has shown to us. When the Holy Spirit comes in He makes us as 'light,' and our righteousness will exceed the righteousness of the most moral upright natural man because the supernatural has been made natural in us. BP. 222

If the Holy Ghost is indwelling a man or woman, no matter how sweet, how beautiful, how Christ-like they are, the lasting thought you go away with is—What a wonderful Being the Lord Jesus Christ is. BSG. 33

It is not what we feel, or what we know, but ever what we *receive* from God—and a fool can receive a gift. "If ye then, being evil, know how to give good gifts unto your children, how much more shall your heavenly Father give the Holy Spirit to them that ask Him?" It is so simple that everyone who is not simple misses it. DI. 20

It is extraordinary how things fall off from a man like autumn leaves once he comes to the place where there is no rule but that of the personal domination of the Holy Spirit. DI. 20

The biggest blessing in your life was when you came to the end of trying to be a Christian, the end of reliance on natural devotion, and were willing to come as a pauper and receive the Holy Spirit. The humiliation is that we have to be quite sure we need Him, so many of us are quite sure we don't need Him. DI. 20

There is nothing so still and gentle as the checks of the Holy Spirit; if they are yielded to, emancipation is the result; but let them be trifled with, and there will come a hardening of the life away from God. Don't 'quench the Spirit.' DI. 22

The Holy Spirit does not obliterate a man's personality; He lifts it to its highest use, viz., for portrayal of the Mind of God. DI. 22

There is one thing we cannot imitate: we cannot imitate being full of the Holy Ghost. DI. 24

The way you will want the baptism of the Holy Ghost and fire is when you begin to see the Lord Jesus; when you see Him, the great heart-hunger, the great longing of the life will be, 'I want to be like Him.' But remember, you must come to Him; it is His prerogative to baptize with the Holy Ghost. It is not a blessing we gain by faith, not a blessing we merge into by devotion and fasting, it is the supernaturally natural result of coming to Jesus as the true Baptizer. GW. 22

The first descent of the Holy Spirit was upon the Son of Man—that is, the whole human race represented in one Person, and that Person the historic Jesus Christ who was God Incarnate. HGM. 9

The second mighty descent of the Holy Spirit was on the Day of Pentecost, when the power of God came in Person. HGM. 10

The Holy Spirit works in no other way than to glorify Jesus Christ. HGM. 10

All that Jesus Christ came to do is made experimentally ours by the Holy Spirit; He does *in* us what Jesus did *for* us. HGM. 11

If we want to be baptized with the Holy Ghost that we may be of use, it is all up; or because we want peace and joy and deliverance from sin, it is all up. "He shall baptize you with the Holy Ghost," not for anything for ourselves at all, but that we may be witnesses unto Him. God will never answer the prayer to be baptized with the Holy Ghost for any other reason than to make us witnesses to Jesus. HGM. 30

When we are baptized with the Holy Ghost we are no longer isolated believers but part of the Mystical Body of Christ. Beware of attempting to live a holy life alone, it is impossible. HGM. 25

We are baptized with the Holy Ghost not *for* anything at all, but entirely, as Our Lord puts it, to be His witnesses, those with whom He can do exactly what He likes. HGM. 130

God does not withhold the best, He cannot give it until we are ready to receive it. Receive the Holy Spirit and let your reason be lifted out of images and out of the good, and instantly you will be lifted into the best. IWP. 77

The Spirit of God does not dazzle and startle and amaze us into worshipping God; that is why He takes such a long while, it is bit by bit, process by process, with every power slowly realizing and comprehending "with all saints. . . ." We cannot comprehend it alone; the 'together' aspect of the New Testament is wonderful. IWP. 88

There are many to-day who are sincere, but they are not real; they are not hypocrites, but perfectly honest and earnest and desirous of fulfilling what Jesus wants of them, but they *really* cannot do it, the reason being that they have not received the Holy Spirit Who will make them real. LG. 109

Ask God on the authority of Jesus to give you the Holy Spirit, and He will do so; but you will never ask until you have struck the bottom board of your need. LG. 117

The Holy Spirit is absolutely honest, He indicates the things that are right and the things that are wrong. LG. 121

The Spirit of God is always the spirit of liberty; the spirit that is not of God is the spirit of bondage, the spirit of oppression and depression. The Spirit of God convicts vividly and tensely, but He is always the Spirit of liberty. God Who made the birds never made bird-cages; it is men who make bird-cages, and after a while we become cramped and can do nothing but chirp and stand on one leg. When we get out into God's great free life, we discover that that is the way God means us to live "the glorious liberty of the children of God." MFL. 92

The Holy Spirit cannot be located as a Guest in a house, He invades everything. MUH. 102

"The love of God"—not the power to love God, but *the love of God*—"is shed abroad in our hearts by the Holy Ghost which is given unto us." The Holy Ghost is the gift of the ascended Christ. OBH. 57

"Grieve not the Holy Spirit." He does not come with a voice of thunder, but with a voice so gentle that it is easy to ignore it. OBH. 68

Our great need is to ask for and receive the Holy Ghost in simple faith in the marvellous Atonement of Jesus Christ, and He will turn us into passionate lovers of the Lord. It is this passion for Christ worked out in us that makes us witnesses to Jesus wherever we are, men and women in whom He delights, upon whom He can look down with approval; men and women whom He can put in the shadow or the sun; men and women whom He can put upon their beds or on their feet; men and women whom He can send anywhere He chooses. PH. 33

The Holy Spirit is honest, and we know intuitively whether we have or have not been identified with the death of Jesus, whether we have or have not given over our self-will to the holy will of God. PH. 160

When we ask God for the Holy Spirit, we receive the very nature of God, *Holy* Spirit. PR. 13

The Holy Spirit does *in* us what Jesus Christ did *for* us. PR. 14

The great need for men and women is to receive the Holy Spirit. Our creeds teach us to believe in the Holy Spirit; the New Testament says we must *receive* Him. PR. 112

The Holy Ghost destroys my personal private life and turns it into a thoroughfare for God. RTR. 42

God does not give us the Holy Spirit until we come to the place of seeing that we cannot do without Him. SA. 38

The great mystic work of the Holy Spirit is in the dim regions of our personality where we cannot go. SHL. 49

When the Holy Spirit comes in He is unmistakable in the direction of His work, He goes direct to the thing that keeps us from believing in Jesus Christ. The work of the Holy Spirit is to make us realize the meaning of the Redemption. As long as we believe it on the outside it does not upset our complacency, but we don't want to be perturbed on the inside. SHL. 59

Week 23

INCARNATION

The Word became flesh and dwelt among us.
—John 1:14

In the Incarnation we see the amalgam of the Divine and the human. Pure gold cannot be used as coin, it is too soft; in order to make gold serviceable for use it must be mixed with an alloy. The pure gold of the Divine is of no use in human affairs; there must be an alloy, and the alloy does not stand for sin, but for that which makes the Divine serviceable for use. God Almighty is nothing but a mental abstraction to me unless He can become actual, and the revelation of the New Testament is that God did become actual: "the Word was made flesh." Jesus Christ was not pure Divine, He was unique: Divine and human. BE. 51

The great message of the Incarnation is that there the Divine and the human became one, and Jesus Christ's claim is that He can manifest His own life in any man if he will co-operate with Him. BE. 54

Almighty God is nothing but a mental abstraction unless He becomes concrete and actual, because an ideal has no power unless it can be realized. The doctrine of the Incarnation is that God did become actual, He manifested Himself on the plane of human flesh, and 'Jesus Christ' is the name not only for God and Man in one, but the name of the personal Saviour who makes the way back for every man to get into a personal relationship with God. BFB. 90

In the Incarnation God proves Himself worthy in the sphere in which we live, and this is the sphere of the revelation of the Self-giving of God. BFB. 98

By the sheer force of the tremendous integrity of His Incarnation, Jesus Christ hewed a way straight through sin and death and hell right back to God, more than conqueror over all. BP. 29

In the Redemption, it was not God the Son paying a price to God the Father: it was God the Father, God the Son, and God the Holy Ghost surrendering this marvellous Being, the Lord Jesus Christ, for one definite purpose. Never separate the Incarnation from the Atonement. The Incarnation is for the sake of the Atonement. In dealing with the Incarnation, we are dealing with a revelation fact, not with a speculation. BP. 33

The whole purpose of the Incarnation is the Redemption, viz., to overcome the disasters of the fall and produce a being more noble than the original Adam. BP. 34

The Incarnation was not for the Self-realization of God, but for the purpose of removing sin and reinstating humanity into communion with God. BSG. 14

Jesus Christ became Incarnate for one purpose, to make a way back to God that man might stand before Him as he was created to do, the friend and lover of God Himself. BSG. 14

Jesus Christ was God Incarnate for one purpose, not to reveal God to us, that is simply one of the outcomes of the Incarnation; the one great purpose of His coming was to bring back the whole human race into oneness with God. BSG. 46

According to the Bible, the Son of God became incarnate in order to bear away the sin of the human race. Before a man can take on him the sin of a family, he must be a member of it; and Jesus Christ took on Him the form of the human family that was cursed with sin, and in that human form He lived a spotlessly holy life, and by means of His death He can introduce the shamed members of the human family into the life He lived. Our Lord made human solidarity His own: He represents the vilest sinner out of hell and the purest saint out of heaven. He stands as the one great Representative of the human race, atoning for its sin. It beggars language to describe what He did—He went into identification with the depths of damnation that the human race might be delivered. BSG. 51

In the Incarnation Jesus Christ came down to the lowest rung possible, He came on to the plane where Adam was originally, and He lived on that plane in order to show what God's normal man was like. And then He did what no man could ever do—He made the way for man to get back to the position he had lost. By the sheer might of the Atonement we can be reinstated in God's favour—that is the marvel. BSG. 77

It takes God Incarnate to wash feet properly. It takes God Incarnate to do anything properly. GW. 9

The great revelation the Bible gives of God is the opposite of what we are apt to imagine Him to be, it is a revelation not of the majestic power of God, but of the fact that God was 'manifested in the flesh'; that God became Incarnate as a Baby in the Person of His Son. That is the last reach of Self-limitation. GW. 30

We may talk about God as the Almighty, the All-powerful, but He means nothing to us unless He has become incarnated and touched human life where we touch it; and the revelation of Redemption is that God's Thought did express itself in Jesus Christ, that God became manifest on the plane on which we live. HGM. 95

The purpose of the Incarnation was not to reveal the beauty and nobility of human nature, but in order to remove sin from human nature. MFL. 104

In the Incarnation the Eternal God was so majestically small that He was not detected, the world never saw Him. NKW. 98

The whole meaning of the Incarnation is the Cross. Beware of separating *God manifest in the flesh* from *the Son becoming sin.* The Incarnation was for the purpose of Redemption. God became incarnate for the purpose of putting away sin; not for the purpose of Self-realization. The Cross is the centre of Time and of Eternity, the answer to the enigmas of both. MUH. 97

Just as our Lord came into human history from the outside, so He must come into us from the outside. PR. 29

The tremendous revelation of Christianity is not the Fatherhood of God, but the Babyhood of God—God became the weakest thing in His own creation, and in flesh and blood He levered it back to where it was intended to be. No one helped Him; it was done absolutely by God manifest in human flesh. God has undertaken not only to repair the damage, but in Jesus Christ the human race is put in a better condition than when it was originally designed. It is necessary to understand these things if you are to be able to battle for your faith. SA. 27

The doctrine of the Incarnation means that God became the weakest thing in His own creation, a Baby. SA. 69

The great purpose of Jesus Christ's coming is that He might put man on a line where sin in him can be destroyed. SA. 69

Week 24

JOY

These things I have spoken to you, that My joy may remain in you, and that your joy may be full.

—John 15:11

The end and aim of human life is not happiness, but 'to glorify God and enjoy Him for ever.' Holiness of character, chastity of life, living communion with God—that is the end of a man's life, whether he is happy or not is a matter of moonshine. BE. 14

A man never knows joy until he gets rightly related to God. Satan's claim is that he can make a man satisfied without God, but all he succeeds in doing is to give happiness and pleasure, never joy. BSG. 54

It is an insult to God and to human nature to have as our ideal a happy life. Happiness is a thing that comes and goes, it can never be an end in itself; holiness, not happiness, is the end of man. BSG. 54

The joy of Jesus was the absolute Self-surrender and Self-sacrifice of Himself to the will of His Father, the joy of doing exactly what the Father sent Him to do. "I delight to do Thy will," and He prays that His disciples may have this joy fulfilled in themselves. BSG. 55

The Bible talks plentifully about joy, but it nowhere speaks about a 'happy' Christian. Happiness depends on what happens; joy does not. Remember, Jesus Christ had joy, and He prays "that they might have My joy fulfilled in themselves." BP. 115

Oh the joy of that life with God and in God and for God! It takes a sharp discipline for many of us to learn that 'my goal is God Himself, not joy, nor peace, nor even blessing, but Himself my God.' GW. 121

God can take any man and put the miracle of His joy into Him, and enable him to manifest it in the actual details of his life. HGM. 49

A life of intimacy with God is characterized by joy. You cannot counterfeit joy or peace. What is of value to God is what we *are,* not what we affect to be. HGM. 52

We can always know whether we are hearkening to God's voice by whether we have joy or not; if there is no joy, we are not hearkening. HGM. 52

Joy is the great note all through the Bible. We have the notion of joy that arises from good spirits or good health, but the miracle of the joy of God has nothing to do with a man's life or his circumstances or the condition he is in. Jesus does not come to a man and say 'Cheer up,' He plants within a man the miracle of the joy of God's own nature. HGM. 48

The stronghold of the Christian faith is *the joy of God,* not *my joy in God.* HGM. 48

The joy of Jesus is a miracle, it is not the outcome of my doing things or of my being good, but of my receiving the very nature of God. HGM. 48

Happiness is not a sign that we are right with God; happiness is a sign of satisfaction, that is all, and the majority of us can be satisfied on too low a level. Jesus Christ disturbs every kind of satisfaction that is less than delight in God. IWP. 109

The joy of anything, from a blade of grass upwards, is to fulfil its created purpose. ". . . that we should be to the praise of His glory." LG. 63

If Jesus Christ is the life of God and we have to follow Him, we must find out what His joy was. It certainly was not happiness. The joy of the Lord Jesus Christ lay in doing exactly what He came to do. He did not come to save men first of all, He came to do His Father's will. LG. 63

The way God's life manifests itself in joy is in a peace which has no desire for praise. When a man delivers a message which he knows is the message of God, the witness to the fulfilment of the created purpose is given instantly, the peace of God settles down, and the man cares for neither praise nor blame from anyone. That is the joy of the life of God; it is uncrushable life, and there is never life without joy. LG. 65

The sign that we are glorifying God is not that we are happy; happiness is childish, individual and pagan. It is natural for a child to be happy because a child does not face facts, but a Christian who is merely happy is blind. LG. 65

Many will confide to you their secret sorrows, but the last mark of intimacy is to confide secret joys. Have we ever let God tell us any of His joys, or are we telling God our secrets so continually that we leave no room for Him to talk to us? MUH. 155

It is an insult to use the word happiness in connection with Jesus Christ. The joy of Jesus was the absolute self-surrender and self-sacrifice of Himself to His Father, the joy of doing that which the Father sent Him to do. "I delight to do Thy will." Jesus prayed that our joy might go on fulfilling itself until it was the same joy as His. MUH. 244

This earth is like a sick chamber, and when God sends His angels here He has to say—'Now be quiet; they are so sick with sin that they cannot understand your hilarity.' Whenever the veil is lifted there is laughter and joy. These are the characteristics that belong to God and God's order of things; sombreness and gloom, oppression and depression, are the characteristics of all that does not belong to God. NKW. 70

Every bit of knowledge that we have of God fills us with ineffable joy. Remember what Jesus said to His disciples—"That My joy might be in you." What was the joy of Jesus? That He understood the Father. OBH. 43

The joy that a believer can give to God is the purest pleasure God ever allows a saint, and it is very humiliating to realise how little joy we do give Him. PH. 40

'I thought God's purpose was to make me full of happiness and joy.' It is, but it is happiness and joy from God's standpoint, not from ours. PH. 83

The emphasis of the New Testament is on joy, not on happiness. PH. 197

Joy is neither happiness nor brightness, joy is literally the nature of God in my blood, no matter what happens. PR. 132

Thank God, the joy of the Lord is an actual experience now, and it goes beyond any conscious experience, because the joy of the Lord takes us into the consciousness of God, and the honour at stake in our body is the honour of God. PR. 136

It is a tremendous thing to know that God reigns and rules and rejoices, and that His joy is our strength. The confidence of a Christian is that God is never in the sulks ". . . the Father of lights, with Whom can be no variation, neither shadow that is cast by turning." RTR. 65

Happiness means we select only those things out of our circumstances that will keep us happy. It is the great basis of false Christianity. SA. 97

The true energy of life lies in being rightly related to God, and only there is true joy found. SHH. 47

Solomon had everything a man could have in life, he had every means of satisfying himself; he tried the beastly line, the sublime line, the aesthetic line, the intellectual line; but, he says, you cannot find your lasting joy in any of them. Joy is only to be found in your relationship to God while you live on this earth, the earth you came from and the earth you return to. SHH. 67

Solomon rattles the bottom board out of every piece of deception. The only true joy in life, he says, is based on a personal relationship to God. You cannot find joy in being like animals, or in art, or aestheticism, in ruling or being ruled—the whole thing is passed in survey in a most ruthless examination by a man whose wisdom is profounder than the profoundest and has never been excelled, and in summing it all up he says that joy is only found in any of these things when a man is rightly related to God. SHH. 78

The joy of Jesus Christ was in the absolute self-surrender and self-sacrifice of Himself to His Father, the joy of doing what the Father sent Him to do—'I delight to do Thy will,' and that is the joy He prays may be in His disciples. SSY. 98

The Scriptures are full of admonitions to rejoice, to praise God, to sing aloud for joy; but only when one has a cause to rejoice, to praise, and to sing aloud, can these things truly be done from the heart. In the physical realm the average sick man does not take a very bright view of life, and with the sick in soul true brightness and cheer are an impossibility. Until the soul is cured there is always an underlying dread and fear which steals away the gladness and "joy unspeakable and full of glory" which God wishes to be the portion of all His children. WG. 64

Week 25

JUDGMENT

Do not judge according to appearance, but judge with righteous judgment.

—John 7:24

In every life there is one place where God must have 'elbow room.' We must not pass judgment on others, nor must we make a principle of judging out of our own experience. It is impossible for a man to know the views of Almighty God. BFB. 22

The Bible says that a man knows by the way he is made that certain things are wrong, and as he obeys or disobeys the ordinance of God written in his spirit, he will be judged. BP. 240

The judgments of God are a consuming fire whereby He destroys in order to deliver; the time to be alarmed in life is when all things are undisturbed. CHI. 66

The judgments of God leave scars, and the scars remain until I humbly and joyfully recognize that the judgments are deserved and that God is justified in them. CHI. 70

Never say, 'That truth is applicable to So-and-so,' it puts you in a false position. To know that the truth is applicable to another life is a sacred trust from God to you, you must never say anything about it. Restraint in these matters is the way to maintain communion with God. DI. 84

Justification means two things—first, that God's law is just, and second, that every sinner is unjust; therefore if God is to justify a man He can only do it by vindicating the law, and by destroying the sinner out of him. GW. 85

One of the greatest disasters in human life is our wrong standards of judgment, we will judge men by their brains, Jesus never did. Jesus judged men and women by their relationship to His Father, an implicit relationship. HG. 68

One of the most remarkable things about Jesus Christ is that although He was full of love and gentleness, yet in His presence every one not only felt benefited, but ashamed. It is His presence that judges us; we long to meet Him, and yet we dread to. HGM. 42

If we judge ourselves by one another we do not feel condemned . . . ; but immediately Jesus Christ is in the background—His life, His language, His looks, His labours, we feel judged instantly. "It is for judgment that I have come into the world." HGM. 43

Our Lord is unceasingly deliberate, the beginning and the end of His judgment is the same; He will not pass a hasty judgment on us. When He comes He will judge us straightaway, and we shall accept His judgment. HGM. 45

We pronounce judgments, not by our character or our goodness, but by the intolerant ban of finality in our views, which awakens resentment and has none of the Spirit of Jesus in it. Jesus never judged like that. It was His presence, His inherent holiness that judged. Whenever we see Him we are judged instantly. HGM. 46

There is no vindictiveness in Our Lord's judgments; He passes judgment always out of His personal love. HGM. 46

The revelation of Jesus comes in the way He walks on our deeps; He tells us to do something which in the light of our own discernment sounds ridiculous, but immediately we do it, we experience the judgment of Jesus. The judgment is not in what He says, it is Himself. HGM. 91

Life serves back in the coin you pay. You are paid back what you give, not necessarily by the same person; and this holds with regard to good as well as evil. If you have been generous, you will meet generosity again through someone else; if you have been shrewd in finding out the defects of others, that is the way people will judge you. Jesus Christ never allows retaliation, but He says that the basis of life is retribution. HGM. 104

We have to learn to see things from Jesus Christ's standpoint. Our judgment is warped in every particular in which we do not allow it to be illuminated by Jesus Christ. MFL. 125

It takes God a long time to get us out of the way of thinking that unless everyone sees as we do, they must be wrong. MUH. 127

There is no getting away from the penetration of Jesus. If I see the mote in your eye, it means I have a beam in my own. Every wrong thing that I see in you, God locates in me. Every time I judge, I condemn myself. Stop having a measuring rod for other people. MUH. 169

The average Christian is the most penetratingly critical individual. Criticism is part of the ordinary faculty of man; but in the spiritual domain nothing is accomplished by criticism. MUH. 169

Beware of justifying yourself when God alone is the justifier. If ever I can justify myself, I make God unjust. If I am right and morally based in all I do and say, I do not need a Saviour, and God is not justified in the extravagant waste of sending Jesus Christ to die for me. If God judges me a sinner who needs saving, and I can prove that I am just, I make God unjust. NKW. 91

The pronouncement of coming doom is a combining of judgment and deliverance. When God's limit is reached He destroys the unsaveable and liberates the saveable; consequently judgment days are the great mercy of God because they separate between good and evil, between right and wrong. OPG. 19

We bring God to the bar of our judgment and say hard things about Him—'Why does God bring thunderclouds and disasters when we want green pastures and still waters?' Bit by bit we find, behind the clouds, the Father's feet; behind the lightning, an abiding day that has no night; behind the thunder a still small voice that comforts with a comfort that is unspeakable. PH. 83

There are times when the Heavenly Father will look as if He were an unjust Judge, but remember, Jesus says, He is not. PH. 97

God is going to judge us by the times when we have been in living communion with Him, not by what we feel like to-day. God judges us entirely by what we have seen. We are not judged by the fact that we live up to the light of our conscience; we are judged by The Light, Jesus Christ. "I am the light of the world"; and if we do not know Jesus Christ, we are to blame. The only reason we do not know Him is because we have not bothered our heads about Him. PH. 119

It is easy to see the specks and the wrong in others, because we see in others that of which we are guilty ourselves. PH. 121

"This is the judgment," i.e., the critical moment—not the sovereign purpose of God, nor the decree of God, but the critical moment in individual experience—"that the light," Jesus Christ, "is come into the world, and men," individual me, "loved the darkness," their own point of view, their own prejudices and preconceived determinations, "rather than the light." That, says Jesus, is the judgment. PH. 202

The standard for the judgment of Christendom is not the light it has received but the light it ought to have received. PS. 44

The standard for the judgment of Christians is Our Lord. PS. 44

We have judged our fellow men as sinners. If God should judge us like that we would be in hell. God judges us through the marvellous Atonement of Jesus Christ. RTR. 23

We cannot judge ourselves by ourselves or by anyone else, there is always one fact more in everyone's life that we do not know. We cannot put men into types, we are never at the balance of one another's heredity; therefore the judgment cannot lie with us. SHH. 37

It is a great thing to notice the things we cannot answer just now, and to waive our judgment about them. Because you cannot explain a thing, don't say there is nothing in it. SHH. 37

There are dark and mysterious and perplexing things in life, but the prevailing authority at the back of all is a righteous authority, and a man does not need to be unduly concerned. When we do find out the judgment of God, we shall be absolutely satisfied with it to the last degree, we won't have another word to say—"that Thou mightest be justified when Thou speakest, and be clear when Thou judgest." SHH. 37

There is no problem, no personal grief, no agony or distress (and God knows there are some fathomless agonies just now—awful injustices and wrongs and evils and nobility all mixed up together) but will have an overwhelming explanation one day. If we will hang in to the fact that God is true and loving and just, every judgment He passes will find us in agreement with it finally. SHH. 37

It is a great education to try and put yourself into the circumstances of others before passing judgment on them. SHH. 113

Don't glory in men; don't think of men more highly than you ought to think. We always know what the other man should be, especially if he is a Christian. We are all lynx-eyed in seeing what other people ought to be. We erect terrific standards, and then criticise men for not reaching them. SHH. 133

No human being dare criticise another human being, because immediately he does he puts himself in a superior position to the one he criticises. SSM. 76

The counsel of Jesus is to abstain from judging. This sounds strange at first because the characteristic of the Holy Spirit in a Christian is to reveal the things that are wrong, but the strangeness is only on the surface. SSM. 77

Jesus says a disciple can never stand away from another life and criticise it, therefore He advocates an uncritical temper, "Judge not." Beware of anything that puts you in the place of the superior person. SSM. 77

"Judge not, that ye be not judged." If we let that maxim of our Lord's sink into our hearts we will find how it hauls us up. "Judge not"—why, we are always at it! The average Christian is the most penetratingly critical individual, there is nothing of the likeness of Jesus Christ about him. A critical temper is contradiction to all our Lord's teaching. Jesus says of criticism, 'Apply it to yourself, never to anyone else.' "Why dost thou judge thy brother? . . . for we shall all stand before the judgment seat of Christ." SSM. 78

Jesus says regarding judging, *'Don't;* be uncritical in your temper, because in the spiritual domain you can accomplish nothing by criticism.' One of the severest lessons to learn to is leave the cases we do not understand to God. SSM. 78

There is always one fact more in every life of which we know nothing, therefore Jesus says, 'Judge not.' SSM. 79

The measure you mete is measured to you again . . . If you have been shrewd in finding out the defects of others, that will be exactly the measure meted out to you, people will judge you in the same way. SSM. 79

Which of us would dare stand before God and say, 'My God, judge me as I have judged my fellow-men'? We have judged our fellow-men as sinners; if God had judged us like that we would be in hell. God judges us through the marvelous Atonement of Jesus Christ. SSM. 80

We cannot get away from the penetration of Jesus Christ. If I see the mote in my brother's eye, it is because I have a beam in my own. It is a most homecoming statement. If I have let God remove the beam from my own outlook by His mighty grace, I will carry with me the implicit sunlight confidence that what God has done for me He can easily do for you, because you have only a splinter, I had a log of wood! This is the confidence God's salvation gives us, we are so amazed at the way God has altered us that we can despair of no one; 'I know God can undertake for you, you are only a little wrong, I was wrong to the remotest depths of my mind; I was a mean, prejudiced, self-interested, self-seeking person and God has altered me, therefore I can never despair of you, or of anyone.' SSM. 81

Week 26

LIFE AND DEATH

Whoever lives and believes in Me shall never die.

—John 11:26

Our true life is not intellect or morality or bodily eating and drinking; our true life is our relationship to Jesus Christ. If once we recognize that and take care to be identified with Him in the crises of life, God will look after all the rest. If we try to draw out inspiration from elsewhere we will die in the attempt. AUG. 89

A great and glorious fact—to believe in Jesus Christ is to receive God, Who is described to the believer as 'eternal life.' Eternal life is not a gift *from* God, but the gift *of* God, that is, God Himself. AUG. 106

"Let not your heart be troubled: ye believe in God, believe also in Me." Jesus Christ is talking here about what no man knows but Himself, viz. the day after death, and He says, 'Don't be troubled about it.' AUG. 116

No man by nature has the life of the Son of God in him; he has in him the life which God creates in all men, but before he can have in his actual life the life that was in the Son of God, he must be born from above. BE. 42

If I am going to decide for the Spirit, I will crucify the flesh; God cannot do it, I must do it myself. To 'crucify' means to put to death, not counteract, not sit on, not whitewash, but kill. If I do not put to death the things in me which are not of God, they will put to death the things that are of God. BE. 79

There are things in life which are irreparable; there is no road back to yesterday. BFB. 16

We are not intended to understand Life. Life makes us what we are, but Life belongs to God. If I can understand a thing and can define it, I am its master. I cannot understand or define Life; I cannot understand or define God; consequently I am master of neither. BFB. 34

The basis of things is tragic; therefore God must find the way out, or there is no way out. BFB. 60

Our actual life is a disguise, no one expresses what he really is. BFB. 105

All we know about eternal life, about hell and damnation, the Bible alone tells us. BP. 95

. . . we cannot explain life, yet it is a very commonplace fact that we are alive. We cannot explain love; we cannot explain death; we cannot explain sin; yet these are all everyday facts. The world of Nature is a confusion; there is nothing clear about it; it is a confusing, wild chaos. Immediately we receive the Spirit of God, He energizes our spirits not only for practical living but for practical thinking, and we begin to 'discern the arm of the Lord,' i.e., to see God's order in and through all the chaos. BP. 230

Death is not annihilation: we exist in a kingdom of death. BSG. 76

Whenever Jesus speaks about life He is referring to the life which is in Himself, and it is this life which He imparts by means of His death. BSG. 76

. . . let us face life as it is, not as we feel it ought to be, for it never will be what it ought to be until the kingdom of this world is become the kingdom of our Lord, and of His Christ. CD. VOL. 1, 118

We are here for one purpose: "to fill up that which is lacking of the afflictions of Christ"—spoilt for this age, alive to nothing but Jesus Christ's point of view. CHI. 72

Think of the dignity it gives to a man's life to know that God has put His honour in his keeping. Our lives mean more than we can tell, they mean that we are fulfilling some purpose of God about which we know nothing . . . CHI. 112

The problems of life are only explainable by means of a right relationship to God. CHI. 114

Beware of the people who tell you life is simple. Life is such a mass of complications that no man is safe apart from God. Coming to Jesus does not simplify life, it simplifies my relationship to God. DI. 36

People say they are tired of life; no man was ever tired of life; the truth is that we are tired of being half dead while we are alive. What we need is to be transfigured by the incoming of a great and new life. GW. 69

'Except you are crucified with Christ until all that is left is the life of Christ in your flesh and blood, *you have no life in you.*' Except your self-love is flooded away by the inrush of the love of Jesus so that you feel your blood move through you in tender charity as it moved through Him, *you have no life in you.*' 'Except your flesh becomes the temple of His holiness, and you abide in Christ and He in you, *you have no life in you.*' GW. 118

"Be thou faithful unto death, and I will give thee a crown of life." The crown of life means I shall see that my Lord has got the victory after all, even in me. HG. 17

The parable of the ten virgins reveals that it is fatal from our Lord's standpoint to live this life without preparation for the life to come. That is not the exegesis, it is the obvious underlying principle. HG. 74

Experimentally the meaning of life is to attain the excellency of a broken heart, for that alone entails repentance and acceptance, the two great poles of Bible revelation. "The sacrifices of God are a broken spirit"—why, we do not know, but God has made it so. The one thing we are after is to avoid getting brokenhearted. HG. 77

Whenever Our Lord speaks of "life" He means *eternal* life, and He says, "Ye have not (this) life in yourselves." Men have natural life and intellectual life apart from Jesus Christ. HG. 110

Death is the inheritance of the whole human race; since Adam, no man has even been alive to God saving by the supernatural act of re-birth. Do not get the idea that because man did not die suddenly physically, he is not dead. The manifestation of death in the body is simply a matter of time, "For *in the day that thou eatest thereof* thou shalt surely die." The birth of death was in that moment; not the birth of death for one man, but the birth of the death of the whole human race. God's attitude revealed in the Bible towards men is that they are "dead in trespasses and sins"; no touch with God, not alive towards God at all, they are quite indifferent to God's claims. IWP. 24

It is only when we get full of dread about life apart from God that we leave ourselves in His hands. IWP. 37

Death is God's delightful way of giving us life. IWP. 80

Never confound eternal life with immortality. Eternal has reference to the quality of life, not to its duration. Eternal life is the life Jesus exhibited when He was here on earth, with neither time nor eternity in it, because it is the life of God Himself. IWP. 114

Jesus said, "Ye have not (this) life in yourselves." What life? The life He had. Men have moral life, physical life and intellectual life apart from Jesus Christ. IWP. 115

. . . can God do what He likes in your life? Can He help Himself liberally to you? IYA. 44

God showed to man that compliance with His dictates would ever mean eternal bliss and joy unspeakable and life and knowledge for evermore, but that ceasing to comply would mean loss of life with God and eternal death. LG. 11

Jesus did not say that eternal life was satisfaction, but something infinitely grander: "This is life eternal, that they might know Thee." MFL. 30

Get into the habit of saying, "Speak, Lord," and life will become a romance. MUH. 30

The remarkable thing about spiritual initiative is that the life comes after we do the "bucking up." God does not give us overcoming life; He gives us life *as we overcome*. MUH. 47

Eternal Life has nothing to do with Time, it is the life which Jesus lived when He was down here. The only source of Life is the Lord Jesus Christ. MUH. 103

The shallow amenities of life, eating and drinking, walking and talking, are all ordained by God. . . . We are so abominably serious, so desperately interested in our own characters, that we refuse to behave like Christians in the shallow concerns of life. MUH. 327

One individual life may be of priceless value to God's purposes, and yours may be that life. MUH. 335

Life without conflict is impossible, either in nature or in grace. NKW. 36

My actual life is given me by God, and I can live in it either as an atheist or as a worshiper. NKW. 40

To give God my life for death is of no value; what is of value is to let Him have all my powers that have been saved and sanctified, so that as Jesus sacrificed His life for His Father, I can sacrifice my life for Him. 'Present your bodies a *living* sacrifice.' NKW. 125

"As He is, so are we." The sanctified life is a life that bears a strong family likeness to Jesus Christ, a life that exhibits His virtues, His patience, His love, His holiness. Slowly and surely we learn the great secret of eternal life, which is to know God. OBH. 43

In personal life despise these two things—dumps and hurry; they are worse than the devil, and are both excessively culpable. Dumps is an absolute slur against God—I won't look up, I have done all I could but it is all up, and I am in despair. Hurry is the same mood expressed in an opposite way—I have no time to pray, no time to look to God or to consider anything, I must do the thing. Perspiration is mistaken for inspiration. Consequently I drive my miserable little wagon in a rut instead of hitching it to a star and pulling according to God's plan. NKW. 45

Jesus does not ask us to die for Him, but to lay down our lives for Him. Our Lord did not sacrifice Himself for death, He sacrificed His *life,* and God wants our life, not our death. OBH. 59

The Holy Spirit destroys our personal private life and turns it into a thoroughfare for God. NKW. 65

The only supernatural life ever lived on earth was the life of our Lord, and He was at home with God anywhere. Wherever we are not at home with God, there is a quality to be added. We have to let God press through us in that particular until we gain Him, and life becomes the simple life of a child in which the vital concern is putting God first. OBH. 65

The questions that matter in life are remarkably few, and they are all answered by these words, "Come unto Me." Not—'Do this' and 'Don't do that,' but 'Come.' "Come unto Me, all ye that labour and are heavy laden." OBH. 101

Being taught of God is a delightful life, it means the discernment is exercised. God does not put us in His 'show room,' we are here for Him to show His marvelous works in us and to use us in His enterprises. OBH. 113

Jesus Christ is the normal man, and in His relationship to God, to the devil, to sin and to man we see the expression in human nature of what He calls 'eternal life.' PR. 13

Jesus Christ came to give us eternal life, a life in which there is neither time nor space, which cannot be marked with suffering or death; it is the life Jesus lived. PH. 76

As soon as we recognise that life is based on tragedy, we won't be too staggered when tragedy emerges, but will learn how to turn to God. PH. 152

Death to us has become natural, but the Bible reveals it to be abnormal. PR. 11

Self-interest, self-sympathy, self-pity—anything and everything that does not arise from a determination to accept my life entirely from Him will lead to a dissipation of my life. PR. 57

The life of Jesus is the life we have to live here, not hereafter. There is no chance to live this kind of life hereafter, we have to live it here. PR. 80

We do not enter into the life of God by imitation, or by vows, or by ceremonies, or by Church membership; we enter into it by its entering into us at regeneration. The Cross of Jesus Christ is the gateway into His life. PR. 99

If we do not put to death the things in us that are not of God, they will put to death the things that are of God. There is never any alternative, some thing must die in us—either sin or the life of God. PR. 101

Eternal life is the gift of the Lord Jesus Christ. "He that believeth on Me hath everlasting life, i.e., the life He manifested in His human flesh when He was here, and says Jesus, 'Ye have not (that) life in yourselves.'" His life is not ours by natural birth, and it can only be given to us by means of His Cross. Our Lord's Cross is the gateway into His life; His Resurrection means that He has power now to convey that life to us. PR. 111

Eternal life is not a present given to me by God, it is Himself. "The gift *of* God," not *from* God. PR. 114

. . . there is only one purpose in our lives, and that is the satisfaction of the Lord Jesus Christ. PS. 46

Jesus Christ has destroyed the domination of death, and He can make us fit to face every problem of life, more than conqueror all along the line. RTR. 54

Jesus Christ can make the weakest man into a Divine dreadnought, fearing nothing. He can plant within him the life that Time cannot touch. RTR. 54

Jesus Christ can put into the man, whose energy has been sapped by sin and wrong until he is all but in hell, a life so strong and full that Satan has to flee whenever he meets him. Jesus Christ can make any life more than conqueror as they draw on His Resurrection life. RTR. 81

God does not give us overcoming life: He gives life to the man who overcomes. In every case of tribulation, from gnats to the cruelty of the sword, we take the step as though there were no God to assist us, and we find He is there. RTR. 81

To say that reason is the basis of human life is absurd, but to say that the basis of human life is tragedy and that the main purpose of it as far as Jesus Christ is concerned, is holiness, is much nearer the point of view given in the Bible. SA. 32

✓ The only simple thing in human life is our relationship to God in Christ. SA. 67

Within the limits of birth and death I can do as I like; but I cannot make myself un-born, neither can I escape death, those two limits are there. I have nothing to do with placing the limits, but within them I can produce what my disposition chooses. Whether I have a distressful time or a joyful time depends on what I do in between the limits of the durations. SHH. 23

. . . we all die. It is humiliating for our predictions to remember that although the spirit of man is indestructible, the phase of life which we bank on naturally passes. We may have labour in it, and delight and satisfaction in it, but it will all pass. When a beast dies, his body disappears and his soul goes downwards into entire nature; the spirit of a man goes straight back to God Who made it; it is never absorbed into God. SHH. 38

The spell between birth and death is mine, and I along with other human beings make the kind of life I live. SHH. 43

✓ Unless a man can get into a relationship with the God Whom the Bible reveals, life is not worth living. SHH. 44

. . . whatever possessions you have will consume the nobility of the life in an appalling way. SHH. 63

It is a man's personal relationship that tells. When he dies he can take nothing he has done or made in his lifetime with him. The only thing he can take with him is what he *is*. SHH. 65

When death ends the present order, the issue will reveal how you have lived. Only when you live in personal relationship to God does the end explain that you have the right secret of life. SHH. 86

It is in the middle that human choices are made; the beginning and the end remain with God. The decrees of God are birth and death, and in between those limits man makes his own distress or joy. SHH. 86

No education, no culture, no sociology or government can touch the fathomless rot at the basis of human life in its deepest down storey. We live in the twenty-second storey up, and the tragedies we touch are only personal tragedies; only one in a million comes to understand the havoc that underlies everything. SHH. 103

Life is immensely precarious, haphazard. A Christian does not believe that everything that happens is ordained by God; what he believes is that he has to get hold of God's order no matter what happens in the haphazard. SHH. 130

Instead of death being the introduction to a second chance, it is the confirmation of the first chance. SHH. 142

There is no possibility of saying a word in favour of a man after death if he did not do things before his death. SHH. 144

Death is a great dread. SHL. 24

It is the physical calamity of death *plus* the thing behind which no man can grasp, that makes death so terrible. SHL. 24

The Bible reveals that death is inevitable—'and so death passed upon all men.' 'It is appointed unto men once to die.' Repeat that over to yourself. It is appointed to every one of us that we are going to cease to be as we are now, and the place that knows us now shall know us no more. We may shirk it, we may ignore it, we may be so full of robust health and spirits that the thought of death never enters, but it is inevitable. SHL. 25

Life is a far greater danger than death. SHL. 26

Death has no terror for the man who is rightly related to God through Jesus Christ. SHL. 26

It is not within the power of human tongue or archangel's tongue to state what an awful fact death is, and what a still more awful fact life is. But thank God, there is the greatest deliverance conceivable from all that life may bring and from all that death may bring. SHL. 27

One life yielded to God at all costs is worth thousands only touched by God. SHL. 79

The natural life is neither moral nor immoral, I make it moral or immoral by my ruling disposition. Jesus teaches that the natural life is meant for sacrifice, we can give it as a gift to God, which is the only way to make it spiritual. SSM. 36

Week 27

LIGHT AND DARKNESS

The night is far spent, the day is at hand. Therefore let us cast off the works of darkness, and let us put on the armor of light.

—Romans 13:12

God is light and in Him is no darkness at all.

—1 John 1:5

"If we walk in the light, as God is in the light," we have fellowship with everyone else who is in the light. BE. 31

The condemnation is not that a man is born with an heredity of sin; a man begins to get the seal of condemnation when he sees the Light and prefers the darkness. BE. 62

"If therefore the light that is in thee be darkness, how great is that darkness!" Darkness is my own point of view; when once I allow the prejudice of my head to shut down the witness of my heart, I make my heart dark. BP. 138

If Jesus Christ had not come with His light, and the Holy Ghost had not come with His light, men had not known anything about sin. BP. 155

. . . nothing is cleaner or grander or sweeter than light. Light cannot be soiled; a sunbeam may shine into the dirtiest puddle, but it is never soiled. A sheet of white paper can be soiled, so can almost any white substance, but you cannot soil light. BP. 173

There is no variableness in God, no "shadow that is cast by turning." We are told that where there is light and substance, there must be shadow; but there is no shadow in God, none whatever. BP. 219

A searchlight illuminates only what it does and no more; but let daylight come, and you find there are a thousand and one things the searchlight had not revealed. Whenever you get the light of God on salvation it acts like a searchlight, everything you read in the Bible teaches salvation and you say, 'Why, it is as simple as can be!' The same with sanctification, and the Second Coming. When you come to the place where God is the dominant light you find facts you never realised before, facts which no one is sufficient to explain saving the Lord Jesus Christ. BSG. 62

God is a light so bright that the first vision of Himself is dark with excess of light. CD. VOL. 1, 52

If I walk in the light as God is in the light, sin is not. HG. 117

As long as you are in the dark you do not know what God is doing; immediately you get into the light, you discover it. HGM. 53

The trouble with most of us is that we will walk only in the light of our conviction of what the light is. IWP. 82

"Ye are the light of the world." We have the idea that we are going to shine in heaven, but we are to shine down here, "in the midst of a crooked and perverse nation." We are to shine as lights in the world in the squalid places, and it cannot be done by putting on a brazen smile, the light must be there all the time. LG. 45

In actual life we must be always in the light, and we cease to be in the light when we want to explain why we did a thing. The significant thing about Our Lord is that He never explained anything; He let mistakes correct themselves because He always lived in the light. There is so much in us that is folded and twisted, but the sign that we are following God is that we keep in the light. LG. 66

It is better never to have had the light than to refuse to obey it. MFL. 16

If the Spirit of God detects anything in you that is wrong, He does not ask you to put it right; He asks you to accept the light, and He will put it right. A child of the light confesses instantly and stands bared before God; a child of the darkness says—"Oh, I can explain that away." When once the light breaks and the conviction of wrong comes, be a child of the light, and confess, and God will deal with what is wrong; if you vindicate yourself, you prove yourself to be a child of the darkness. MUH. 83

If you do not obey the light, it will turn into darkness. MUH. 240

To walk in the light means that everything that is of the darkness drives me closer into the centre of the light. MUH. 361

If we have entered into the heavenly places in Christ Jesus, the light has shone, and, this is the marvellous thing, as we begin to do what we know the Lord would have us do, we find He does not enable *us* to do it, He simply puts through us all His power and the thing is done in His way. Thank God for everyone who has seen the light, who has understood how the Lord Jesus Christ clears away the darkness and brings the light by showing His own characteristics through us. OBH 40

There is another thing about the possession of light in Jesus Christ: my possession of light is quite different from yours. Each of us has a particular possession of light that no one else can have, and if we refuse to take our possession, everyone else will suffer. OBH. 42

One step in the right direction in obedience to the light, and the manifestation of the Son of God in your mortal flesh is as certain as that God is on His throne. When once God's light has come to us through Jesus Christ, we must never hang back, but obey; and we shall not walk in darkness, but will have the light of life. OBH. 43

God is Light, and He lifts us up in Himself, no matter who we are, and poises us as surely as He established the stars, in the very light that He is in. He makes us meet to be partakers of that wonderful inheritance, and slowly and surely the marvel of the life of the Son of God is manifested in our mortal flesh. OBH. 46

"Let your light so shine before men. . . ." Our light is to shine in the darkness; it is not needed in the light. OBH. 75

"What I tell you in the darkness . . ." Let it be understood that the darkness our Lord speaks of is not darkness caused by sin or disobedience, but rather darkness caused from excess of light. PH. 10

We are not judged by the light we have, but by the light we have refused to accept. God holds us responsible for what we will not look at. A man is never the same after he has seen Jesus. We are judged by our immortal moments, the moments in which we have seen the light of God. PH. 119

We all like the twilight in spiritual and moral matters, not the intensity of black and white, not the clear lines of demarcation—saved and unsaved. We prefer things to be hazy, winsome and indefinite, without the clear light. When the light does come difficulty is experienced, for when a man awakens he sees a great many things. We may feel complacent with a background of drab, but to be brought up against the white background of Jesus Christ is an immensely uncomfortable thing. PH. 198

The unaltered, natural disposition of a man is called by our Lord 'darkness,' that means prejudice against the light. PS. 44

"What I tell you in darkness"—watch where God puts you into darkness, and when you are there, keep your mouth shut. When you are in the dark, listen, and God will give you a very precious message for someone else when you get into the light. RTR. 83

I am not judged by the light I have, but by the light I have refused to accept. SA. 49

Light is the description of clear, beautiful, moral character from God's standpoint, and if we walk in the light, "the blood of Jesus Christ cleanses us from all sin;" God Almighty can find nothing to censure. SA. 52

The light always reveals and guides, and men dislike it, and prefer darkness when their deeds are evil. SSM. 20

"Ye are the light of the world." Light cannot be soiled; you may try to grasp a beam of light with the sootiest hand, but you leave no mark on the light. A sunbeam may shine into the filthiest hovel in the slums of a city, but it cannot be soiled. A merely moral man, or an innocent man, may be soiled in spite of his integrity, but the man who is made pure by the Holy Ghost cannot be soiled, he is as light. SSM. 20

Week 28

LOVE

In this is love, not that we loved God, but that He loved us and sent His Son to be the propitiation for our sins.

—1 John 4:10

Love to be anything at all must be personal; to love without hating is an impossibility, and the stronger and more emphatic the love, the more intense is its obverse, hatred. God loves the world so much that He hates with a perfect hatred the thing that switched men wrong; and Calvary is the measure of His hatred. BE. 32

To love the world as it is is the wrong kind of love, it is that sentiment which is 'the enemy of God', because it means I am the friend of the system of things which does not take God into account. We are to love the world in the way God loves it, and be ready to spend and be spent until the wrong and evil are removed from it. BE. 33

It is of no use to pray, 'O Lord, for more love! give me love like Thine; I do not want to love Thee better,' if we have not begun at the first place, and that is to choose to receive the Holy Spirit Who will shed abroad the love of God in our hearts. BP. 119

We have defined love, in its highest sense, as being the sovereign preference of my person for another person. BP. 134

If my love is first of all God, I shall take no account of the base ingratitude of others, because the mainspring of my service to my fellow-men is love to God. BP. 181

Love never professes; love *confesses*. CD. VOL. 2, 76

Love in the Bible is ONE; it is unique, and the human element is but one aspect of it. It is a love so mighty, so absorbing, so intense that all the mind is emancipated and entranced by God; all the heart is transfigured by the same devotion; all the soul in its living, working, waking, sleeping moments is indwelt and surrounded and en-wheeled in the rest of this love. CD. VOL. 2, 154

The wrath of God abides all the time a man persists in the way that leads away from God; the second he turns, he is faced with His love. Wrath is the dark line in God's face, and is expressive of His hatred of sin. CHI. 14

The love of God and the wrath of God are obverse sides of the same thing, like two sides of a coin. The wrath of God is as positive as His love. God cannot be in agreement with sin. When a man is severed from God the basis of his moral life is chaos and wrath, not because God is angry, like a Moloch, it is His constitution of things. CHI. 14

God's love is wrath towards wrong; He is never tender to that which hates goodness. CHI. 67

Most of us love other people for what they are to us instead of for what God wants them to be. CHI. 69

There is only one Being who loves perfectly, and that is God, yet the New Testament distinctly states that we are to love as God does; so the first step is obvious. If ever we are going to have perfect love in our hearts we must have the very nature of God in us. CHI. 88

A false idea of God's honour ends in misinterpreting His ways. It is the orthodox type of Christian who by sticking to a crude idea of God's character, presents the teaching which says, "God loves you when you are good, but not when you are bad." God loves us whether we are good or bad. That is the marvel of His love. CHI. 115

You don't love a person with your heart and leave the rest of your nature out, you love with your whole being, from the crown of the head to the sole of the foot. GW. 9

The Bible makes no distinction between Divine love and human love, it speaks only of 'love.' The majority of us have an impersonal, ethereal, vague abstraction we call love to God; Jesus says I must love God with all my heart and soul and mind and strength, then my love for my fellow men will be relative to that centre. GW. 39

'Love is of God'; it never came from the devil and never can go to the devil. When I am rightly related to God, the more I love the more blessing does He pour out on other lives. The reward of love is the capacity to pour out more love all the time, 'hoping for nothing again.' That is the essential nature of perfect love. GW. 41

When you are sentimentally interested in a person you are conscious of it; when you are in love with a person you are not conscious of it because the love is deeper than consciousness and is only revealed in a crisis. When you love God you become identified with His interests in other people, and He will bring around you those He is interested in—the sinners, the mean, the ungrateful, and you will soon know by your attitude to them whether you love God. GW. 41

The love of God is spelt on the Cross and nowhere else; there His conscience is satisfied. GW. 86

God loves the un-lovely, and it broke His heart to do it. The depth of the love of God is revealed by that wonderful word, 'whosoever.' HG. 120

You cannot prove that God is love if you have not been born from above, because everything around you disproves it. HGM. 97

Love springs spontaneously, that is, it is not premeditated; but love does not develop like that. Both naturally and spiritually love requires careful developing; love won't stay if it is not sedulously cultivated. If I am not careful to keep the atmosphere of my love right by cultivation, it will turn to lust—'I must have this thing for myself.' HGM. 134

The one characteristic of love is that it thinks of nothing for itself, it is absorbed in God. IWP. 21

Love is the sovereign preference of my person for another person, and Jesus says that other Person must be Himself. IWP. 84

. . . God is Love, not, God is loving. God and love are synonymous. Love is not an attribute of God, it is God; whatever God is, love is. If your conception of love does not agree with justice and judgment and purity and holiness, then your idea of love is wrong. It is not love you conceive of in your mind, but some vague infinite foolishness, all tears and softness and of infinite weakness. LG. 9

God is Love—one brief sentence, you can print it on a ring: it is the Gospel. A time is coming when the whole round world will know that God reigns and that God is Love, when hell and heaven, life and death, sin and salvation, will be read and understood aright at last. LG. 14

—"Keep yourselves in the love of God," not 'keep on loving God,' none can do that. When once you have understood the truth about your own heart's sinfulness, think not again of it, but look at the great, vast, illimitable magnificence of the love of God. LG. 19

'Love is difficult to define, but the working definition I would like to give is that 'Love is the sovereign preference of my person for another person, embracing everyone and everything in that preference.' LG. 21

The love of God is not to be looked for in justice, right, truth, and purity; the love of God *is* Jesus Christ. LG. 69

Love is the sovereign preference of my person for another person, and when the Holy Spirit is in a man, that other Person is Jesus. The only Lover of the Lord Jesus Christ is the Holy Ghost. LG. 122

If human love does not carry a man beyond himself, it is not love. If love is always discreet, always wise, always sensible and calculating, never carried beyond itself, it is not love at all. It may be affection, it may be warmth of feeling, but it has not the true nature of love in it. MUH. 52

We cannot love to order, and yet His word stands—"If any come to Me, and *hate not* his father, and mother, and wife, and children, and brethren, and sisters, yea, and his own life also," (i.e. a hatred of every loyalty that would divide the heart from loyalty to Jesus) "he cannot be My disciple." OBH. 57

Devotion to a Person is the only thing that tells; and no man on earth has the love which Jesus demands, unless it has been imparted to him. We may admire Jesus Christ, we may respect Him and reverence Him; but apart from the Holy Ghost we do not love Him. The only Lover of the Lord Jesus Christ is the Holy Ghost. OBH. 57

The revelation of God's love is that He loved us when He could not possibly respect us—He loved us "while we were yet sinners"; "when we were enemies." OBH. 58

When we receive the nature of God into us, the first thing that happens is that God takes away all pretence and pious pose; and He does it by revealing that He loved us, not because we were lovable, but because it is His nature to love. *"God is love."* OBH. 58

The curious thing about the love of God is that it is the cruellest thing on earth to everything that is not of Him. God hurts desperately when I am far away from Him; but when I am close to Him, He is unutterably tender. OBH. 58

God's love for me is inexhaustible, and His love for me is the basis of my love for others. We have to love where we cannot respect and where we must not respect, and this can only be done on the basis of God's love for us. "This is My commandment, That ye love one another, *as I have loved you*." OBH. 59

The supreme moment of the Cross in actual history is but the concentrated essence of the very nature of the Divine love. God lays down His life for the very creation which men utilise for their own selfish ends. The Self-expenditure of the love of God exhibited in the life and death of our Lord becomes a bridge over the gulf of sin; whereby human love can be imbued by Divine love, the love that never fails. OBH. 60

The greatest love of a man is his love for his friends; the greatest love of God is His love for His enemies; the highest Christian love is that a man will lay down his life for his Friend, the Lord Jesus Christ—"I have called you friends." OBH. 60

God does not give us power to love as He loves; the love of God, the very nature of God, possesses us, and He loves through us. OBH. 100

When the Holy Spirit has shed abroad the love of God in our hearts, then that love requires cultivation. No love on earth will develop without being cultivated. We have to dedicate ourselves to love, which means identifying ourselves with God's interests in other people, and God is interested in some funny people, viz., in you and in me! OBH. 117

An unemotional love is inconceivable. Love for the good must involve displeasure and grief for the evil. OPG. 16

This is the characteristic of the Divine love: not that God lays down His life for His friends, but that He lays down His life for His enemies. That is not human love. It does not mean that no human being has ever laid down his life for his enemies, but it does mean that no human being ever did so without having received the Divine nature through the Redemption of our Lord. PH. 25

The highest Christian love is not devotion to a work or to a cause, but to Jesus Christ. PH. 28

That God is love is a revelation. PH. 64

Jesus has loved me to the end of all my meanness and selfishness and sin; now, He says, show that same love to others. PH. 81

It is the most ordinary business to fall in love; it is the most extraordinary business to abide there. The same thing with regard to the love of our Lord. The Holy Ghost gives us the great power to love Jesus Christ. That is not a rare experience at all; the rare experience is to get into the conception of loving Him in such a way that the whole heart and mind and soul are taken up with Him. PH. 109

If human love is always discreet and calculating, never carried beyond itself, it is not of the true nature of love. The characteristic of love is that it is spontaneous, it bursts up in extraordinary ways; it is never premeditated. PH. 140

Love is not blind. Love has insight, it sees the things that are not seen. We are told that when we are in love with a person we do not see his defects: the truth is that we see what others do not see, we see him in the ideal, in the real relationship. PH. 155

Love is not measured by what it gets, but by what it costs, and our relationship to Jesus Christ can never be on the line of, 'Why shouldn't I do this?' Our Lord simply says, 'If any man will be My disciple, those are the conditions." PR. 93

Unless we are willing to give up good things for Jesus Christ, we have no realisation of Whom He is. 'But really I cannot give up things that are quite legitimate!' Then never mention the word love again in connection with Jesus Christ if you cannot give up the best you have for Him. This is the essential nature of love in the natural life, otherwise it is a farce to call it love, it is not love, but lust; and when we come to our relationship with Jesus Christ, this is the love He demands of us. PR. 103

When we preach the love of God there is a danger of forgetting that the Bible reveals not first the love of God but the intense, blazing holiness of God, with His love as the centre of that holiness. PS. 20

To know that God is love, God is holy, God is near, is pure delight to man in his innocent relationship to God, but a terror extreme since the fall. God can never leave a man until He has burned him as pure as He is Himself. It is God's love that forbids He should let him go. PS. 61

The springs of love are in God, that means they cannot be found anywhere else. It is absurd for us to try and find the love of God in our hearts naturally, it is not there any more than the life of Jesus Christ is there. Love and life are in God and in Jesus Christ and in the Holy Spirit whom God gives us, not because we merit Him, but according to His own particular graciousness. RTR. 34

God has loved me to the end of all my sinfulness, of all my self-will, all my stiff-neckedness, all my pride, all my self-interest; now He says—"love one another, as I have loved you." I am to show to my fellow men the same love that God showed me. That is Christianity in practical working order. RTR. 46

The love of God in Christ Jesus is such that He can take the most unfit man—unfit to survive, unfit to fight, unfit to face moral issues—and make him not only fit to survive and to fight, but fit to face the biggest moral issues and the strongest power of Satan, and come off more than conqueror. RTR. 55

We have to love where we cannot respect and where we must not respect, and this can only be done on the basis of God's love for us. "This is My commandment, that you love one another, as I have loved you." RTR. 56

"Love never faileth!" What a wonderful phrase that is! but what a still more wonderful thing the reality of that love must be; greater than prophecy—that vast forth-telling of the mind and purpose of God; greater than the practical faith that can remove mountains; greater than philanthropic self-sacrifice; greater than the extraordinary gifts of emotions and ecstacies and all eloquence; and it is this love that is shed abroad in our hearts by the Holy Ghost which is given unto us. RTR. 67

In the Cross we may see the dimensions of Divine love. The Cross is not the cross of a man, but an exhibition of the heart of God. At the back of the wall of the world stands God with His arms outstretched, and every man driven there is driven into the arms of God. The Cross of Jesus is the supreme evidence of the love of God. RTR. 88

'Love . . . taketh not account of evil'; it does not ignore the fact that there is evil, but it does not take it into calculations. SHL. 93

The marvel of the Divine love is that God exhibits His love not only to good people but to bad people. SSM. 50

The love of God is not like the love of a father or a mother, it is the love *of* God. SSM. 51

No one could have had a more sensitive love in human relationship than Jesus; and yet He says there are times when love to father and mother must be hatred in comparison to our love for Him. SSY. 52

Love is difficult to define, although simple to know; life is difficult to define, although simple to have. .SSY. 158

Love cannot be defined. Try and define your love for Jesus Christ, and you will find you cannot do it. Love is the sovereign preference of my person for another person, and Jesus Christ demands that that other person be Himself. That does not mean we have no preference for anyone else, but that Jesus Christ has the sovereign preference; within that sovereign preference come all other loving preferences, down to flowers and animals. The Bible makes no distinction between Divine love and human love, it speaks only of love. SSY. 158

'Things are not happening in the way I expected they would, therefore I am going to give it all up.' To talk like that is a sure sign that we are not possessed by love for Him, but only by love for ourselves. SSY. 170

MAN

A man's steps are of the Lord; How then can a man understand his own way?

—Proverbs 20:24

Immorality has its seat in every one of us, not in some of us. If a man is not holy, he is immoral, no matter how good he may seem. Immorality is at the basis of the whole thing; if it does not show itself outwardly, it will show itself before God. AUG. 45

Personality is the characteristic of the spiritual man as individuality is the characteristic of the natural man. BE. 31

There is no subject more intimately interesting to modern people than man's relationship to man; but men get impatient when they are told that the first requirement is that they should love God first and foremost. BE. 124

God created a unique being, not an angel, and not God Himself; He created man. BP. 5

Man was created out of the earth, and related to the earth, and yet he was created in the image of God, whereby God could prove Himself more than a match for the devil by a creation a little lower than the angels, the order of beings to which Satan belongs. This is, as it were, God's tremendous experiment in the creation of man. BP. 5

All through the New Testament the Spirit of God has foretold that we are going to have the worship of man installed, and it is in our midst to-day. We are being told that Jesus Christ and God are ceasing to be of importance to the modern man, and what we are worshipping more and more now is 'Humanity,' and this is slowly merging into a new phase; all the up-to-date minds are looking towards the manifestation of this "superman," a being much greater than the being we know as man . . . BP. 7

Man is the climax of creation. He is on a stage a little lower than the angels, and God is going to overthrow the devil by this being who is less than angelic. BP. 8

Not only is Man the head and climax of the six days' work, but he is the beginning of, and stands at the threshold of, the Sabbath of God. God's heart is, as it were, absolutely at rest now that He has created man; even in spite of the fact of the fall, and all else, God is absolutely confident that everything will turn out as He said it would. The devil has laughed at God's hope for thousands of years, and has ridiculed and scorned that hope, but God is not upset or alarmed about the final issue; He is certain that man will bruise the serpent's head. This has reference to those who are born again through Jesus Christ's amazing Atonement. BP. 9

. . . the Bible reveals that our Redeemer entered into the world through the woman. Man, as man, had no part whatever in the Redemption of the world; it was "the seed of the woman." BP. 19

Character is the whole trend of a man's life, not isolated acts here and there, and God deals with us on the line of character building. BP. 109

The path of peace for us is to hand ourselves over to God and ask Him to search us, not what we think we are, or what other people think we are, or what we persuade ourselves we are or would like to be, but 'Search *me* out, O God, explore *me* as I really am in Thy sight.' BFB. 158

Character is the sum total of a man's actions. You cannot judge a man by the good things he does at times; you must take all the times together, and if in the greater number of times he does bad things, he is a bad character, in spite of the noble things he does intermittently. BP. 205

The marvel of the creation of man is that he is made "of the earth, earthy." God allowed the enemy to work on this creation of man in a way he cannot work on any other creation, but ultimately God is going to overthrow the rule of His enemy by a being "a little lower than the angels," viz., man. BP. 216

Man as God created him is a revelation fact, not a fact we get at by our commonsense. We have never seen Man. God *created* the earth and "*formed* man of the dust of the ground," that is, God did not make man's body by a creative fiat, He deliberately builded it out of the dust of created matter according to a design in the Divine mind. Adam and Jesus Christ both came direct from the hand of God. We are not creations of God, we are pro-created through progenitors, the heredity of the human race is mixed; that accounts for all the perplexities. "And the Lord God formed man of the dust of the ground"—there is nothing the matter with matter; what has gone wrong is the infection of material things by sin, which is not material. Sin is not in matter and material things; if it were, it would be untrue to say that Jesus Christ, who "was made in the likeness of men," was "without sin." CHI. 12

When I realize that there is something between God and me, it is at the peril of my soul I don't stop everything and get it put right. Immediately a thing makes itself conscious to me, it has no business there. CHI. 74

There is a potential hero in every man—and a potential skunk. CHI. 97

It is an appalling fact that our features tell our moral character unmistakably to those who can read them, and we may be very thankful there are few who can; our safety is in other people's ignorance. In spite of the disguise of refinement, sensuality, selfishness and self-indulgence speak in our features as loud as a thunder-clap. Our inner spirit tells with an indelible mark on every feature, no matter how beautiful or how ugly the features may be. Let us remember that that is how God sees us. DI. 33

Man was created to be the friend and lover of God and for no other end, and until he realizes this he will go through turmoil and upset.

Human nature must rise to its own Source, the bosom of God, and Jesus Christ by His Redemption brings it back there. GW. 40

. . . what makes Christ's glory is His severity, i.e., His love for God's holy law rather than His love for man: Jesus Christ stood on God's side against man. GW. 85

If you want to know God's original design for man, you see it in Jesus Christ; He was easily Master of the life on the earth, in the air and in the sea, not as God, but as Man; it was the human in Jesus that was master. HGM. 60

The whole of creation was designed for man, and God intended man to be master of the life upon the earth, in the air and in the sea; the reason he is not master is because of sin, but he will yet be. HGM. 82

If you want to know the most marvellous thing in the whole of creation, it is not the heavens, the moon and the stars, but—"What is man that Thou art mindful of him? Thou madest him to have dominion over the works of Thy hands." HGM. 82

One of the most subtle errors is that God wants our possessions; they are not any use to Him. God does not want our possessions, He wants us. IWP. 120

The strength of a *real* man or *real* woman cannot be estimated. HGM. 122

Our natural virtues are remnants of what God created man to be, not promises of what he is going to be. The natural virtues cannot be patched up to come anywhere near God's demands, and the sign that God is at work in us is that He corrupts our confidence in the natural virtues. IWP. 57

Immediately man begins to examine himself, he finds he is inscrutable; there are possibilities below the threshold of his life which no one knows but God. MFL. 43

No man is virtuous because he cannot help it; virtue is acquired. MUH. 339

God is a perplexing Being to man because He is never in the wrong, and through the process of allowing every bit of man's wrongdoing to appear right at the time, He proves Himself right ultimately. Beware of the conception that God has to use His wits to keep Himself from being outwitted by man and the devil. NKW. 55

God never hastens and He never tarries. He works His plans out in His own way, and we either lie like clogs on His hands or we assist Him by being as clay in the hands of the potter. NKW. 58

Don't only make room for God, but believe that God has room enough for you. NKW. 66

God cannot come to me in my way, He can only come in His own way—in ways man would never dream of looking for Him. NKW. 98

Men are apt to cry to God to stop—'If only God would leave me alone!" God never will. His passionate, inexorable love never allows Him to leave men alone, and with His children He will shake everything that can be shaken till there is nothing that can be shaken any more; then will abide the consuming fire of God until the life is changed into the same image from glory to glory, and men see that strong family likeness to Jesus that can never be mistaken. OBH. 38

"A double minded man," i.e. a discreet man, diplomatic and wise—"is unstable in all his ways." The man who does not put God first in his calculations is always double minded. 'If I do,' 'Supposing,' and 'But'—these are all in the vocabulary of the double minded man. OBH. 53

Character is the way we have grown to act with our hands and our feet, our eyes and our tongue, and the character we make always reveals the ruling disposition within. If any man is in Christ, there is a new creation. OBH. 81

The virtuous man or woman is the one who has gone through the fight and has added virtue, added it on the basis of the Divine nature, not on the basis of human determination. OBH. 106

These two things, dust and Divinity, make up man. That he is made of the dust of the ground is man's glory, not his shame—it is only his shame in so far as he is a sinner, because in it he is to manifest the image of God. We are apt to think because we are "of the earth, earthy," that this is our humiliation, but it is not so; it is the very thing God's word makes most of. OPG. 4

If I maintain my right to my natural self I will begin to degenerate and get out of God's purpose. What happens in my personal life when I am born from above is that the Son of God is born in me, then comes in this law of the sacrifice of the natural to the spiritual, and the possibility of degeneration. If I refuse to sacrifice the natural, the God-life in me is killed. OPG. 47

A man is what he is in the dark. PH. 76

Virtue is not in the man who has not been tempted, neither is purity. When a man is tempted and remains steadfastly unspotted, then he is virtuous. PH. 148

God created man a splendid moral being, fitted to rule the earth and air and sea, but he was not to rule himself; God was to be his Master, and man was to turn his natural life into a spiritual life by obedience. PR. 11

No one on earth is more mean than I am, no one more capable of doing wrong, and yet we are always more afraid of the other fellow than of ourselves. PH. 224

A man's character is what he habitually is. SA. 50

God put man in the garden with the tree of knowledge of good and evil, and said, "Ye shall not eat of it." God did not say they were not to know good and evil, but that they were not to know good and evil by eating of the tree. They were intended to know evil in the way Jesus Christ knew it, viz., by contrast with good. They did eat of the tree, consequently the human race knows good by contrast with evil. Adam knew evil positively and good negatively, and none of us knows the order God intended. SA. 71

God made man a mixture of dust and Deity. SHH. 57

Modern wisdom says that man is a magnificent promise of what he is going to be. If that point of view is right, then there is no need to talk about sin and Redemption, and the Bible is a cunningly devised fable. But the Bible point of view seems to cover most of the facts. SHH. 76

One of the most difficult things to do is to place men. A man who knows men and can place them rightly is worth his weight in gold. SHH. 136

. . . a description of Old Age in its frailty. The keepers of the house (arms) and the strong men (legs) are weak and trembling; the grinders cease (teeth) and the windows are darkened (eyesight dimmed), the doors shut (ears are deaf), the grinding low (slow and tedious mastication), the easily startled nerves, and the loss of voice, the inability to climb, and the fear of highway traffic; the whitened hair like the almond tree in blossom, when any work seems a burden, and the failing natural desire, all portray the old man nearing the end of his earthly journey. SHH. 151

It is a marvellous moment in a man's life when he knows he is explored by God. SHL. 47

A man's character tells over his head all the time. SHH. 139

We have to learn that God is not meant for us, it is we who are meant for God. SSY. 166

Week 30

NEW BIRTH

If anyone is in Christ, he is a new creation; old things have passed away; behold, all things have become new.

—2 Corinthians 5:17

Being born again of the Spirit is an unmistakable work of God, as mysterious as the wind. Beware of the tendency to water down the supernatural in religion. AUG. 47

After being born again a man experiences peace, but it is a militant peace, a peace maintained at the point of war. BE. 78

Jesus Christ's salvation works first at the centre, not at the circumference. No one is capable of thinking about being born, or of how they will live when they are born, until they are born; we have to be born into this world first before we can think about it. "Marvel not that I said unto thee, Ye must be born again,"—'you must be born into a new world first, and if you want to know My doctrine, do My will' said Jesus. A right relation to God first is essential. BP. 144

What takes place at new birth is an 'explosion' on the inside (a literal explosion, not a theoretical one) that opens all the doors which have been closed and life becomes larger, there is the incoming of a totally new point of view. BSG. 62

No man ought to need to be born again; the fact that he does indicates that something has gone wrong with the human race. CHI. 19

It is the 'preaching of the cross' that produces the crisis we call New Birth. We are in danger of preaching the new birth instead of proclaiming that which produces the new birth, viz., the preaching of Jesus Christ, and Him crucified. GW. 17

The creation performed by God is what the Apostle Paul calls it—a *new* creation; it is not the bringing out of something already there, but the creating of something which was never there before, an entirely new creation, as unlike anything born in a man by nature as Jesus Christ is unlike anything produced by the human race throughout its history. GW. 63

"Marvel not that I said unto thee, Ye must be"—not developed, not educated, but "born again"—'fundamentally made all over again, before you can see the kingdom of God and enter into it.' HGM. 12

The conception of new birth in the New Testament is not of something that springs out of us, what modern psychology calls 'a subliminal uprush,' but of something that comes into us. HGM. 13

Some teachers make new birth a simple and natural thing, they say it is necessary, but a necessity along the line of natural development. When Jesus Christ talks about it He implies that the need to be born again is an indication of something radically wrong—"Marvel not that I said unto thee. Ye must be born again." It is a crisis. HGM. 54

"If any man is in Christ there is a new creation," everything becomes amazingly simple, not easy, but simple with the simplicity of God. HGM. 73

The only way we can be born again is by renouncing all other good. The 'old man,' or the man of old, means all the things which have nothing to do with the new life. It does not mean sins, any coward among us will give up wrong things, but will he give up right things? Will we give up the virtues, the principles, the recognition of things that are dearer to the 'Adam' life than the God life? The nature of the 'Adam' disposition in us rebels against sacrificing natural good. Jesus says, 'If you don't sacrifice natural good, you will barter the life I represent.' IWP. 99

Being born again of the Spirit is not contrary to God's original plan; for a time it has to be apparently contrary to it because Adam refused to sacrifice the life of nature to the will of God and transform it into a spiritual life by obeying the voice of God. IWP. 101

New birth refers not only to a man's eternal salvation, but to his being of value to God in this order of things; it means infinitely more than being delivered from sin and from hell. The gift of the essential nature of God is made efficacious in us by the entering in of the Holy Spirit; He imparts to us the quickening life of the Son of God, and we are lifted into the domain where Jesus lives. LG. 114

Every man has need of new birth. LG. 116

The conception of new birth in the New Testament is not a conception of something that springs out of us, but of something that enters into us. Just as our Lord came into human history from without, so He must come into us from without. Our new birth is the birth of the life of the Son of God into our old human nature, and our human nature has to be transfigured by the indwelling life of the Son of God. LG. 116

Being born again of the Spirit is an unmistakable work of God, as mysterious as the wind, as surprising as God Himself. We do not know where it begins, it is hidden away in the depths of our personal life. Being born again from above is a perennial, perpetual and eternal beginning; a freshness all the time in thinking and in talking and in living, the continual surprise of the life of God. MUH. 20

When God re-creates us in Christ Jesus He does not patch us up; He makes us *"a new creation."* MFL. 102

God does not discard the old and create something entirely new; He creates something in the old until the old and the new are made one. NKW. 58

We preach to men as if they were conscious of being dying sinners; they are not, they are having a good time, and our talk about being born again is from a domain of which they know nothing. The natural man does not want to be born again. PR. 12

The phrase "born from above" as our Lord used it does not mean being saved from hell or from sin, but that I am born into the realm in which He lives. PH. 151

In new birth God does three impossible things, impossible, that is, from the rational standpoint. The first is to make a man's past as though it had never been; the second, to make a man all over again, and the third, to make a man as certain of God as God is of Himself. New birth does not mean merely salvation from hell, but something more radical, something which tells in a man's actual life. PH. 183

The 'natural' has not life in itself, therefore we must be born from above. PR. 14

The meaning of New Birth is that we know God by a vital relationship, not only by our intellect. PR. 28

Our human nature is just the same after new birth as before, but the mainspring is different. Before new birth we sin because we cannot help it; after new birth we need not sin. PR. 35

We make the blunder of imagining that when we are born from above, we cease to be ordinary human beings, whereas we become much more ordinary human beings than we were before. Our human nature goes on all the time. PR. 38

The life of Jesus is the life of the normal man of God, but we cannot begin to live it unless we are born from above. PR. 90

Nothing has any power to alter a man save the incoming of the life of Jesus, and that is the only sign that he is born again. RTR. 76

We make character out of our disposition. Character is what we make, disposition is what we are born with; and when we are born again we are given a new disposition. A man must make his own character, but he cannot make his disposition; that is a gift. Our natural disposition is gifted to us by heredity; by regeneration God gives us the disposition of His Son. SSM. 29

Week 31

OBEDIENCE

Not everyone who says to Me, Lord, Lord, shall enter the kingdom of heaven, but he who does the will of My Father in heaven.

—Matthew 7:21

Spiritually, we are built not to command, but to obey. Always beware of the tendency to want to have things explained; you may take it as an invariable law that when you demand an explanation in connection with a moral problem it means you are evading obedience. BE. 12

Obey the Spirit of God and the word of God, and it will be as clear as a sunbeam what you have to do; it is an attitude of will towards God, an absolute abandon, a glad sacrifice of the soul in unconditional surrender. BE. 89

God will have us discern what He is doing, but it takes time because we are so slow to obey, and only as we obey do we perceive morally and spiritually. BFB. 52

Obedience to God will mean that some time or other you enter into desolation . . . CHI. 69

The gathering in of God's salvation around a man means that he is checked at first by the merest zephyr touch: there is nothing so gentle as the check of the Holy Spirit; if he obeys, emancipation is at once, if he does not obey, the zephyr touch will turn into a destructive blow from which there is no escape. CHI. 74

It is not our power to love God that enables us to obey, but the presence of the very love of God in our heart which makes it so easy to obey Him that we don't even know we are obeying. As you recall to your mind the touchings of the love of God in your life—they are always few—you will never find it impossible to do anything He asks. CHI. 89

If I am going to know who Jesus is, I must obey Him. The majority of us don't know Jesus because we have not the remotest intention of obeying Him. DI. 4

There are some questions God cannot answer until you have been brought by obedience to be able to stand the answer. Be prepared to suspend your judgment until you have heard God's answer for yourself. DI. 13

How long it takes for all the powers in a Christian to be at one depends on one thing only, viz., obedience. DI. 31

The virtue of our Redemption comes to us through the obedience of the Son of God—"though He were a Son, yet learned He obedience by the things which He suffered . . ." Our view of obedience has become so distorted through sin that we cannot understand how it could be said of Jesus that He 'learned' obedience; He was the only One of whom it could be said, because He was *"without sin."* He did not learn obedience in order to *be* a Son: He came *as* Son to redeem mankind. DI. 55

Weighing the *pros and cons* for and against a statement of Jesus Christ's means that for the time being I refuse to obey Him. DI. 71

It is not a question of being willing to go straight through, but of *going* straight through. Not a question of saying, 'Lord, I will do it,' but of *doing* it. There must be the reckless committal of everything to Him with no regard for the consequences. GW. 79

We get the life of God all at once, but we do not learn to obey all at once; we only learn to obey by the discipline of life. HG. 38

The curious thing about Our Lord is that He never insists on our obedience. HGM. 130

God never insists on our obedience; human authority does. Our Lord does not give us rules and regulations; He makes very clear what the standard is, and if the relation of my spirit to Him is that of love, I will do all He wants me to do without the slightest hesitation. If I begin to object it is because I love someone else in competition with Him, viz., myself. HGM. 148

"I am crucified with Christ; nevertheless I live; yet not I, but Christ liveth in me." These words mean the breaking of my independence and surrendering to the supremacy of the Lord Jesus. No one can do this for me, I must do it myself. There is no possibility of debate when once I am there. It is not that we have to do work for God, we have to be so loyal to Jesus Christ that He does His work through us. We learn His truth by obeying it. HGM. 148

In order to be able to wield the sword of the Spirit, which is the Word of God, we must obey, and it takes the courageous heart to obey. IYA. 35

The term 'obey' would be better expressed by the word 'use.' For instance, a scientist, strictly speaking, 'uses' the laws of nature; that is, he more than obeys them, he causes them to fulfil their destiny in his work. That is exactly what happens in the saint's life, he 'uses' the commands of the Lord and they fulfil God's destiny in his life. MFL. 53

Jesus Christ's first obedience was to the will of His Father, and our first obedience is to be to Him. The thing that detects where we live spiritually is the word 'obey.' The natural heart of man hates the word, and that hatred is the essence of the disposition that will not let Jesus Christ rule. MFL. 114

"Consider the lilies of the field"—they grow where they are put. Many of us refuse to grow where we are put, consequently we take root nowhere. Jesus says that if we obey the life God has given us, He will look after all the other things. MUH. 26

Spiritual muddle is only made plain by obedience. Immediately we obey, we discern. MUH. 258

The questions that matter in life are remarkably few, and they are all answered by the words—"Come unto Me." Not—Do this, or don't do that: but—"Come unto Me." MUH. 163

In the Bible obedience is based on the relationships of equals, that of a son with his father. Our Lord was not God's servant, He was His son. "*Though He were a Son,* yet learned He obedience . . ." MUH. 266

Our Lord never enforces obedience; He does not take means to make me do what He wants. At certain times I wish God would master me and make me do the thing, but He will not; in other moods I wish He would leave me alone, but He does not. MUH. 266

"I suppose I shall understand these things some day!" You can understand them now. It is not study that does it, but obedience. The tiniest fragment of obedience, and heaven opens and the profoundest truths of God are yours straight away. God will never reveal more truth about Himself until you have obeyed what you know already. Beware of becoming "wise and prudent." MUH. 284

All God's revelations are sealed until they are opened to us by obedience. You will never get them open by philosophy or thinking. Immediately you obey, a flash of light comes. Let God's truth work in you by soaking in it, not by worrying into it. The only way you can get to know is to stop trying to find out and by being born again. Obey God in the thing He shows you, and instantly the next thing is opened up. One reads tomes on the work of the Holy Spirit, when one five minutes of drastic obedience would make things as clear as a sunbeam. MUH. 284

In spiritual relationship we do not grow step by step; we are either there or we are not. God does not cleanse us more and more from sin, but when we are in the light, walking in the light, we *are* cleansed from all sin. It is a question of obedience, and instantly the relationship is perfected. Turn away for one second out of obedience, and darkness and death are at work at once. MUH. 284

Jesus Christ will not help me to obey Him, I must obey Him and when I do obey Him, I fulfil my spiritual destiny. MUH. 307

Our Lord never insists upon obedience; He tells us very emphatically what we ought to do, but He never takes means to make us do it. MUH. 307

In the spiritual domain nothing is explained until we obey, and then it is not so much an explanation as an instant discernment. NKW. 17

Right feeling is produced by obedience, never vice versa. NKW. 39

There are things God tells us to do without any light or illumination other than just the word of His command, and if we do not obey it is because we are independently strong enough to wriggle out of obeying. NKW. 57

The spirit of obedience gives more joy to God than anything else on earth. NKW. 126

There is no possibility of questioning on my part when God speaks, if He is speaking to His own nature in me; prompt obedience is the only result. NKW. 127

We read some things in the Bible three hundred and sixty-five times and they mean nothing to us, then all of a sudden we see what they mean, because in some particular we have obeyed God, and instantly His character is revealed. NKW. 128

We have to stop hesitating and take the first step; and the first step is to stop hesitating! "How long halt ye between two opinions?" There are times when we wish that God would kick us right over the line and *make* us do the thing; but the remarkable thing about God's patience is that He waits until we stop hesitating. Some of us hesitate so long that we become like spiritual storks; we look elegant only as long as we stand on one leg; when we stand on two we look very ungraceful. OBH. 52

If God tells us to do something and we hesitate over obeying, we endanger our standing in grace. OBH. 53

'Obedience of the heart is the heart of obedience.' Whenever we obey, the delight of the supernatural grace of God meets our obedience instantly. Absolute Deity is on our side at once every time we obey, so that natural obedience and the grace of God coincide. OBH. 112

It is the glory of God to conceal His teaching in obedience: we only know as we obey. "If any man willeth to do His will, he shall know of the teaching . . ." It is only by way of obedience that we understand the teaching of God. PH. 82

There is only one golden rule for spiritual discernment, and that is obedience. We learn more by five minutes' obedience than by ten years' study. PR. 22

God never takes away our power to disobey; if He did, our obedience would be of no value, for we should cease to be morally responsible. PR. 35

When we are born from above and the Son of God is formed in us, it is not the passing of the years that matures His life in us, but our obedience. PR. 39

Woe be to you if you hanker for a second after the thing about which God has said 'No' to you. If you do, you will put to death the life of God in you. PR. 54

We can never get into touch with God by our own effort; but we must maintain touch with God by our own effort. Jesus Christ can take anyone, no matter who he is, and presence him with His wonderful Divine salvation. The nature of God is shed abroad in our hearts by the Holy Ghost, but we have to maintain contact with His nature by obedience. PR. 123

Jesus Christ's life must work through our flesh, and that is where we have to obey. So many go into raptures over God's supernatural salvation, over the wonderful fact that God saves us by His sovereign grace (and we cannot do that too much), but they forget that now He expects us to get ourselves into trim to obey Him. PR. 123

Divine silence is the ultimate destiny of the man who refuses to come to the light and obey it. PS. 46

The possibility of disobedience in a child of God makes his obedience of amazing value. PS. 50

Whenever God's will is in the ascendant all compulsion is gone. When we choose deliberately to obey Him, then with all His almighty power He will tax the remotest star and the last grain of sand to assist us. RTR. 29

"If God so clothe the grass of the field . . . how much more . . ." Jesus says that if we obey the life God has given us, He will look after all the other things. Has Jesus Christ told us a lie? If we are not experiencing the "much more" it is because we are not obeying the life God has given us; we are taken up with confusing considerations. RTR. 30

Obedience to Jesus Christ is essential, but never compulsory. In the early stages we have the notion that the Christian life is one of freedom; and so it is, but freedom for one thing only—freedom to obey our Master. RTR. 35

Never try to explain God until you have obeyed Him. The only bit of God we understand is the bit we have obeyed. RTR. 75

When you are identified with Jesus Christ you become a new creation in the same surroundings. SA. 30

"Why don't You tell us plainly who You are?" Jesus Christ could not, because He could only be discerned through moral obedience. SA. 58

If I am going to find out a thing scientifically, I must find it out by curiosity; but if I want to find out anything on the moral line, I can only do it by obedience. SA. 71

Moral insight is gained only by obedience. The second I disobey in personal bodily chastity, I hinder everyone with whom I come in contact; if in moral integrity I disobey for one second, I hinder everyone; and if as a Christian I disobey in spiritual integrity, others will suffer too. SA. 90

Moral problems are only solved by obedience. We cannot see what we see until we see it. Intellectually things can be worked out, but morally the solution is only reached by obedience. One step in obedience is worth years of study, and will take us into the centre of God's will for us. SA. 112

The essential element in moral life is obedience and submission. If you want spiritual truth, obey the highest standard you know. SHH. 88

One of the great secrets of life is that obedience is the key to spiritual life as curiosity is the key to intellectual life. In the spiritual domain curiosity is not only of no use but is a direct hindrance. When once a man learns that spiritual knowledge can only be gained by obedience, the emancipation of his nature is incalculable. SHH. 123

The only way to find out things in the moral universe is by obedience. SHL. 62

The great cure for infidelity is obedience to the Spirit of God. SSM. 72

If we could not disobey God, our obedience would not be worth anything. SSM. 104

If for one whole day, quietly and determinedly, we were to give ourselves up to the ownership of Jesus and to obeying His orders, we should be amazed at its close to realize all He had packed into that one day. SSY. 129

Week 32

PRAYER

If you abide in Me, and My words abide in you, you will ask what you desire, and it shall be done for you.

—John 15:7

The essential meaning of prayer is that it nourishes the life of the Son of God in me and enables Him to manifest Himself in my mortal flesh. BE. 46

Certain things can only be dealt with by ignoring them; if you face them you increase their power. It is absurd to say, Pray about them; when once a thing is seen to be wrong, don't pray about it, it fixes the mind on it; never for a second brood on it, destroy it by neglect. BE. 47

Jesus Christ did not say, 'Ask what you like, and it shall be done unto you', but 'ask what you *will*, ask when your will is in, the thing that is a real problem to you', and God has pledged His honour that you will get the answer every time. BFB. 77

We do not ask, we worry, whereas one minute in prayer will put God's decree at work, viz., that He answers prayer on the ground of Redemption. BFB. 77

Prayer is the instrument of the life of worship, it is not worship itself. CD. VOL. 2, 10

In regard to prayer, we are apt to be apologetic and apathetic, complex and confused; yet what a splendid audacity a childlike child has! and that is what our Lord taught us to have. CD. VOL. 2, 17

Our Lord did not say it was wrong to pray in the corners of the street, but He did say it was wrong to have the motive to be *"seen of men."* CD. VOL. 2, 18

It is not wrong to pray in the early morning, but it is wrong to have the motive that it should be known. CD. VOL. 2, 18

Do it now, *"enter into thy closet;"* and remember, it is a place selected to pray in, not to make little addresses in, or for any other purpose than to pray in, never forget that. CD. VOL. 2, 33

The real reason for prayer is intimacy of relation with our Father. CD. VOL. 2, 36

Prayer is simple, as simple as a child making known its wants to its parents; prayer is stupid, because it is not according to common sense; it is certain that God does things in answer to prayer, and this, common sense naturally says, is ridiculous; prayer is supernatural because it relies entirely on God. CD. VOL. 2, 43

Our prayers should be in accordance with the nature of God, therefore, the answers are not in accordance with our nature but with His. We are apt to forget this and to say without thinking that God does not answer prayer; but He always answers prayer, and when we are in close communion with Him we know that we have not been misled. CD. VOL. 2, 45

Intercessory prayer is part of the sovereign purpose of God. If there were no saints praying for us, our lives would be infinitely balder than they are, consequently the responsibility of those who never intercede and who are withholding blessing from other lives is truly appalling. CD. VOL. 2, 57

Jesus Christ carries on intercession for us in heaven; the Holy Ghost carries on intercession in us on earth; and we the saints have to carry on intercession for all men. CD. VOL. 2, 60

'Asking' in prayer is at once the test of three things—simplicity, stupidity, and certainty of God. DI. 39

Spiritual certainty in prayer is God's certainty, not a side-eddy of sanctimoniousness. DI. 40

The very powers of darkness are paralysed by prayer. No wonder Satan tries to keep our minds fussy in active work till we cannot think to pray. DI. 40

The reason for intercession is not that God *answers* prayer, but that God tells us to pray. DI. 40

Prayer is the vital breath of the Christian; not the thing that makes him alive, but the evidence that he *is* alive. DI. 40

The greatest answer to prayer is that I am brought into a perfect understanding with God, and that alters my view of actual things. DI. 41

By intercessory prayer we can hold off Satan from other lives and give the Holy Ghost a chance with them. No wonder Jesus put such tremendous emphasis on prayer! DI. 41

If I pray that someone else may be, or do, something which I am not, and don't intend to do, my praying is paralysed. DI. 41

Never try to make people agree with your point of view, begin the ministry of intercession. The only Being worth agreeing with is the Lord Jesus Christ. DI. 42

The meaning of prayer is that I bring power to bear upon another soul that is weak enough to yield and strong enough to resist; hence the need for strenuous intercessory prayer. DI. 42

See that you do not use the trick of prayer to cover up what you know you ought to do. DI. 42

—tell God what you know He knows in order that you may get to know it as He does. GW. 20

Intercessory prayer is the test of our loyalty. GW. 61

Prayer is God's ordained way, the insignificant way of prayer. GW. 99

We have to pray with our eyes on God, not on the difficulties. GW. 99

There is always a suitable place to pray, to lift up your eyes to God; there is no need to get to a place of prayer, pray wherever you are. HG. 22

We cannot talk to God unless we walk with Him when we are not talking. HGM. 73

A prayer offered by the humblest and most obscure saint on the ground of the Redemption of Jesus Christ demands the complete attention of God and the performance of His programme. HGM. 80

Any soul who has not that solitary place alone with God is in supreme peril spiritually. HGM. 115

One of the first lessons learnt in the Ministry of the Interior is to talk things out before God in soliloquy—tell Him what you know He knows in order that you may get to know it as He does. HGM. 127

The knowledge of where people are wrong is a hindrance to prayer, not an assistance. HGM. 128

Jesus Christ does not pay any attention to the gift of 'religious gab,' and His words—"But when ye pray, use not vain repetitions, as the heathen do: for they think that they shall be heard for their much speaking," refer not to the mere repetition and form of words, but to the fact that it is never our earnestness that brings us into touch with God, but our Lord Jesus Christ's vitalizing death. IYA. 12

It is not so true that "Prayer changes things" as that prayer changes *me,* and then I change things; consequently we must not ask God to do what He has created us to do. IYA. 14

Prayer is not a question of altering things externally, but of working wonders in a man's disposition. IYA. 14

God answers prayer on the ground of Redemption and on no other ground. IYA. 17

There is only one kind of person who can really pray, and that is the childlike saint, the simple, stupid, supernatural child of God; I do mean 'stupid.' Immediately you try to explain why God answers prayer on the ground of reason, it is nonsense; God answers prayer on the ground of Redemption and no other ground. IYA. 17

. . . what makes prayer easy is not our wits or our understanding, but the tremendous agony of God in Redemption. A thing is worth just what it costs. Prayer is not what it costs us, but what it cost God to enable us to pray. It cost God so much that a little child can pray. It cost God Almighty so much that anyone can pray. But it is time those of us who name His Name knew the secret of the cost, and the secret is here, "My soul is exceeding sorrowful, even unto death." IYA. 22

Prayer imparts the power to walk and not faint, and the lasting remembrance of our lives is of the Lord, not of us. IYA. 28

When we pray easily it is because Satan is completely defeated in his onslaughts; when we pray difficultly it is because Satan is gaining a victory. We have not been continuously practising, we have not been facing things courageously, we have not been taking our orders from our Lord. Our Lord did not say, 'Go' or 'Do'; He said, "Watch and pray." IYA. 31

There is nothing a rationally-minded being can ridicule more easily than prayer. "Praying always"—the unutterable simplicity of it! No panic, no flurry, always at leisure from ourselves on the inside. IYA. 36

There is a difference in the prayers of the Old and the New Testament. In the Old Testament the prophet bases his prayer on the character of God, and appeals to God's great mercies. In the New Testament, prayer is based on a relationship with God through Jesus Christ: "When ye pray, say, Our Father." IYA. 38

Never make the blunder of trying to forecast the way God is going to answer your prayer. IYA. 39

When through Jesus Christ we are rightly related to God, we learn to watch and wait, and wait wonderingly. 'I wonder how God will answer this prayer.' 'I wonder how God will answer the prayer the Holy Ghost is praying in me.' 'I wonder what glory God will bring to Himself out of the strange perplexities I am in.' 'I wonder what new turn His providence will take in manifesting Himself in my ways.' IYA. 42

A great many people do not pray because they do not feel any sense of need. The sign that the Holy Ghost is in us is that we realise, not that we are full, but that we are empty, there is a sense of absolute need. IYA. 60

God's silences are His answers. If we only take as answers those that are visible to our senses, we are in a very elementary condition of grace. IYA. 48

Some prayers are followed by silence because they are wrong, others because they are bigger than we can understand. IYA. 49

It will be a wonderful moment for some of us when we stand before God and find that the prayers we clamoured for in early days and imagined were never answered, have been answered in the most amazing way, and that God's silence has been the sign of the answer. If we always want to be able to point to something and say, 'This is the way God answered my prayer,' God cannot trust us yet with His silence. IYA. 49

As long as we have the idea only that God will bless us in answer to prayer, He will do it, but He will never give us the grace of a silence. If He is taking us into the understanding that prayer is for the glorifying of His Father, He will give us the first sign of His intimacy—silence. The devil calls it unanswered prayer. IYA. 52

The whole meaning of prayer is that we may know God. IYA. 59

Prayer is not an exercise, it is the life. IYA. 60

Inarticulate prayer, the impulsive prayer that looks so futile, is the thing God always heeds. The habit of ejaculatory prayer ought to be the persistent habit of each one of us. IYA. 63

"Your Father knoweth what things ye have need of, before ye ask Him." Then why pray? To get to know your Father. It is not sufficient for us to say, 'Oh yes, God is love,' we have to know He is love, we have to struggle through until we do see He is love and justice, then our prayer is answered. IYA. 87

Prayer is simple, prayer is supernatural, and to anyone not related to our Lord Jesus Christ, prayer is apt to look stupid. IYA. 93

When we pray for others the Spirit of God works in the unconscious domain of their being that we know nothing about, and the one we are praying for knows nothing about, but after the passing of time the conscious life of the one prayed for begins to show signs of unrest and disquiet. We may have spoken until we are worn out, but have never come anywhere near, and we have given up in despair. But if we have been praying, we find on meeting them one day that there is the beginning of a softening in an enquiry and a desire to know something. It is that kind of intercession that does most damage to Satan's kingdom. It is so slight, so feeble in its initial stages that if reason is not wedded to the light of the Holy Spirit, we will never obey it, and yet it is that kind of intercession that the New Testament places most emphasis on, though it has so little to show for it. It seems stupid to think that we can pray and all that will happen, but remember to Whom we pray, we pray to a God Who understands the unconscious depths of a personality about which we know nothing, and He has told us to pray. The great Master of the human heart said, "Greater works than these shall he do. . . . And whatsoever ye shall ask in My name, that will I do." IYA. 94

There is only one field of service that has no snares, and that is the field of intercession. All other fields have the glorious but risky snare of publicity; prayer has not. IYA. 96

In the matter of intercession, when we pray for another the Spirit of God works in the unconscious domain of that one's being about which we know nothing, and about which the one we pray for knows nothing, and after a while the conscious life of the one prayed for begins to show signs of softening and unrest, of enquiry and a desire to know something. It seems stupid to think that if we pray all that will happen, but remember to Whom we pray; we pray to a Being Who understands the unconscious depths of a man's personality, and He has told us to pray. MFL. 20

Ask yourself how much time you have taken up asking God that you may not do the things you do. He will never answer, you have simply not to do them. Every time God speaks, there is something we must obey. We should do well to revise what we pray about. Some of the things we pray about are as absurd as if we prayed, 'O Lord, take me out of this room,' and then refused to go. MFL. 40

The majority of us are unable to fix our thoughts in prayer, we lie abroad before God and do not rouse ourselves up to lay hold of Him, consequently we have wandering thoughts continually. God will not bring every thought and imagination into captivity; we have to do it, and that is the test of spiritual concentration. MFL. 79

The greatest barrier to intercession is that we take ourselves so seriously, and come to the conclusion that God is reserved with us; He is not. God has to ignore things we take so seriously until our relationship to Him is exactly that of a child. MFL. 83

If God were human, how sick to the heart and weary He would be of the constant requests we make for our salvation, for our sanctification. We tax His energies from morning till night for things for ourselves—something for *me* to be delivered from! When we touch the bedrock of the reality of the Gospel of God, we shall never bother God any further with little personal plaints. MUH. 32

There are certain things we must not pray about—moods, for instance. Moods never go by praying, moods go by kicking. A mood nearly always has its seat in the physical condition, not in the moral. It is a continual effort not to listen to the moods which arise from a physical condition, never submit to them for a second. We have to take ourselves by the scruff of the neck and shake ourselves, and we will find that we can do what we said we could not. The curse with most of us is that we *won't*. The Christian life is one of incarnate spiritual pluck. MUH. 141

Jesus never mentioned unanswered prayer, He had the boundless certainty that prayer is always answered. MUH. 147

The real business of your life as a saved soul is intercessory prayer. Wherever God puts you in circumstances, pray immediately, pray that His Atonement may be realized in other lives as it has been in yours. Pray for your friends *now;* pray for those with whom you come in contact *now*. MUH. 172

We are not here to prove God answers prayer; we are here to be living monuments of God's grace. MUH. 219

The idea of prayer is not in order to get answers from God; prayer is perfect and complete oneness with God. MUH. 219

God always hears the prayers of His Son, and if the Son of God is formed in me the Father will always hear my prayers. MUH. 222

We must have a selected place for prayer and when we get there the plague of flies begins—This must be done, and that. "Shut thy door." A secret silence means to shut the door deliberately on emotions and remember God. God is in secret, and He sees us from the secret place; He does not see us as other people see us, or as we see ourselves. MUH. 236

When we live in the secret place it becomes impossible for us to doubt God, we become more sure of Him than of anything else. Your Father, Jesus says, is in secret and nowhere else. Enter the secret place, and right in the centre of the common round you find God there all the time. MUH. 236

Our ordinary views of prayer are not found in the New Testament. We look upon prayer as a means of getting things for ourselves; the Bible idea of prayer is that we may get to know God Himself. MUH. 241

Naturally, prayer is not practical, it is absurd; we have to realize that prayer is stupid from the ordinary common-sense point of view. MUH. 290

The Spirit of God needs the nature of the believer as a shrine in which to offer His intercession. MUH. 313

Intercession is the one thing that has no snares, because it keeps our relationship with God completely open. MUH. 348

If you ask me to pray for you and I am not complete in Christ, I may pray but it avails nothing; but if I am complete in Christ my prayer prevails all the time. MUH. 351

Prayer is the supreme activity of all that is noblest in our personality, and the essential nature of prayer is faith. NKW. 79

Repetition in intercessory importunity is not bargaining, but the joyous insistence of prayer. NKW. 79

Prayer is not a question of altering things externally, but of working wonders in a man's disposition. OBH. 116

Never *say* you will pray about a thing; *pray about it*. OBH. 116

If we are abiding in Jesus and His words are abiding in us, then Jesus says God will answer our prayers. OBH. 122

It is much easier to ask God to do our work for us than to do it ourselves—'Oh well, I will pray and ask God to clean this thing up for me.' God won't. We must do our own work. PH. 98

Prayer is always a temptation to bank on a miracle instead of a moral issue until we are disciplined. God will do more than we can do, but only in relationship to our spiritual growth. PH. 98

The prayers of some people are more efficacious than those of others, the reason being that they are under no delusion, they do not rely on their own earnestness, they rely absolutely on the supreme authority of the Lord Jesus Christ. PR. 126

Jesus Christ is asking God to save Him *out of* the hour, not *from* it. All through, that is the inner attitude of Jesus Christ, He received Himself in the fires of sorrow; it was never 'Do not let the sorrow come.' That is the opposite of what we do, we pray, 'Oh, Lord, don't let this or that happen to me'; consequently all kinds of damaging and blasphemous things are said about answers to prayer. PH. 191

Every time we pray our horizon is altered, our attitude to things is altered, not sometimes but every time, and the amazing thing is that we don't pray more. PH. 215

Prayer means that we get into union with God's view of other people. Our devotion as saints is to identify ourselves with God's interests in other lives. God pays no attention to our personal affinities; He expects us to identify ourselves and *His* interests in others. PR. 97

Do not ask others to pray for you; our Lord says, 'Pray yourself, *ask*.' PR. 126

I think sometimes we will be covered with shame when we meet the Lord Jesus and think how blind and ignorant we were when He brought people around us to pray for, or gave us opportunities of warning, and instead of praying we tried to find out what was wrong. We have no business to try and find out what is wrong, our business is to pray, so that when the awakening comes Jesus Christ will be the first they meet. PS. 35

Intercession leaves you neither time nor inclination to pray for your own "sad sweet self." The thought of yourself is not kept out because it is not there to keep out, you are completely and entirely identified with God's interest in other lives. RTR. 29

Whenever the insistence is on the point that God answers prayer, we are off the track. The meaning of prayer is that we get hold of God, not of the answer. RTR. 31

Prayer imparts the power to walk and not faint. RTR. 50

God never answers prayer to prove His own might. RTR. 53

Mental wool-gathering can be stopped immediately the will is roused. Prayer is an effort of will, and the great battle in prayer is the overcoming of mental wool-gathering. We put things down to our own inability to concentrate. "My soul, wait thou only upon God," i.e. pull yourself together and be silent unto God. RTR. 66

Prayer alters a man on the inside, alters his mind and his attitude to things. The point of praying is not that we get things from God, but that we learn by prayer to detect the difference between God's order and God's permissive will. God's order is—no pain, no sickness, no devil, no war, no sin: His permissive will is all these things, the "soup" we are in just now. What a man needs to do is to get hold of God's order in the kingdom on the inside, and then he will begin to see how to handle the riddle of the universe on the outside. SHH. 19

The prayer Our Lord taught us is full of wisdom along this line, "Give us this day our daily bread." That does not mean that if we do not pray we shall not get it. The word "give" has the sense of "receiving." When we become children of God we receive our daily bread from Him, the basis of blessing lies there, otherwise we take it as an animal with no discernment of God. SHH. 64

We are all agnostic about God, about the Spirit of God, and prayer. It is nonsense to call prayer reasonable; it is the most super-reasonable thing there is. SHH. 97

Prayer is never heard on the ground of earnestness, but only on the ground of the Redemption. SHH. 137

It is far more rare to find a sincere soul than one might suppose. No one but a fool or a sincere soul would ever pray this prayer—'Search me, O God, search me right out to the remotest depths, to the innermost recesses of my thoughts and imaginations; scrutinize me through and through until I know that Thou dost know me utterly, that I may be saved from my own ways and brought into Thy way.' Any soul who prays that prayer will be answered. SHL. 46

We are ill-taught if we look for results only in the earthlies when we pray. A praying saint performs far more havoc among the unseen forces of darkness than we have the slightest notion of. SHL. 55

It is impossible to live the life of a disciple without definite times of secret prayer. You will find that the place to enter in is in your business, as you walk along the streets, in the ordinary ways of life, when no one dreams you are praying, and the reward comes openly, a revival here, a blessing there. SSM. 58

You are born into this world and will probably never know to whose prayers your life is the answer. SSY. 15

How God works in answer to prayer is a mystery that logic cannot penetrate, but that He does work in answer to prayer is gloriously true. SSY. 24

Prayer is the answer to every problem there is. SSY. 131

Week 33

PREACHING

How shall they hear without a preacher? And how shall they preach unless they are sent?

—Romans 10:14, 15

◆

The one calling of a New Testament preacher is to uncover sin and reveal Jesus Christ as Saviour, consequently he cannot be poetical, he has to be surgical. We are not sent to give beautiful discourses which make people say, 'What a lovely conception that is; but to unearth the devil and his works in human souls. AUG. 20

. . . preaching is God's ordained method of saving the world. AUG. 36

The reason some of us have no power in our preaching, no sense of awe, is that we have no passion for God, but only a passion for Humanity. The one thing we have to do is to exhibit Jesus Christ crucified, to lift Him up all the time. AUG. 56

To-day the preacher is tested, not by the building up of saints but on the ground of his personality. AUG. 83

An orator rouses human nature to do what it is asleep over: the New Testament preacher has to move men to do what they are dead-set against doing, viz., giving up the right to themselves to Jesus Christ; consequently the preaching of the Gospels awakens a terrific longing, but an equally intense resentment. BE. 52

If you have the Spirit of God in you, the preaching of the Cross is according to the wisdom of God: if you have not the Spirit of God in you, the preaching of Christ crucified is foolishness. BP. 264

We are nowhere told to preach salvation, or sanctification, or Divine healing; we are told to lift up Jesus, who is the Redeemer, and He will produce His redemptive results in the souls of men. If I preach only the effects of the Redemption, describe in persuasive speech what God has done for me, nothing will happen. It is only when I am humble enough, and stupid enough, to preach the Cross that the miracle of God takes place. The "preaching of the Cross" creates that which enables a man to believe in God, because the Cross *is* the manifestation of the Redemption. The Cross "condemns men to salvation." The "foolishness of preaching" is the way God has chosen to make the Redemption efficacious in human lives. You can't *persuade* a man to believe in God; belief in God is not an act of the intellect, it is a moral creation produced by the interaction of God's Spirit and my spirit in willing obedience; intellect comes in afterwards to explain what has happened. In preaching the Cross we use our intellect, not to prove that Jesus died, but to present the fact of His death. CHI. 35

The preacher's duty is not to convict men of sin, or to make them realize how bad they are, but to bring them into contact with God until it is easy for them to believe in Him. DI. 43

The life of a preacher speaks louder than his words. DI. 44

There is far more wrought by the Word of God than we will ever understand, and if I substitute anything for it, fine thinking, eloquent speech, the devil's victory is enormous, but I am of no more use than a puff of wind. DI. 45

We have to preach something which to the wisdom of this world is foolishness. If the wisdom of this world is right, then God is foolish; if God is wise, the wisdom of this world is foolishness. Where we go wrong is when we apologize for God. DI. 45

A clever exposition is never right because the Spirit of God is not clever. Beware of cleverness; it is the great cause of hypocrisy in a preacher. DI. 45

The determination to be a fool if necessary is the golden rule for a preacher. DI. 45

To whom is our appeal? To none but those God sends you to. You can't get men to come; nobody could get you to come until you came. "The wind bloweth where it listeth, . . . so is everyone that is born of the Spirit." DI. 46

A joyous, humble belief in your message will compel attention. DI. 49

If any man's preaching does not make me brace myself up and watch my feet and my ways, one of two things is the reason—either the preacher is unreal, or I hate being better. DI. 49

To talk about 'getting a message', is a mistake. It is preparation of myself that is required more than of my message. DI. 50

"The heart of the righteous studieth to answer." To give your congregation extemporaneous thinking, i.e., thinking without study, is an insult—ponderous 'nothings.' The preacher should give his congregation the result of strenuous thinking in un-studied, extemporaneous speech. DI. 50

In impromptu speaking, begin naturally, and the secret of beginning naturally is to forget you are religious. Many wear a crushing religious garb. DI. 51

Beware of detaching yourself from your theme in order to heed the way you present it. Never be afraid of expressing what is really *you*. DI. 51

Don't preach salvation; don't preach holiness; don't preach the baptism of the Holy Ghost; preach Jesus Christ and everything else will take its right place. GW. 48

God's word is as a seed. The 'seed-thought' idea is one that preachers and evangelists need to remember. We imagine we have to plough the field, sow the seed, reap the grain, bind it into sheaves, put it through the threshing machine, make the bread—all in one discourse. GW. 94

The great condemnation of much of cur modern preaching is that it conveys no sense of the desperate tragedy of conviction of sin. When once the real touch of conviction of sin comes, it is hell on earth—there is no other word for it. HG. 98

If I preach a particularly searching discourse and never give the people a chance to act according to their inspired instincts at the time, their blood is on my head before God. If I make the issue clear and give them the opportunity to act, I clear my soul from their blood, whether they answer or not. The devil's counterfeit for this is wanting to see how many people we can get out to the penitent form. As preachers and teachers we have to bring people to the point of doing something. MFL. 15

We may see no result in our congregation, but if we have presented the truth and anyone has seen it for one second, he can never be the same again, a new element has come into his life. It is essential to remember this and not to estimate the success of preaching by immediate results. MFL. 20

In the teachings of Jesus Christ the element of judgment is always brought out, it is the sign of God's love. Never sympathize with a soul who finds it difficult to get to God, God is not to blame. It is not for us to find out the reason why it is difficult, but so to present the truth of God that the Spirit of God will show what is wrong. The great sterling test in preaching is that it brings everyone to judgment. The Spirit of God locates each one to himself. MUH. 126

The preaching of to-day is apt to emphasize strength of will, beauty of character—the things that are easily noticed. The phrase we hear so often, Decide for Christ, is an emphasis on something Our Lord never trusted. He never asks us to decide for Him, but to yield to Him—a very different thing. MUH. 234

If by your preaching you convince me that I am unholy, I resent your preaching. The preaching of the gospel awakens an intense resentment because it must reveal that I am unholy; but it also awakens an intense craving. God has one destined end for mankind, viz., holiness. MUH. 245

It seems so remote from actual things to say that the preaching of the Cross conveys the Presence of God, but God has chosen to save in this way. "It was God's good pleasure through the foolishness of the preaching to save them that believe," because behind the preaching of the Gospel is the creative Redemption of God at work in the souls of men. That is the miracle of God. If you can tell how a corn of wheat put into the ground will bring forth what it never was before, you can also tell how the Word of God put into a man's soul will bring forth what was not there before—a new life. The same God is the Author of both. PH. 136

Jesus did not say—'Go out and spread propaganda,' but "Feed My sheep." They are not our sheep, but His. PH. 160

A preacher has no business to stir up emotions without giving his hearers some issue of will on which to transact. PH. 210

Be as stern and unflinching as God Almighty in your preaching, but as tender and gentle as a sinner saved by grace should be when you deal with a human soul. PS. 81

A man can never be the same again, I don't care who he is, after having heard Jesus Christ preached. He may say he pays no attention to it; he may appear to have forgotten all about it, but he is never quite the same, and at any moment truths may spring up into his consciousness that will destroy all his peace and happiness. RTR. 77

To terrorise a man into believing in God is never the work of God, but the work of human expediency. If we want to convince a congregation of a certain thing, we may use terror to frighten them into it; but never say that is God's way, it is our way. If we do not get conversions one way, then we preach hell fire and produce terror; we don't care what we preach as long as we dominate. To call that God's method is a travesty of the character of God. The methods God uses are indicated in Jesus Christ, and He never terrorised anyone. SHH. 29

Man cannot order the seasons or make the seed to grow; and as preachers and teachers we are powerless to make saints. SHL. 113

God honours His word no matter who preaches it. SSM. 103

We are apt to have the idea that a man called to the ministry is called to be a different kind of being from other men. According to Jesus Christ, he is called to be the "doormat" of other men; he is their spiritual leader, but never their superior. SSY. 22

Never water down the word of God to the understanding of your people. WG. 78

Week 34

REASON

Come now, and let us reason together, Says the Lord.

—Isaiah 1:18

To "believe also" in Jesus means that we submit our intelligence to Him as He submitted His intelligence to His Father. This does not mean that we do not exercise our reason, but it does mean that we exercise it in submission to Reason Incarnate. AUG. 105

Rationalism fundamentally is rotten. The boldness of rationalism is not in what it does, but in the way it criticizes. The basis of things is not rational, it is tragic; there is something wrong at the heart of life that reason cannot account for. BE. 53

Reason is our guide among the facts of life, but it does not give us the explanation of them. Sin, suffering, and the Book of God all bring a man to the realization that there is something wrong at the basis of life, and it cannot be put right by his reason. Our Lord always dealt with the 'basement' of life, i.e., with the real problem; if we only deal with 'the upper storey' we do not realize the need of the Redemption. BFB. 17

There are people who can silence you with their logic while all the time you know, although you cannot prove it, that they are wrong. This is because the basis of things is not logical, but tragic. Logic and reasoning are only methods of dealing with things as they are; they give no explanation of things as they are. BFB. 22

You cannot get at the basis of things by disputing. Our Lord Himself comes off second best every time in a logical argument, and yet you know that He has in reality come off 'more than conqueror.' BFB. 35

When a so-called rationalist points out sin and iniquity and disease and death, and says, 'How does God answer that?' you have always a fathomless answer—the Cross of Christ. DI. 12

A logical position is satisfying to intellect, but it can never be true to life. Logic is simply the method man's intellect follows in making things definable to himself, but you can't define what is greater than yourself. DI. 83

The way the serpent beguiled Eve through his subtlety was by enticing her away from personal faith in God to depend on her reason alone. GW. 108

Men must reason according to their god, and the god of to-day is common sense; that is why Jesus Christ's teaching is ruled out of court. HG. 86

If I believe in God I pray on the ground of Redemption and things happen; it is not reasonable, it is Redemptive. Where reason says 'There is a mountain, it is impossible', I do not argue and say 'I believe God can remove it', I do not even see the mountain; I simply set my face unto the Lord God and make my prayer, and the mountain ceases to be. HGM. 71

A child of faith must never limit the promise of God by what seems good to him, but must give to the power of God the preference over his own reason. God never contradicts reason. He transcends it always. NKW. 75

There is no logic for faith or for suffering. The region in which God deals with us is the region of implicit life that cannot be put into words. PH. 76

We cannot enter into the kingdom of heaven head first. PH. 185

In spiritual matters logical processes do not count. Curiosity does not count, nor argument, nor reasoning; these are of no avail for spiritual discernment. PR. 22

Logic and reasoning are methods of expounding Reality, but we do not get at Reality by our intellect. Reality is only got at by our conscience. PR. 22

The basis of things is not rational, but tragic. Reason is our guide among facts as they are, but reason cannot account for things being as they are. This does not mean that a man is not to use his reason; reason is the biggest gift he has. The rationalist says that everything in between birth and death is discernible by human reason; but the actual experience of life that things do not run in a reasonable way, there are irrational elements to be reckoned with. SHH. 3

Reason and logic and intellect have to do with the time between birth and death, but they can give no explanation of before birth or after death. All we infer of either is speculation; it may be interesting but it is apt to blind us to true facts. SHH. 39

Things cannot be worked out on a logical line, there is always something incalculable. SHH. 124

The rationalist demands an explanation of everything. The reason I won't have anything to do with God is because I cannot define Him. If I can define God, I am greater than the God I define. SHH. 144

Our Lord never talks on the basis of reason. He talks on the basis of Redemption. What is nonsense rationally is Redemptive Reality. SSY. 165

Week 35

REDEMPTION

You were not redeemed with corruptible things, like silver or gold, . . . but with the precious blood of Christ.

—1 Peter 1:18, 19

The Redemption means a great deal more than my personal salvation and yours, that is a mere outcome; pseudo-evangelism is apt to make it the great thing. The great thing according to the New Testament is not that the Redemption touches *me*, but that it avails for the whole human race. BE. 65

The whole purpose of the Redemption is to give back to man the original source of life, and in a regenerated man this means "Christ formed in you." BE. 80

If there is no tragedy at the back of human life, no gap between God and man, then the Redemption of Jesus Christ is 'much ado about nothing.' BFB. 16

There is nothing simple under heaven saving a man's relationship to God on the ground of the Redemption. BFB. 17

The basis of things is not rational, common sense tells him it is not; the basis of things is tragic, and the Bible reveals that the only way out is through the Redemption. BFB. 17

The New Testament never says that Jesus Christ came primarily to teach men: it says that He came to reveal that He has put the basis of human life on Redemption, that is, He has made it possible for any and every man to be born into the Kingdom where He lives. BFB. 19

If Redemption is not the basis of human life, and prayer man's only resource, then we have 'followed cunningly devised fables.' BFB. 33

The reason the experience of Redemption is so easy is because it cost God so much. If my religion slips easily into my life it is because someone else has paid the price for it. BFB. 74

There is a gap and a wildness in things and if God does not step in and adjust it, there is no hope; but God has stepped in by the Redemption, and our part is to trust confidently in Him. BFB. 83

On the ground of the Redemption I am saved and God puts His Holy Spirit into me, then He expects me to react on the basis of that relationship. I can evade it by dumping my responsibility on to a Church, or a Book or a creed, forgetting what Jesus said—"Ye search the Scriptures, because ye think that in them ye have eternal life; and these are they which bear witness of Me; and ye will not come to Me, that ye may have life." BFB. 91

Redemption is not going to be finished: it is finished. Believing does not make a man redeemed; believing enables him to realize that he is redeemed. BSG. 53

Redemption is the great outside fact of the Christian faith; it has to do not only with a man's experience of salvation, but with the basis of his thinking. The revelation of Redemption means that Jesus Christ came here in order that by means of His Death on the Cross He might put the whole human race on a redemptive basis, so making it possible for every man to get back into perfect communion with God. "I have finished the work which Thou gavest Me to do." What was finished? The redemption of the world. CHI. 8

Men are not *going* to be redeemed; they *are* redeemed. "It is finished." It was not the salvation of individual men and women like you and me that was finished: the whole human race was put on the basis of Redemption. CHI. 8

The Redemption is not only for mankind, it is for the universe, for the material earth; everything that sin and the devil have touched and marred has been completely redeemed by Jesus Christ. There is a day coming when the redemption will be actually manifested, when there will be "a new heaven and a new earth," with a new humanity upon it. CHI. 9

Through the Redemption we have deliverance from the disposition of sin which is within us, and severance from the body of sin to which we are connected by our "old man"; that is, we are absolutely and completely delivered from sin both in disposition and domination. CHI. 10

Unless the universality of sin is recognized we will never understand the need for the Redemption. What the Redemption deals with is the sin of the whole human race, not primarily with the sins of individuals, but something far more fundamental, viz., the heredity of sin. CHI. 10

If you look upon Jesus Christ from the common-sense standpoint you will never discern who He is; but if you look upon Him as God "manifested in the flesh" for the purpose of putting the whole human race back to where God designed it to be, you get the meaning of Redemption. The great marvellous revelation of Redemption is that it atones for everyone; men are "condemned to salvation." CHI. 11

The great thing about the Redemption is that it deals with *sin,* i.e., my claim to my right to myself, not primarily with man's sins. It is one of the most flattering things to go and rescue the degraded, one of the social passions of mankind, but not necessarily the most Christian: it is quite another thing to tell men who are among the best of men that what Jesus Christ asks of them is that they give up the right to themselves to Him DI. 54

Belief in the Redemption is difficult because it needs self-surrender first. DI. 56

Redemption is the Reality which alters inability into ability. DI. 57

The mighty Redemption of God is made actual in my experience by the living efficacy of the Holy Ghost. DI. 57

Beware of preaching a Redemption that is past; it *is* past, but it must be seen to be ever-present, and I can only make it an ever-present reality be becoming a new creation in Christ Jesus. GW. 18

Through the forces that are against him God is making a finer type of man than the first Adam, a man more worthy to be His son. That is the meaning of His marvellous Redemption. Everything that Satan and sin have marred is going to be reconstructed and readjusted. GW. 102

Unless we have faith in the Redemption, all our activities are fussy impertinences which tell God He is doing nothing. HG. 95

We can never expound the Redemption, but we must have strong unshaken faith in it so that we are not swept off our feet by actual things. That the devil and man are allowed to do as they like is a mere episode in the providence of God. Everything that has been touched by sin and the devil has been redeemed; we are to live in the world immovably banked in that faith. HG. 95

Jesus Christ is not working out the Redemption, it is complete; we are working it out, and beginning to realize it by obedience. HG. 95

We must make a distinction in our minds between the revelation of Redemption and conscious participation in it. When we are born again we consciously enter into participation of the Redemption. We do not help God to redeem the world: we realize that God has redeemed it. Redemption is not dependent on our experience of it. The human race is redeemed; we have to be so faithful to God that through us may come the awakening of those who have not yet realized that they are redeemed. HG. 95

If the Redemption of Christ cannot go deeper down than hell, it is not redemption at all. HG. 98

When the Redemption is effective in me, I am a delight to God, not to myself. I am not meant for myself, I am meant for God. HG. 120

If the Redemption cannot get hold of the worst and vilest, then Jesus Christ is a fraud. HGM. 65

The basis of human life is Redemption. There is nothing more certain in Time or Eternity than what Jesus Christ did on the Cross. He switched the whole of the human race back into right relationship to God, and any one of us can get into touch with God *now,* not presently. HGM. 105

Redemption means that Jesus Christ can give me His own disposition, and all the standards He gives are based on that disposition. *Jesus Christ's teaching is for the life He puts in.* LG. 125

Everything that sin and Satan have touched and blighted, God has redeemed; Redemption is complete. We are not working *for* the redemption of the world, we are working *on* the Redemption, which is a very different thing. OBH. 61

God is a holy God, and the marvel of the Redemption is that God the Holy One puts into me, the unholy one, a new disposition, the disposition of His Son. PH. 65

A man cannot save his own soul, or forgive his sins, or get hold of God in prayer, or sanctify himself; but Jesus reveals that God has done all this in Redemption. PH. 225

The Redemption of the human race does not necessarily mean the salvation of every individual. Redemption is of universal application, but human responsibility is not done away with. Jesus Christ states emphatically that there are possibilities of eternal damnation for the man who positively neglects or positively rejects His Redemption. PR. 79

Nothing that happens can upset God or the almighty reality of Redemption. RTR. 51

The whole claim of the Redemption of Jesus is that He can satisfy the last aching abyss of the human soul, not only hereafter, but here and now. RTR. 60

According to the Bible, the basis of things is tragedy, and the way out is the way made by God in Redemption. SA. 14

Redemption is not a man's bit. SA. 16

The great fundamental revelation regarding the human race is that God has redeemed us; and Redemption enters into our lives when we are upset enough to see we need it. SA. 17

Redemption is a moral thing, Jesus Christ does not merely save from hell; "He shall save his people from their sins," i.e., make totally new moral men. Jesus Christ did not come to give us pretty ideas of God, or sympathy with ourselves; He came from a holy God to enable men, by the sheer power of His Redemption, to become holy. SA. 18

Redemption does not amount to anything to a man until he meets an agony; until that time he may have been indifferent; but knock the bottom board out of his wits, bring him to the limit of his moral life, produce the supreme suffering worthy of the name of agony, and he will begin to realize that there is more in Redemption than he had ever dreamed, and it is at that phase that he is prepared to hear Jesus Christ say, "Come unto Me." Our Lord said, "I did not come to call the man who is all right; I came to call the man who is at his wits' end, the man who has reached the moral frontier." SA. 28

He did not go to heaven from the Mount of Transfiguration because He had Redemption to fulfill. He emptied Himself of His glory a second time, and came down into the world again to identify Himself with the sin of man. SA. 47

If the human race apart from Jesus Christ is all right, then the Redemption of Jesus Christ is a useless waste. SA. 120

God has put the whole human race on the basis of Redemption. A man cannot redeem himself; Redemption is absolutely finished and complete; its reference to individual men is a question of their individual action. SA. 121

No man can redeem his own soul, or give himself a new heredity; that is the work of the sovereign grace of God. Man has nothing to do with Redemption, it is God's "bit"; but God cannot give a man a good character, that is not God's business, nor is it an inevitable thing. God will give us what we cannot give ourselves, a totally new heredity. SHH. 94

An understanding of Redemption is not necessary to salvation any more than an understanding of life is necessary before we can be born into it. SSM. 49

When I realize what Jesus Christ has done for me, then I am a debtor to every human being until they know Him too, not for their sake, not because they will otherwise be lost, but because of Jesus Christ's Redemption. SSY. 23

We have to beware of becoming the advocate of a certain view of the limitless. The Redemption avails for everyone—'The Lamb of God which taketh away the sin of the world!' not the sin of those who belong to any particular country, but the sin *of the world*. The words are worthy only of Almighty God's wisdom, not of man's. SSY. 145

The only final thing in the world is the Redemption of Jesus Christ. SSY. 145

Week 36

RELIGION

Pure and undefiled religion before God and the Father is this: to visit orphans and widows in their trouble, and to keep oneself unspotted from the world.

—James 1:27

If I have for my religious ideal a good social life lived among the societies of men, that is to be 'of' the world, no matter how religious it may be in terms. BE. 34

I can 'mouth' my salvation, I can thank God for it, but if I do not produce 'goods up to sample' my religious life is a travesty. BE. 62

If my religion is based on my right to myself, that spells 'Satan' in my soul; I may be right-living, but I am anti-God. 'If you are going to be My disciple,' Jesus says, 'you must give up your right to yourself.' BE. 63

We are not to worship reminiscences; this is the characteristic of all other religions, saving the Bible religion. The Bible religion is one of eternal progress, an intense and militant going on. CD. VOL. 1, 25

The citadel of true religion is personal relationship to God, let come what will. CHI. 111

'What has my religion done for me I could not do for myself?' That is a question every man is forced to ask. Religion ostensibly is faith in Someone, or a form of belief in some power, I would be the poorer if I did not have, and I should be able to state in what way I would be poorer. DI. 37

If my religion is not based on a personal history with Jesus it becomes something I suffer from, not a joyous thing, but something that keeps me from doing what I want to do. DI. 37

Religion is never intellectual, it is always passionate and emotional; but the curious thing is that it is religion that leads to emotion, not emotion to religion. If religion does not make for passion and emotion, it is not the true kind. When you realize that you are saved, that God has forgiven your sins, given you the Holy Spirit, I defy you not to be carried away with emotion. Religion which makes for logic and reason is not religion, but to try to make religion out of emotion is to take a false step. HG. 33

The religion of Jesus Christ is not a religion of ethical truth, but of Redemption. HG. 96

Spirituality is what God is after, not religiosity. IWP. 64

There is no value whatever in religious externals, the only thing that is of value is spiritual reality, and this is spiritual reality—that I allow God to work in me to will and to do of His good pleasure, and then work out what He has worked in, being carefully careless about everything saving my relationship to God. IWP. 64

Unless the blessings of God can deal with our bodies and make them the temples of the Holy Ghost, then the religion of Jesus Christ is in the clouds. PH. 130

Many of us are supernaturally solemn about our religion because it is not real. Immediately our religion becomes real, it is possible to have humour in connection with it. PH. 217

We carry our religion as if it were a headache, there is neither joy nor power nor inspiration in it, none of the grandeur of the unsearchable riches of Christ about it, none of the passion of hilarious confidence in God. PH. 223

Unless our salvation works out through our finger tips and everywhere else, there is nothing to it, it is religious humbug. PR. 101

It is easy to turn our religious life into a cathedral for beautiful memories, but there are feet to be washed, hard flints to be walked over, people to be fed. Very few of us go there, but that is the way The Son of God went. RTR. 8

Have you never met the person whose religious life is so exact that you are terrified to come near him? Never have an exercise of religion which blots God clean out. RTR. 78

The religion of Jesus Christ means that a man is delivered from sin into something which makes him forget all about himself. SA. 84

The trick of pseudo-evangelism is that it drives a man into concentrated interest in himself. The curse of much modern religion is that it makes us desperately interested in ourselves, overweeningly concerned about our own whiteness. SA. 84

The stupendous difference between the religion of Jesus Christ and every other religion under heaven is that His religion is one which brings help to the bottom of hell, not a religion that can deal only with what is fine and pure. SA. 119

If a man cannot prove his religion in the valley, it is not worth anything. SHH. 18

Don't be fanatically religious and don't be irreverently blatant. Remember that the two extremes have to be held in the right balance. If your religion does not make you a better man, it is a rotten religion. The test of true religion is when it touches these four things—food, money, sex and mother earth. These things are the test of a right sane life with God, and the religion that ignores them or abuses them is not right. SHH. 99

Religion is a matter of taste, a matter in which a man's religious life and his actuual life do not necessarily agree. In spiritual life that could never be; spiritual life means the real life, and it is significant that whenever Jesus talks about discipleship He speaks of it in actual terms. SHL. 105

Jesus Christ did not come to found religion, nor did He come to found civilisation, they were both here before He came; He came to make us spiritually real in every domain. In Jesus Christ there was nothing secular and sacred, it was all real, and He makes His disciples like Himself. SSM. 49

The main idea in the region of religion is, Your eyes on God, not on men. SSM. 56

Unless your religion will go to the lowest and the worst and the most desperate case you know of, your religion is of no use. There are a great many forms of belief which cannot begin to touch the worst of mankind, they can only deal with cultured minds and hearts. Jesus Christ's religion goes down to the lowest of the low as well as up to the highest of the high, and to all in between. The marvel of Jesus Christ is that He takes facts as they are. He Himself is the answer to every problem of heart and mind and life. WG. 39

There are only two religions that accept gloom as a fact (I mean by gloom, sin, anguish and misery, the things that make people feel that life is not worth living), viz., Buddhism and Christianity. Every other religion ignores it. WG. 63

Week 37

REPENTANCE

Godly sorrow produces repentance leading to salvation, not to be regretted; but the sorrow of the world produces death.

—2 Corinthians 7:10

Repentance is the blood of sanctification, the exhibition of a real gift of God; not only am I sorry for my sin, that is human, but in the sorrow for sin God slips in something else—the power never to do the thing again. BE. 64

The only repentant man is the holy man, and the only holy man is the one who has been made so by the marvel of the Atonement. BE. 117

The bedrock of Christianity is repentance. BFB. 103

Because a man has altered his life it does not necessarily mean that he has repented. A man may have lived a bad life and suddenly stop being bad, not because he has repented, but because he is like an exhausted volcano. The fact that he has become good is no sign of his having become a Christian. BFB. 103

The only repentant man is the holy man, i.e., the one who becomes the opposite of what he was because something has entered into him. Any man who knows himself knows that he cannot be holy, therefore if he does become holy, it is because God has 'shipped' something into him; he is now 'presenced with Divinity,' and can begin to bring forth 'fruits meet for repentance.' BFB. 103

Strictly speaking, repentance is a gift of God. No man can repent when he chooses. A man can be remorseful when he chooses, but remorse is a lesser thing than repentance. Repentance means that I show my sorrow for the wrong thing by becoming the opposite. BFB. 108

That a man stops being bad and becomes good may have nothing to do with salvation; the only one sign that a man is saved is repentance. CHI. 25

Repentance is the experimental side of Redemption and is altogether different from remorse or reformation. "Repentance" is a New Testament word and cannot be applied outside the New Testament. We all experience remorse, disgust with ourselves over the wrong we have done when we are found out by it, but the rarest miracle of God's grace is the sorrow that puts an end for ever to the thing for which I am sorry. Repentance involves the receiving of a totally new disposition so that I never do the wrong thing again. CHI. 26

Repentance brings us to the place where we are willing to receive any punishment under heaven so long as the law we have broken is justified. That is repentance, and I think I am right in saying that very few of us know anything at all about it. We have the idea nowadays that God is so loving and gentle and kind that all we need do is to say we feel sorry for the wrong we have done and we will try to be better. That is not repentance; Repentance means that I am remade on a plane which justifies God in forgiving me. CHI. 27

The last delusion God delivers us from is the idea that we don't deserve what we get. Once we see ourselves under the canopy of God's overflowing mercy we are dissolved in wonder, love and praise. That is the meaning of repentance, which is the greatest gift God ever gives a man. CHI. 70

Salvation from sin is frequently confounded with deliverance from sins. A man can deliver himself from sins without any special work of God's grace. The bedrock of New Testament salvation is repentance, and repentance is based on relationship to a Person. DI. 65

Watch Jesus Christ whenever there is the tiniest sign of repentance, He is the incarnation of forgiving and forgetting, and He says that is God's nature. HG. 79

Self-knowledge is the first condition of repentance. HG. 79

Jesus Christ is not an individual Who died twenty centuries ago; He is God and mankind centred in His Cross. The Cross is the revelation of the deepest depth in Almighty God. What should be the reaction of that in my life? Holiness, rugged, fierce holiness in every detail of the life. That is the meaning of New Testament repentance. HG. 102

Repentance means that we recognize the need for forgiveness—'hands up, I know it.' HGM. 101

Scriptural repentance leads to positive salvation and sanctification; the only truly repentant man is the holy man. HGM. 118

Repentance does not bring a sense of sin, but a sense of unutterable unworthiness. MUH. 235

To *admit* instead of *confess* is to trample the blood of the Son of God under foot, but immediately we allow the Holy Spirit to give us the gift of repentance, the shed blood of Christ will purge our conscience from dead works and send us into heart-spending service for God with a passionate devotion. OBH. 71

The 'repenting' of God in individual cases means that God remains true to His purpose and must mean my condemnation, and my condemnation causes Him grief and agony. It is not that God won't overlook wrong, it is that He cannot, His very love forbids it. OPG. 16

The new life will manifest itself in conscious repentance and unconscious holiness, never the other way about. The bedrock of Christianity is repentance. If ever you cease to know the virtue of repentance, you are in darkness. RTR. 51

When God handles the wrong in a man it makes him turn to God and his life becomes a sacrament of experimental repentance. SA. 121

The disposition of the Son of God can only enter my life by the road of repentance. SA. 121

There is a difference between a man altering his life, and repenting. A man may have lived a bad life and suddenly stop being bad, not because he has repented, but because he is like an exhausted volcano; the fact that he has become good is no sign that he is a Christian. SA. 121

Repentance means that I estimate exactly what I am in God's sight, and I am sorry for it, and on the basis of Redemption I become the opposite. SA. 121

Repentance is not a reaction, remorse is. Remorse is—I will never do the thing again. Repentance is that I deliberately become the opposite to what I have been. SHH. 53

The prodigal son had his self-love wounded; he was full of shame and indignation because he had sunk to such a level. There was remorse, but no repentance yet, no thought of his father.

'I will arise and go to my father, and will say unto him, Father I have sinned against heaven and in thy sight and am no more worthy to be called thy son: And he arose and came to his father.' That is repentance. The surgery of Providence had done its work, he was no longer deluded about himself. A repentant soul is never allowed to remain long without being gripped by the love of God. SHL. 82

Week 38

SAINT

Beloved of God, called to be saints.

—Romans 1:7

In the Christian life the saint is ever young; amazingly and boisterously young, certain that everything is all right. AUG. 90

A saint is not an ethereal creature too refined for life on this earth; a saint is a mixture of the Divine and the human that can stand anything. BE. 52

The truly godly person is one who is entirely sanctified, and he or she is never sanctimonious, but absolutely natural. The characteristic of a saint is freedom from anything in the nature of self-consciousness. BE. 83

It is a crime for a saint to be weak in God's strength. BE. 97

You may put a saint in tribulation, amid an onslaught of principalities and powers, in peril, pestilence or under the sword, you may put a saint anywhere you like, and he is 'more than conqueror' every time. Why? Because his heart being filled with the love of God, he has the power to perceive and understand that behind all these things is God making them 'work together for good.' BP. 111

Once let God's honour be slandered, and instantly there is something else to deal with in your 'meek' saint. BP. 114

As saints, we should smart and suffer keenly whenever we see pride and covetousness and self-realization, because these are the things that go against the honour of God. BP. 185

Character in a saint means the disposition of Jesus Christ persistently manifested. BP. 205

The work of Jesus is the creation of saints; He can take the worst, the most misshapen material, and make a saint. BSG. 55

A saint is a creature of vast possibilities, knit into shape by the ruling personality of God. CD. VOL. 1, 9

The production of a saint is the grandest thing earth can give to Heaven. A saint is not a person with a saintly character: a saint *is* a saintly character. Character, not ecstatic moods, is the stuff of saintliness. A saint is a living epistle written by the finger of God, known and read of all men. CD. VOL. 1, 99

The vocation of a saint is to be in the thick of it "for Thy sake." Whenever Jesus Christ refers to discipleship or to suffering, it is always, "for My sake." The deep relationship of a saint is a personal one, and the reason a saint can be radiant is that he has lost interest in his own individuality and has become absolutely devoted to the Person of the Lord Jesus Christ. CD. VOL. 1, 156

The mark of the saint is the good right thing he has the privilege of not doing. There are a hundred and one right and good things which, if you are a disciple of Jesus, you must avoid as you would the devil although there is no devil in them. DI. 35

The Lord can never make a saint out of a good man, He can only make a saint out of three classes of people—the godless man, the weak man, and the sinful man, and no one else, and the marvel of the Gospel of God's grace is that Jesus Christ can make us naturally what He wants us to be. HG. 76

We are all possible saints or possible devils. HGM. 40

As saints we are called to go through the heroism of what we believe, not of stating what we believe, but of standing by it when the facts are dead against God. HGM. 80

. . . nothing clings to us more closely than trying to live up to the ideas we have got from saintly people. We have nothing to do with saintly people, we have only to do with 'looking to Jesus.' HGM. 144

We must be able to mount up with wings as eagles, but we must know also how to come down. It is the coming down and the living down that is the power of the saint. LG. 58

There is only one lodestar to the saint, the Lord Jesus Christ. LG. 73

The saint is at home anywhere on Mother Earth; he dare be no longer parochial or denominational; he belongs to Jesus Christ. LG. 131

A saint's life is in the hands of God as a bow and arrow in the hands of an archer. God is aiming at something the saint cannot see; He stretches and strains, and every now and again the saint says: 'I cannot stand any more.' But God does not heed; He goes on stretching until His purpose is in sight, then He lets fly. We are here for God's designs, not for our own. LG. 132

We have to learn that this is the dispensation of the humiliation of the saints. The Christian Church has blundered by not recognizing this. In another dispensation the manifestation of the saints will take place, but in this dispensation we are to be disciples of Jesus Christ, not following our own convictions but remaining true to Him. LG. 132

The essential element in life of a saint is simplicity—"thy whole body shall be full of light." MFL. 114

The weakest saint can experience the power of the Deity of the Son of God if once he is willing to "let go." Any strand of our own energy will blur the life of Jesus. We have to keep letting go, and slowly and surely the great full life of God will invade us in every part, and men will take knowledge of us that we have been with Jesus. MUH. 103

Pride is the deification of self, and this to-day in some of us is not of the order of the Pharisee, but of the publican. To say "Oh, I'm no saint," is acceptable to human pride, but it is unconscious blasphemy against God. It literally means that you defy God to make you a saint, "I am much too weak and hopeless, I am outside the reach of the Atonement." Humility before men may be unconscious blasphemy before God. Why are you not a saint? It is either that you do not want to be a saint, or that you do not believe God can make you one. It would be all right, you say, if God saved you and took you straight to heaven. That is just what He will do! "We will come unto him, and make our abode with him." Make no conditions, let Jesus be everything, and He will take you home with Him not only for a day, but for ever. MUH. 164

A saint is never consciously a saint; a saint is consciously dependent on God. MUH. 320

God wants to do with the saints what His Son prayed He would do—make them one with Himself. NKW. 149

The dominant thing about a saint is not self-realisation, but the Lord Himself; consequently a saint can always be ignored because to the majority of eyes our Lord is no more noticeable in the life of a saint that He was to men in the days of His flesh. But when a crisis comes the saint is the one to whom men turn; and the life which seemed colourless is seen to be the white light of God. OBH. 65

To say "Oh I'm no saint; I can't stand the folks who testify that they are sanctified" is acceptable with men; they will say it is true humility to talk in that way. But say this before God, and though it may sound humble, it is blasphemy because it means God cannot make me a saint. OBH. 80

The reason I am not a saint is either that I do not want to be a saint or I do not believe God can make me one. OBH. 103

. . . the only standard for judging the saint is Jesus Christ, not saintly qualities. OPG. 29

A saint must measure his life by self-expenditure, that is, by what God pours through him. PH. 138

The attitude of a saint is that he is related to God through Jesus Christ, consequently the spring of his life is other than the world sees. PH. 163

If the saint is paying attention to the Source, Jesus Christ, out of him and unconsciously to him are flowing the rivers of living water wherever he goes. Men are either getting better or worse because of us. PR. 44

. . . the curse of the saint is his goodness! PS. 22

If God were to remove from us as saints the possibility of disobedience there would be no value in our obedience, it would be a mechanical business. PS. 50

We lose saintliness whenever we take our eyes for one second off the Source of our life, the Lord Jesus Christ. PS. 52

. . . the life of God within the saint produces agony every now and again, because God won't leave us alone, He won't say, 'Now that will do.' He will keep at us, blazing and burning us, He is a 'consuming fire.' PS. 66

Around the saints is the great power of God which keeps watch and ward over them so that 'that wicked one toucheth them not.' PS. 75

Beware of the storms of spiritual misgiving. The security of the saint's life is his relationship to Jesus and obedience to His Word. RTR. 10

A saint is one who, on the basis of the Redemption of Jesus Christ, has had the centre of his life radically altered, and has deliberately given up his right to himself. This is the point where the moral issue comes, the frontier whereby we get in contact with God. SA. 39

A saint does not mean a man who has not enough sin to be bad, but a man who has received from Jesus Christ a new heredity that turns him into another man. SA. 50

God made His own Son to be sin that He might make the sinner a saint. SA. 120

Not only does God waste His saints according to the judgments of men, He seems to bruise them most mercilessly. You say, 'But it could never be God's will to bruise me': if it pleased the Lord to bruise His own Son, why should He not bruise you? SHL. 121

The saints who satisfy the heart of Jesus are the imperial people of God for ever, nothing deflects them, they are super-conquerors, and in the future they will be side by side with Jesus. 'He that overcometh, I will give to him to sit down with Me in My throne, even as I also overcame, and sat down with My Father, in His throne.' SHL. 123

When a man is born from above, he does not need to pretend to be a saint, he cannot help being one. SSM. 30

We do not need the grace of God to stand crises; human nature and our pride will do it. We can buck up and face the music of a crisis magnificently, but it does require the supernatural grace of God to live twenty-four hours of the day as a saint, to go through drudgery as a saint, to go through poverty as a saint, to go through an ordinary, unobtrusive, ignored existence as a saint, unnoted and unnoticeable. SSY. 69

Week 39

SALVATION

Thanks be to God for His indescribable gift!

—2 Corinthians 9:15

As Christian workers we must never forget that salvation is God's thought, not man's; therefore it is an unfathomable abyss. AUG. 58

Most of us take our salvation much too cheaply. BFB. 26

The Bible does not only teach the way of salvation, but the way of spiritual sanity. BP. 240

The measure of the salvation of Jesus is not that it does for the best man we know, but that it does for the worst and most sin-stained. BSG. 14

The emphasis to-day is being put on the fact that we have to save men; we have not. We have to exalt the Saviour Who saves men, and then make disciples in His Name. BSG. 28

Salvation is an immense marvel to me—I, a sinner, can be made into a saint; but it is only possible because of what Jesus Christ did. BSG. 53

Salvation means that if a man will turn—and every man has the power to turn, if it is only a look towards the Cross, he has the power for that—if a man will but turn, he will find that Jesus is able to deliver him not only from the snare of the wrong disposition within him, but from the power of evil and wrong outside him. CHI. 97

When a man experiences salvation it is not his belief that saves him; teaching goes wrong when it puts a man's belief as the ground of his salvation. Salvation is God's 'bit' entirely. DI. 54

Salvation is based on the *revelation* fact that God has redeemed the world from the possibility of condemnation on account of sin. The *experience* of salvation means that a man can be regenerated, can have the disposition of the Son of God put into him, viz., the Holy Spirit. DI. 56

No man can be saved by praying, by believing, by obeying, or by consecration; salvation is a free gift of God's almighty grace. We have the sneaking idea that we earn things and get into God's favour by what we do—by our praying, by our repentance: the only way we get into God's favour is by the sheer gift of His grace. GW. 11

We are apt to have the idea that salvation is a kind of watertight compartment and if we enter in all our liberty will be destroyed. That is not our Lord's conception; He says he 'shall go in and go out.' GW. 110

There is nothing so secure as the salvation of God; it is as eternal as the mountains, and it is our trust in God that brings us the conscious realization of this. HG. 28

Many of us are saved by the skin of our teeth, we are comfortably settled for heaven, that is all we care for, now we can make a pile on earth. HG. 83

Jesus Christ's salvation deals not only with the outcast and downtrodden, it deals with clean-living, upright, sterling men and women, and immediately you present the Gospel as Jesus presents it, it is this class you clash with. HGM. 13

It is impossible to locate the 'soul-saving' idea in the New Testament. The glory of the Lord's disciples is not the saving of souls; but the 'soul of salvation' expressed in personal lives. It is God's work to save souls. HGM. 28

If we get taken up with salvation or with holiness or Divine healing instead of with Jesus Christ, we will be disillusioned. HGM. 110

It is possible to be grossly selfish in absorbing the salvation of Jesus, to enjoy all its benedictions, and never follow Him one step. IWP. 57

When once you let the God of peace grip you by salvation and squeeze the suspicion out of you till you are quiet before Him, the believing attitude is born, there is no more suspicion, you are in moral agreement with God about everything He wants to do. IYA. 70

If there is one point where we say 'I won't' then we shall never know His salvation. LG. 143

Salvation is sudden, but the working out of salvation in our life is never sudden. It is moment by moment, here a little and there a little. The Holy Spirit educates us down to the scruple. MFL. 46

The salvation of Jesus is not a Divine anticipation, it is an absolute fact. People talk about the magnificent ideals that are yet to be; but the marvel of being born from above is that the reality is infinitely more wonderful than all we have imagined. MFL. 60

There is a difference between the way we try to appreciate the things of God and the way in which the Spirit of God teaches. We begin by trying to get fundamental conceptions of the creation and the world; why the devil is allowed; why sin exists. When the Spirit of God comes in He does not begin by expounding any of these subjects. He begins by giving us a dose of the plague of our own heart; He begins where our vital interests lie—in the salvation of our souls. MFL. 98

Salvation is sudden, but the working of it out in our lives is never sudden. It is moment by moment, here a little and there a little. God educates us down to the scruple. MFL. 120

Salvation is not merely deliverance from sin, nor the experience of personal holiness; the salvation of God is deliverance out of self entirely into union with Himself. My experimental knowledge of salvation will be along the line of deliverance from sin and of personal holiness; but salvation means that the Spirit of God has brought me into touch with God's personality, and I am thrilled with something infinitely greater than myself, I am caught up into the abandonment of God. MUH. 73

There is a difference between conscious and unconscious salvation. To be consciously saved means that we become of immense practical value to God in this order of things. NKW. 19

Salvation will never be actual until you physically commit yourself to it. NKW. 71

We cannot do anything for our salvation, but we must do something to manifest it; we must work it out. OBH. 81

"Work out your own salvation. . . ." We have not to work out that which tells for our salvation, but to work out in the expression of our lives the salvation which God has worked in. What does my tongue say? What things do my ears like to listen to? What kind of bodily associates do I like to be with? OBH. 131

When I am saved by God's almighty grace I realize that I am delivered completely from what He has condemned—and *that* is salvation; I don't palliate it any longer, but agree with God's verdict on it on the Cross. At the back of all the condemnation of God put 'Calvary.' OPG. 16

Salvation to be experimental in me is always a judgment inasmuch as it is concerned with some kind of separation. 'The Cross condemns men to salvation.' OPG. 20

It is God who is the Architect of salvation, therefore salvation is not a common-sense design; what we have to do is to get inside that salvation. If I put my faith in any erection of my own, my vows and decisions, my consecration, I am building something for myself; I must co-operate with God in His plan of salvation. OPG. 20

Salvation is not an edict of God; salvation is something wrought out on the human plane through God becoming Man. OPG. 24

God does not ask us to believe that men can be saved; we cannot pull men out of hell by believing that we can pull them out. When we see a man in hell, every attitude of our souls and minds are paralysed; we cannot believe he can be saved. God does not ask us to believe that he can be saved; He asks us whether we will believe that Jesus believes He can save him. PH. 32

Have patience with yourself, and remember that this is salvation not for the hereafter, but for here and now. PH. 67

Salvation is so wonderful, so full of ease and power, because of what it cost Jesus Christ. PH. 88

The test of Jesus Christ's salvation is that it produces Christ-likeness, a life of absolute simplicity before God. Let us be what will satisfy His heart. PH. 90

There is a difference between being saved and being a disciple. Some of us are saved, "yet so as through fire." We are grateful to God for saving us from sin, but we are of no use to Him in so far as our actual life is concerned. We are not spiritual disciples. PH. 132

If you are religious, beware lest you are keener on the plan of salvation than on the Saviour. PH. 230

Unless our salvation works out through our finger tips and everywhere else, there is nothing to it, it is religious humbug. PH. 101

The centre of salvation is the Cross of Jesus Christ, and why it is so easy to obtain salvation is because it cost God so much; and why it is so difficult to experience salvation is because human conceit will not accept, nor believe, nor have anything to do with unmerited salvation. PR. 107

Salvation means the incoming into human nature of the great characteristics that belong to God, and there is no salvation that is not supernatural. PR. 121

Salvation is always supernatural. The Holy Ghost brings me into union with God by dealing with that which broke the union. It is dangerous to preach a persuasive gospel, to try and persuade men to believe in Jesus Christ with the idea that if they do, He will develop them along the natural line. PR. 122

Jesus Christ can take anyone, no matter who he is, and presence him with His wonderful Divine salvation. PR. 123

If sin is a radical twist with a supernatural originator, salvation is a radical readjustment with a supernatural Originator. To present salvation as less than that is deplorable. PS. 15

The purpose of the sword is to destroy everything that hinders a man being delivered. The first thing in salvation is the element of destruction, and it is this that men object to. PS. 24

Salvation is the biggest, gladdest word in the world; it cannot mean pretence in any shape or form, therefore suppression is no element of the word, neither is counteraction. Salvation is God's grace to sinful men, and it takes a lifetime to say the word properly. Most of us restrict the meaning of salvation, we use it to mean New Birth only, or something limited. PS. 24

Thank God, salvation does not mean that God turns us into milksops; God's salvation makes us for the first time into men and women. PS. 29

If you have a passion for souls it is because your salvation has made such a practical change in you that you would part with your right hand to get every man there too. RTR. 16

Thank God for His safeguarding, for His salvation which keeps us, waking and sleeping, conscious and unconscious, in danger and out of it. RTR. 55

Unless we are damnable, we are not worth saving. If we cannot go to the devil, we cannot go to God. The measure of the depth to which a man can fall is the height to which he can rise. Virtue is the outcome of conflict, not of necessity. SHH. 101

If you have been making a great profession in your religious life but begin to find that the Holy Spirit is scrutinizing you, let His searchlight go straight down, and He will not only search you, He will put everything right that is wrong; He will make the past as though it had never been; He will 'restore the years the cankerworm hath eaten'; He will 'blot out the handwriting of ordinances that is against you'; He will put His Spirit within you and cause you to walk in His ways; He will make you pure in the deepest recesses of your personality. Thank God, Jesus Christ's salvation is a flesh-and-blood reality! SHL. 51

Salvation means not only a pure heart, an enlightened mind, a spirit right with God, but that the whole man is comprehended in the manifestation of the marvellous power and grace of God, body, soul, and spirit are brought into fascinating captivity to the Lord Jesus Christ. SSM. 88

The salvation of God not only saves a man from hell, but alters his actual life. SSM. 92

"Enter ye in at the strait gate . . ." If a man tries to enter into salvation in any other way than Jesus Christ's way, he will find it a broad way, but the end is distress. SSM. 93

Salvation is of universal application, but human responsibility is not done away with. SSY. 106

SANCTIFICATION

This is the will of God, your sanctification.

—1 Thessalonians 4:3

Sanctification means not only that we are delivered from sin, but that we start on a life of stern discipline. It is not a question of praying but of performing, of deliberately disciplining ourselves. BE. 48

When we are sanctified we do not get something like a landslide of holiness from heaven; we are introduced into a relationship of oneness with God, and as Our Lord met antagonistic forces and overcame them, so must we. The life Jesus lived is the type of our life after sanctification. We are apt to make sanctification the end; it is only the beginning. Our holiness as saints consists in the exclusive dedication to God of all our powers. BSG. 37

"Jesus Christ is made unto us sanctification," that is, *He* is the holy nature which we receive. CHI. 22

There is no difficulty in getting sanctified if my will and affections have at their heart the earnest desire for God's glory. CHI. 54

If I am willing for God to strangle in me the thing that makes me everlastingly hanker after my own point of view, my own interests, my own whiteness—if I am willing for all that to be put to death, then "the God of peace will sanctify me wholly." CHI. 54

The process of sanctification begins at the moment of birth from above and is consummated on the unconditional surrender of my right to myself to Jesus Christ. CHI. 81

The time that elapses between new birth and entire sanctification depends entirely on the individual. CHI. 81

After sanctification it is difficult to state what your aim in life is, because God has taken you up into His purposes. CHI. 95

The test of sanctification is not our talk about holiness and singing pious hymns; but, what are we like where no one sees us? with those who know us best? DI. 60

If I exalt Sanctification, I preach people into despair; but if I lift up Jesus Christ, people learn the way to be made holy. DI. 60

The sanctification of the Bible never fixes you on the fact that you are delivered from sin: it fixes you on the One who *is* Sanctification. Sanctification is not something Jesus Christ gives me, it is Himself in me. GW. 48

The value to God of one man or woman right out in supreme sanctification is incalculable. GW. 126

To imagine that Jesus Christ came to save and sanctify *me* is heresy: He came to save and sanctify me *into Himself* . . . HGM. 130

Numbers of people say, 'I have asked God to sanctify me and He has not done it.' Of course He has not! Do we find one word in the Bible which tells us to pray, 'Lord, sanctify me'? What we do read is that God sanctifies what we give. IWP. 17

The more people there are who enter into sanctification through Jesus Christ, the more is Satan's dominance ruined. IWP. 28

Sanctification may take a few moments of realized transaction, but all the rest of the life goes to prove what that transaction means. IWP. 85

To coin a phrase, Jesus Christ 'sanctified His sanctification,' that is, He determinedly sacrificed His holy Self to His Father. Jesus Christ separated, or sanctified, Himself by sacrificing His holy Self to the will of His Father; He sanctified His intelligence by submitting His intelligence to the word of His Father, and He sanctified His will by submitting His will to the will of His Father. As the sanctified children of God we need to bear in mind that after the experience of sanctification we have to separate our holiness to God. We are not made holy for ourselves, but for God, there is to be no insubordination about us. IYA. 66

Are we prepared for what sanctification will cost? It will cost an intense narrowing of all our interests on earth, and an immense broadening of our interest in God. IYA. 67

Some people pray and long and yearn for the experience of sanctification, but never get anywhere near it; others enter in with a sudden marvellous realisation. Sanctification is an instantaneous, continuous work of grace; how long the approach to it takes depends upon ourselves, and that leads some to say sanctification is not instantaneous. The reason why some do not enter in is because they have never allowed their minds to realise what sanctification means. IYA. 67

People say, 'I don't understand this doctrine of sanctification.' Well, get into the experience first. You only get home by going there. You may think about getting there, but you will never get there till you go. IYA. 69

The majority of us have never allowed our minds to dwell as they should on these great massive truths; consequently sanctification has been made to mean a second dose of conversion. Sanctification can only be named in the presence of God, it is stamped by a likeness to Christ. IYA. 71

Sanctification means that God keeps my whole spirit and soul and body undeserving of censure in His sight. LG. 138

To say that the doctrine of sanctification is unnatural is not true, it is based on the way God has made us. MFL. 72

Sanctification must never be made synonymous with purification; Jesus Christ has no need of purification, and yet He used the word 'sanctify.' In the words, "I sanctify Myself," Jesus gives the key to the saint's life. MFL. 107

We take the term sanctification much too lightly. Are we prepared for what sanctification will cost? It will cost an intense narrowing of all our interests on earth, and an immense broadening of all our interests in God. Sanctification means intense concentration on God's point of view. MUH. 39

We talk as if it were the most precarious thing to live the sanctified life; it is the most secure thing, because it has Almighty God in and behind it. The most precarious thing is to try and live without God. If we are born again it is the easiest thing to live in right relationship to God and the most difficult thing to go wrong, if only we will heed God's warnings and keep in the light. MUH. 359

Obedience to the supremacy of the Lord Jesus is the only legitimate outcome of sanctification. Thank God, He wants us to be human, not spooks! NKW. 133

Sanctification does not put us into the place that Adam was in and require us to fulfil the will of God as He makes it known to us; sanctification is something infinitely more than that. In Jesus Christ is perfect holiness, perfect patience, perfect love, perfect power over all the power of the enemy, perfect power over everything that is not of God, and sanctification means that all that is ours in Him. OBH. 13

Sanctification does not mean that the Lord gives us the ability to produce by a slow, steady process a holiness like His; it is *His* holiness in us. OBH. 14

The Spirit of God conveys to the initiated, to those who are born again, what a marvellous thing sanctification is. The perfections of Jesus—ours by the sheer gift of God. God does not give us power to imitate Him: He gives us His very Self. OBH. 16

The great mighty work of God's grace in sanctification is a Divine work. OBH. 30

Sanctification is the impartation to us of the holy qualities of Jesus Christ. It is His patience, His love, His holiness, His faith, His purity,

His godliness that are manifested in and through every sanctified soul. The presentation that God by sanctification plants within us His Spirit, and then setting Jesus Christ before us says—'There is your Example, follow Him and I will help you, but you must do your best to follow Him and do what He did,' is an error. It is not true to experience, and, thank God, it is not true to the wonderful Gospel of the grace of God. The mystery of sanctification is "*Christ in you, the hope of glory.*" "That which hath been made was life in Him," that is, Jesus Christ can create in us the image of God even as it was in Himself. OBH. 31

By sanctification we enter into the kingdom of perfect oneness with Jesus Christ; everything He is, we are by faith. OBH. 88

A sanctified saint remains perfectly confident in God, because sanctification is not something the Lord gives me, sanctification is *Himself in me.* PH. 41

The Lord Jesus Christ is the beginning, the middle and the end. Many are willing to accept sanctification, but they do not want the One Who is sanctification. PH. 45

. . . when I think I can define what sanctification is, I have done something God refuses to do. Books about sanctification are much more clearer that the Bible. The Bible is uncommonly confusing, so is human life. There is only one thing that is simple, ant that is our relationship to Jesus Christ. PH. 87

Sanctification means being identified with Jesus until all the springs of our being are in Him. PH. 225

. . . after the work of sanctification, when the life of a saint really begins, God lifts His hand off and lets the world, the flesh, and the devil do their worst, for He is assured that "greater is He that is in you, than he that is in the world." PR. 75

After sanctification the characteristic of the life is clear—Jesus Christ first, Jesus Christ second and Jesus Christ third, all that the Lord wants; the life goes on with a flood of intense energy, adoration unspeakable. PS. 37

Sanctification is the gateway to real union with God, which is life unutterable. PS. 47

To say after sanctification, 'Now I can do what I like,' is a perilously dangerous statement. If it were true, it would never have been recorded that "even Christ pleased not Himself." PS. 50

Sanctification means intense concentration on God's point of view. It means every power of body, soul and spirit chained and kept for God's purpose only. RTR. 31

Sanctification is the work of Christ in me, the sign that I am no longer independent, but completely dependent upon Him. SHL. 88

If our experience of sanctification ends in pious sentiment, the reason is that it has never dawned on us that we must deliberately set our sanctified selves apart for God's use as Jesus did. SSY. 95

We take our salvation and our sanctification too cheaply, without realising that Jesus Christ went through the deep waters of uttermost damnation that we might have it. SSY. 102

SATAN

Whose minds the god of this age has blinded, who do not believe, lest the light of the gospel of the glory of Christ, who is the image of God, should shine on them.

—2 Corinthians 4:4

The devil is the adversary of God in the rule of man and Satan is his representative. BFB. 8

Satan counterfeits the Holy Spirit. BFB. 8

One of the most cunning travesties is to represent Satan as the instigator of external sins. The satanically-managed man is moral, upright, proud and individual; he is absolutely self-governed and has no need of God. BFB. 8

According to the Bible, man is responsible for the introduction of Satan: Satan is the result of a communication set up between man and the devil. BFB. 8

Satan is to be humiliated by man, by the Spirit of God in man through the wonderful regeneration of Jesus Christ. BP. 8

Satan thwarted God's purpose, and then laughed his devilish laugh against God, but the Bible says that God will laugh last. "The Lord shall laugh at him: for He seeth that His day is coming." BP. 16

The pretensions of Satan are clear. He is the god of this world and he will not allow relationship to the true God. Satan's attitude is that of a pretender to the throne, he claims it as his right. Wherever and whenever the rule of God is recognized by man, Satan proceeds to instil the tendency of mutiny and rebellion and lawlessness. BP. 20

Satan's pretension is that he is equal with God. His perversion is two-fold: he tries to pervert what God says to us, and also to pervert God's mind about us. BP. 22

Satan is an awful being, he is able to deceive us on the right hand and on the left, and the first beginnings of his deceptions are along the lines of self-pity. Self-pity, self-conceit, and self-sympathy will make us accept slanders against God. BP. 22

Satanic anarchy is conscious and determined opposition to God. Wherever God's rule is made known, Satan will put himself alongside and oppose it. Satan's sin is at the summit of all sins; man's sin is at the foundation of all sins, and there is all the difference in the world between them. BP. 24

Men are responsible for doing wrong things, and they do wrong things because of the wrong disposition in them. The moral cunning of our nature makes us blame Satan when we know perfectly well we should blame ourselves; the true blame for sins lies in the wrong disposition in us. In all probability Satan is as much upset as the Holy Ghost is when men fall into external sin, but for a different reason. When men go into external sin and upset their lives, Satan knows perfectly well that they will want another Ruler, a Saviour and Deliverer; as long as Satan can keep men in peace and unity and harmony apart from God, he will do so. BP. 24

Satan's sin is dethroning God. BP. 24

Satan, . . . is as subtle as God is good, and he tries to counterfeit everything God does, and if he cannot counterfeit it, he will limit it. Do not be ignorant of his devices! BP. 101

Satan uses the problems of this life to slander God's character; he tries to make us think that all the calamities and miseries and wrongs spring from God. BP. 134

"Resist the devil," not attack him. BSG. 29

Every temptation of Satan is perfectly wise. The wisest, shrewdest, subtlest things are said by Satan, and they are accepted by everybody as the acme of human philosophy; but when the Spirit of God is at work in a man, instantly the hollow mockery at the heart of what Satan is trying to do, is seen. When we understand the inwardness of the temptation we see how Satan's strategy is turned into confusion by the Spirit of God. BSG. 30

Health and happiness is what is wanted to-day and Jesus Christ is simply exploited. We who name the Name of Christ, are we beginning to discern what Satan is after? He is trying to fatigue out of us what God has put in, viz., the possibility of being of value to God. Our only safety is to watch Our Lord and Saviour. BSG. 31

Satan did not tempt Jesus to sin, as we think of sin; he knew better. The one thing Satan aims at is that we put ourselves as master instead of God. BSG. 31

Satan does not come as "an angel of light" to anybody but a saint. DI. 19

If Satan in his malice and cunning can slander God to His own children, he will do it because that is his whole aim. GW. 98

In the Bible the devil is represented as the antagonist of Deity; Satan represents the self-interest of humanity. Our Lord's words "Get thee hence, Satan" refer to the interests of humanity in conflict with God's interests. HGM. 60

Satan is not removed now from the presence of the saints, but the saint is still kept in the world where the evil one rules, consequently the saint is continually being badgered by the evil one. Jesus prayed, not that we should be taken out of the world, but that we should be "kept from the evil one." IWP. 28

The only soul Satan cannot touch is the soul whose spiritual life and rational life and physical life is hid with Christ in God; that soul is absolutely secure. IWP. 35

When a man has received the Holy Spirit, the watching of Satan is keen, his whole desire is to split up the personality. IWP. 39

The devil is a bully, but he cannot stand for a second before God. IYA. 32

Satan does not come on the line of tempting us to sin, but on the line of making us shift our point of view, and only the Spirit of God can detect this as a temptation of the devil. LG. 153

God does not deal with Satan direct, man must deal with Satan because man is responsible for his introduction. That is why God became Incarnate. Put it in any other way—why God could banish Satan in two seconds; but it is man who, through the Redemption, is to overcome Satan, and much more than overcome him, he is to do that which will exhibit the perfect fulfilment of this prophecy. Jesus Christ, the last Adam, took on Him our human form, and it is through His seed in that human form that Satan is to be overcome. OPG. 9

Satan's great aim is to deflect us from the centre. He will allow us to be devoted 'to death' to any cause, any enterprise, to anything but the Lord Jesus. PH. 17

Satan is to be overcome and conquered by human beings. That is why God became Incarnate. It is in the Incarnation that Satan is overcome. PR. 62

The devil does not tempt us to do wrong things; he tries to make us lose what God has put into us by regeneration, the possibility of being of value to God. When we are born from above the central citadel of the devil's attack is the same in us as it was in our Lord—viz., to do God's will in our own way. PR. 63

Satan tried to put Jesus Christ on the way to becoming King of the world and Saviour of men in a way other than that pre-determined by God. PR. 63

The prince of this world and Satan are synonymous terms. Satan is the manifestation of the devil for which man is held responsible, that is, Satan is the result of a communication between man and the devil. PR. 104

For a thing to be Satanic does not mean that it is abominable and immoral. The satanically managed man is moral, upright, proud, and individual; he is absolutely self-governed and has no need of God. PR. 105

The disposition of self-realisation is the manifestation in us of the devil as Satan, and when we come to the Cross we leave Satan outside, Satan cannot take one step inside the Cross. PR. 105

The onslaught of Satan in Gethsemane was that Jesus Christ would never get through His agony as Son of Man. As Son of God, Satan could not prevent His getting through, but his challenge was that he would prevent Jesus Christ bringing one soul through with Him—and Satan was hopelessly defeated. PR. 111

The sin of Satan is revealed only dimly, but the dim outline indicates that it was the summit of all sin, full, free, conscious, spiritual sin; he was not entrapped into it, he was not ensnared into it, he sinned with the full clear understanding of what he was doing. PS. 11

Satan had the possibility of disobedience and when the temptation producing the dilemma came, he inclined to rebellion against God. PS. 55

Satan is never represented in the Bible as being guilty of sins, of doing wrong things; he is *a wrong being*. PS. 59

Satan has no power to dispossess God of me. RTR. 50

There is a difference between the Devil and Satan. The Bible holds man responsible for the introduction of Satan. Adam started a communication with another of God's creations, and the result was Satan. Jesus Christ calls the self-realization point of view, "Satan," anti-Christ. SA. 86

For a thing to be Satanic does not mean that it is abominable and immoral; the Satanically-managed man is absolutely self-governed and has no need of God. SHL. 42

When Satan rules the hearts of natural men under the inspiration of the devil, they are not troubled, they are at peace, entrenched in clean worldliness, and before God can rule a man's kingdom He must first overthrow this false rule. SHL. 42

One of the most cunning travesties of Satan is to say that he is the instigator of drunkenness and external sins. Man himself is responsible for doing wrong things, and he does wrong things because of the wrong disposition that is in him. The true blame for sin lies in the wrong disposition, and the cunning of our nature makes us blame Satan when we should blame ourselves. SHL. 43

Week 42

SELF

If anyone desires to come after Me, let him deny himself, and take up his cross daily, and follow Me.

—Luke 9:23

The term self-denial has come to mean giving up things; the denial Jesus speaks of is a denial right out to my right to myself, a clean sweep of all the decks to the mastership of Jesus. AUG. 53

What is the best God has given you? Your right to yourself. 'Now,' He says, 'sacrifice that to Me.' If you do, He will make it yours and His for ever. If you do not, it will spell death to you. AUG. 88

Jesus Christ is always unyielding on one point, viz., that I must give up my right to myself to Him. BE. 48

The relationship set up between Adam and the devil was self-realization, not immorality and vice, but, my claim to my right to myself, whether it is manifested in clean living or unclean living is a matter of indifference; sin is the fundamental relationship underneath. BE. 62

Self-realization and God cannot live together. BE. 64

From man's standpoint, self-realization is full of light and wisdom; from God's standpoint, it is the dark night of the soul. BE. 81

God's right to me is killed by the incoming of my self-conscious right to myself—'I can do without God.' BE. 82

We only know ourselves as God searches us. 'God knows me' is different from 'God is omniscient'; the latter is a mere theological statement; the former is a child of God's most precious possession—'O Lord, Thou hast searched *me,* and known *me.*' BE. 85

As long as my right to myself remains, I respect it in you, you respect it in me, and the devil respects it in the whole crowd, and amalgamates humanity under one tremendous rule which aims at blotting the one true God off His throne. BE. 115

Redemption is easy to experience because it cost God everything, and if I am going to be regenerated it is going to cost me something. I have to give up my right to myself. BFB. 76

The true centre for self is Jesus Christ. BP. 180

Self . . . is not to be annihilated, but to be rightly centered in God. *Self*-realization has to be turned into *Christ*-realization. Our Lord never taught "Deeper death to self"; He taught death right out to my right to myself, to self-realization. He taught that the principal purpose of our creation is "to glorify God and to enjoy Him forever"; that the sum total of my self is to be consciously centred in God. BP. 183

As long as we are flippant and stupid and shallow and think that we know ourselves, we shall never give ourselves over to Jesus Christ; but when once we become conscious that we are infinitely more than we can fathom, and infinitely greater in possibility either for good or bad than we can know, we shall be only too glad to hand ourselves over to Him. BP. 258

Any man would have known without His coming that it was wrong to take life, the law is written in him; any man would have known that immorality was wrong; but no man apart from Jesus Christ would believe that 'my right to myself' is the very essence of sin. BSG. 12

When we realize what Jesus means when He says, 'If you would be My disciple, give up your right to yourself to Me,' we begin to understand that "the carnal mind is enmity against God." 'I will not give up my right to myself; I will serve God as I choose.' Jesus Christ came to remove this disposition of self-realization. BSG. 12

There is nothing more highly esteemed among men that self-realisation, but it is the one thing of which Jesus Christ is the enemy because its central citadel is independence of God. CHI. 17

It is well to remember that our examination of ourselves can never be unbiased or unprejudiced, so that we are only safe in taking the estimate of ourselves from our Creator instead of from our own introspection, whether conceited or depressed. DI. 30

Naturally, a man regards his right to himself as the finest thing he has, yet it is the last bridge that prevents Jesus Christ having His way in a life. DI. 34

The approaches to Jesus are innumerable; the result of coming to Him can be only one—the dethroning of my right to myself, or I stop short somewhere. DI. 34

My right to myself is not merely something I claim, but something that continually makes me insist on my own way. DI. 62

God is the only One who has the right to myself and when I love Him with all my heart and soul and mind and strength, self in its essence is realized. GW. 40

Self is not to be absorbed into God, it is to be centred in God. GW. 40

The true import of love is the surrender of my self, I got out of myself in order to live in and for God. To be indwelt by the Spirit of Jesus means I am willing to quit my own abode from the self-interested standpoint and live only in and for God. It is not the surrender to a conqueror, but the surrender of love, a sovereign preference for God. I surrender myself—not because it is bad, self is the best thing I have got, and I give it to God; then self-realization is lost in God-realization. GW. 41

I may be under conscious apprehension for discipleship, and I go through the form of being willing to give up my right to myself, but the Holy Spirit reveals that I have never really done it—'I will spend myself for Jesus,' 'I will do everything He asks me to do'—but not one thing, and it is the only thing I can do, viz., give up my right to myself to Him. GW. 42

The word translated 'soul' or 'life' may be equally well translated 'himself,' and the verses mean just what they say. Jesus is not defining the great fundamental doctrine of personality, He is talking about the man himself, the person who lives, and with whom we come in contact. Jesus says if a man gains himself, he loses himself; and if he loses himself for His sake, he gains himself. HG. 62

So many of us get depressed about ourselves, but when we get to the point where we are not only sick of ourselves, but sick to death, then we shall understand what the Atonement of the Lord Jesus Christ means. It will mean that we come to Him without the slightest pretence, without any hypocrisy, and say, 'Lord, if You can make anything of me, do it,' and He will do it. HG. 76

Jesus Christ revealed that men were evil, and that He came that He might plant in them the very nature that was in Himself. He cannot, however, begin to do this until a man recognizes himself as Jesus sees him. HG. 87

"I don't mind being saved from hell and receiving the Holy Spirit, but it is too much to expect me to give up my right to myself to Jesus Christ, to give up my manhood, my womanhood, all my ambitions." HG. 99

God can do nothing for me if I am sufficient for myself. HGM. 16

Wherever there is self-realization, the voice of God is a continual embarrassment. HGM. 51

There is nothing more highly esteemed among men than self-realization, but Jesus says that "that which is highly esteemed among men is abomination in the sight of God." HGM. 74

. . . the meaning of sacrifice is the deliberate giving of the best I have to God that He may make it His and mine for ever: if I cling to it, I lose it, and so does God. HGM. 75

Wherever Christian experience is proving unsatisfactory it is because the Holy Spirit is still battling around this one point, my right to myself, and until that is deliberately given over by me to Jesus Christ I will never have the relationship to Him He asks for. HGM. 140

We have no business to bring in that abomination of the lower regions that makes us think too little of ourselves; to think too little of ourselves is simply the obverse side of conceit. If I am a disciple of Jesus, He is my Master, I am looking to Him, and the thought of self never enters. IWP. 111

We do not object to being delivered from sin, but we do not intend to give up the right to ourselves; it is this point that is baulked. Jesus will never make us give up our right to ourselves; we must do it of our own deliberate choice. LG. 123

Jesus Christ said it was impossible for the man who is self-centred in his particular impression of himself to believe in Him. MFL. 14

By heeding the reality of God's grace within us we are never bothered again by the fact that we do not understand ourselves, or that other people do not understand us. If anyone understood me, he would be my god. The only Being Who understands me is the Being Who made me and Who redeems me, and He will never expound me to myself; He will only bring me to the place place of reality, viz., into contact with Himself, and the heart is at leisure from itself for ever afterwards. MFL. 63

Self is not sinful; if it were, how could Jesus say "I sanctify Myself"? Jesus Christ had no sin to deny, no wrong self to deny; He had only a holy Self. It was that Self He denied all the time, and it was that Self that Satan tried to make Him obey. MFL. 107

It was the denying of His holy Self that made the marvellous beauty of our Lord's life. MFL. 108

Many of us are after our own ends, and Jesus Christ cannot help Himself to our lives. MUH. 55

The little "I am" always sulks when God says *do*. Let the little "I am" be shrivelled up in God's indignation—"I AM THAT I AM hath sent thee." He must dominate. Is it not penetrating to realize that God knows where we live, and the kennels we crawl into! He will hunt us up like a lightning flash. No human being knows human beings as God does. MUH. 278

Determinedly take no one seriously but God, and the first person you find you have to leave severely alone as being the greatest fraud you have ever known, is yourself. MUH. 327

We have to get rid of all notions about ourselves and our own standards, and keep in front what God puts in front, viz., Our Lord Himself, then we will not be tempted to delusion about ourselves. NKW. 89

'To obey is better than sacrifice.' It is a great deal better to fulfil the purpose of God in your life by discerning His will than it is to perform great acts of self-sacrifice. OBH. 119

To be found out by yourself is a terrible thing. OPG. 52

When we are told we must give up our right to ourselves to Jesus Christ, we are bound to ask—if we do not ask, we have not grasped the situation thoroughly—'Who is it that asks this tremendous devotion? Is there any principle, any cause, any enterprise on the face of the earth of such importance that a man has to give the very highest he has, viz., his right to himself, for it?' The only Being Who dare ask of me this supreme sacrifice is the Lord Jesus Christ. PH. 16

Everyone has to begin with this struggle for self, and striving to enter in at the strait gate is a picture of the struggle. Anything that does not enter in at the strait gate, e.g., selfishness, self-interest, self-indulgence, ends in destruction. The struggle to enter in, no matter with what it may be in connection, braces us morally. Self-indulgence is a refusal to struggle, a refusal to make ourselves fit. PH. 79

A self indwelt by Jesus becomes like Him. PH. 81

It takes a long time to realise what Jesus is after, and the person you need most patience with is yourself. PH. 102

We cannot go on spiritually if we are self-assertive. PH. 169

Jesus Christ did not say, 'He that believeth on Me, in himself shall realise the blessing of the fulness of God,' but 'out of him shall escape everything he has received.' Our Lord always preaches anti-self-realisation; He is not after developing a man at all, He is after making a man exactly like Himself, and the measure of the Son of God is self-expenditure. PH. 127

"If any man will come after Me, let him deny himself," i.e., let him give up his right to himself. No one can bring us to this denial, even God Himself cannot, we must come there of our own accord, and the length of time it takes to do so depends entirely on whether we want to come or not. If we give way to the play of our emotions and do not intend deliberately to come to the point of identification, we will get off on to spiritual sentimentality and end nowhere. PH. 158

It is no longer my claim to my right to myself that rules my personal life—I am not dead, but the old disposition of my right to myself has gone, it is Jesus Christ's right to me that rules me now, "and that life which I now live in the flesh" I live from that centre. PH. 163

We cannot receive ourselves in success, we lose our heads; we cannot receive ourselves in monotony, we grouse; the only way we can find ourselves is in the fires of sorrow. Why it should be so I do not know, but that it is so is true not only in Scripture, but in human life. PH. 192

We are apt to imagine that the cross we have to carry means the ordinary troubles and trials of life, but we must have these whether we are Christians or not. Neither is our cross suffering for conscience' sake. Our cross is something that comes only with the peculiar relationship of a disciple to Jesus Christ; it is the evidence that we have denied our right to ourselves. PR. 102

The right to ourselves is the only thing we have to give to God. We cannot give our natural possessions, because they have been given to us. If we had not our right to ourselves by God's creation of us, we should have nothing to give, and consequently could not be held responsible. PR. 102

How many of us are of any worth to Jesus Christ? Our attitude is rather that we are much obliged to God for saving us, but the idea of giving up our chances to realise ourselves in life is too extravagantly extreme. Some of us will take all God has to give us while we take good care not to give Him anything back. PR. 103

Naturally, a man regards his right to himself as the finest thing he has, yet it is the last bridge that prevents Jesus Christ having His way in that life. RTR. 38

Beware of the pious fraud in you which says—"I have no misgivings about Jesus, only about myself." No one ever had misgivings about himself! RTR. 53

The first thing to do in examining the power that dominates me is to take hold of the unwelcome fact that I am responsible for being thus dominated because I have yielded. If I am a slave to myself, I am to blame for it because at a point, away back, I yielded myself to myself. Likewise, if I obey God, I do so because I have yielded myself to Him. RTR. 83

The problem of the universe is not mine but the Almighty's; the problem I am up against is the muddle inside. SA. 68

The disposition of sin is not immorality or wrongdoing, but my claim to my right to myself. SA. 104

It may take four minutes or forty years to be identified with Jesus Christ; it depends on whether I am willing to face the music, i.e., forgo my hereditary right to my claim to myself and let Him take His claim to me. SA. 108

Any fool will give up wrongdoing and the devil, if he knows how to do it; but it takes a man in love with Jesus Christ to give up the best he has for Him. Jesus Christ does not demand that I give up the wrong, but the right, the best I have for Him, viz., my right to myself. SA. 112

We have no business to be ignorant about ourselves. If any of us have come to manhood or womanhood with the idea that we have a holy innocence on the inside, we are desperately deluded. SHL. 48

People say, 'Oh, I can't understand myself!' Of course you cannot. 'No one else understands me!' Of course they don't; if they did, we would not be worth understanding. There is only one Being Who understands us, and that is our Creator. SHL. 54

The modern jargon is all for self-realization; we educate ourselves for the purpose of self-realization, we select our friendships for self-realization purposes. Jesus says, 'Whosoever will lose his life for My sake'—deliberately fling it away—'shall find it.' SHL. 78

To say, 'Oh, I'm sick of myself,' is a sure sign that we are not. When we really are sick of ourselves we will never say so, but will gladly come to the end of ourselves. So long as we say, 'I'm tired of myself,' it is a sign that we are profoundly interested in ourselves. SHL. 79

The way God brings us to know ourselves is by the kind of people He brings round us. What we see to condemn in others is either the discernment of the Holy Ghost or the reflection of what we are capable of ourselves. We always notice how obtuse other people are before we notice how obtuse we ourselves are. If we see meanness in others, it is because we ourselves are mean. SHL. 81

The Holy Spirit continually urges us to sign away our right to our individual self to Jesus. SHL. 84

If you have to calculate what you are willing to give up for Jesus Christ, never say that you love Him. Jesus Christ asks us to give up the best we have to Him, our right to ourselves. There is only this one crisis, and in the majority of lives it has never been reached, we are brought up to it again and again, and every time we go back. SHL. 86

Self-realization must be renounced in order that Jesus Christ may realize Himself in us. SHL. 86

Most of us have no ear for anything but ourselves, anything that is not 'me' we cannot hear. SSY. 10

Week 43

SERVICE

Not with eyeservice, as men-pleasers, but as bondservants of Christ, doing the will of God from the heart,

—Ephesians 6:6

The stamp of the worker gripped by God is that, slowly and surely, one here and another there is being won for God. AUG. 9

The only way to be sent is to let God lift us right out of any sense of fitness in ourselves and place us where He will. AUG. 26

The intensity of the moments spent under the shadow of the Almighty is the measure of your usefulness as a worker. AUG. 27

Don't get dissipated; determine to develop your intellect for one purpose only—to make yourself of more use to God. AUG. 36

The Cross is the great opening through which all the blood of Christian service runs. AUG. 55

The only way to keep true to God is by a steady persistent refusal to be interested in Christian work and to be interested alone in Jesus Christ. AUG. 64

May God save us from Christian service which is nothing more than the reaction of a disappointed, crushed heart; seeking surcease from sorrow in social service. Christian service is the vital, unconscious result of the life of a believer in Jesus. AUG. 107

Beware of the tendency of trying to do what God alone can do, and of blaming God for not doing what we alone can do. BP. 119

. . . our service is not to be that of pity, but of personal, passionate love to God, and a longing to see many more brought to the centre where God has brought us. BP. 184

I have no business in God's service if I have any personal reserve, I am to be broken bread and poured-out wine in His hands. DI. 47

We are saved and sanctified not for service, but to be absolutely Jesus Christ's, the consuming passion of the life is for Him. DI. 61

Christian service is not our work; loyalty to Jesus is our work. DI. 85

The value of our work depends on whether we can direct men to Jesus Christ. DI. 85

Whenever success is made the motive of service infidelity to our Lord is the inevitable result. DI. 85

Nothing hoodwinks us more quickly than the idea that we are serving God. DI. 88

It is much easier to do Christian work than to be concentrated on God's point of view. DI. 89

The worker whose work tells for God is the one who realizes what God has done in him. GW. 48

The only way we can be sent is by God deliberately lifting us out of any sense of fitness in ourselves; I realize I am utterly weak and powerless, and that if I am to be of any use for God, He must do it in me all the time. GW. 48

The greatest service we can render God is to fulfil our spiritual destiny. It is the despised crowd God is counting on, insignificant but holy. GW. 126

Social service that is not based on the Cross of Christ is the cultured blasphemy of civilized life against God, because it denies that God has done anything, and puts human effort as the only way whereby the world will be redeemed. HG. 100

Never look at the work of God in and through you; never look at the way God uses you in His service; immediately you do, you put your mind away from where Jesus Christ wants to get it. IWP. 44

If you are right with God, you will be amazed at what other people get in the way of real spiritual help out of what you say; but never think about it. The temptation comes all along to say, 'It is because I brooded that God gave me that thought.' The right attitude is to keep the mind absolutely concentrated on God and never get off on the line of how you are being used by Him. IWP. 45

If we are paying attention to the Source, rivers of living water will pour out of us, but immediately we stop paying attention to the Source, the outflow beings to dry up. We have nothing to do with our 'usability,' but only with our relationship to Jesus Christ, nothing must be allowed to come in between. IWP. 45

So many of us put prayer and work and consecration in place of the working of God; we make ourselves the workers. God is the Worker, we work out what He works in. IWP. 63

There is only one service that has no snares, and that is prayer. Preaching has snares to the natural heart; so has public service. Prayer has no snare because it is based on the Redemption of the Lord Jesus Christ made efficacious all the time by the Holy Spirit. IYA. 36

God does not expect us to work *for* Him, but to work *with* Him. IYA. 56

. . . if we are to be of use to God in the world we must be useful from God's standpoint, not from our own standpoint or the standpoint of other people. LG. 55

We slander God by our very eagerness to work for Him without knowing Him. LG. 58

The people who are of absolutely no use to God are those who have sat down and have become overgrown with spiritual mildew; all they can do is to refer to an experience they had twenty or thirty years ago. That is of no use whatever, we must be vitally at it all the time. With Paul it was never 'an experience I once had,' but *"the life which I now live."* MFL. 99

We have a way of saying—'What a wonderful power that man or woman would be in God's service.' Reasoning on man's broken virtues makes us fix on the wrong thing. The only way any man or woman can ever be of service to God is when he or she is willing to renounce all their natural excellencies and determine to be weak in Him—'I am here for one thing only, for Jesus Christ to manifest Himself in me.' That is to be the steadfast habit of a Christian's life. MFL. 106

Beware of anything that competes with loyalty to Jesus Christ. The greatest competitor of devotion to Jesus is service for Him. It is easier to serve than to be drunk to the dregs. The one aim of the call of God is the satisfaction of God, not a call to do something for Him. We are not sent to battle for God, but to be used by God in His battlings. MUH. 18

Jesus Christ calls service what we are to Him, not what we do for Him. MUH. 171

The tendency to-day is to put the emphasis on service. Beware of the people who make usefulness their ground of appeal. If you make usefulness the test, then Jesus Christ was the greatest failure that ever lived. The lodestar of the saint is God Himself, not estimated usefulness. It is the work that God does through us that counts, not what we do for Him. MUH. 243

Jesus Christ says, in effect, Don't rejoice in successful service, but rejoice because you are rightly related to Me. MUH. 243

Spend plenty of time with God; let other things go, but don't neglect Him. And beware of practical work. NKW. 137

If we are going to be used by God, He will take us through a multitude of experiences that are not meant for us at all, but meant to make us useful in His hands. PH. 34

The stars do their work without fuss; God does His work without fuss, and saints do their work without fuss. PH. 41

The only way we can serve God is by having "no confidence in the flesh." PH. 69

If you are devoted to the cause of humanity, you will soon be exhausted and have your heart broken by ingratitude, but if the mainspring of your service is love for Jesus, you can serve men although they treat you as a door-mat. PH. 80

With us, Christian service is something we do; with Jesus Christ it is not what we *do for* Him, but what we *are to* Him that He calls service. Our Lord always puts the matter of discipleship on the basis of devotion not to a belief or a creed, but to Himself. There is no argument about it, and no compulsion, simply—'If you would be My disciple, you must be devoted to Me.' PH. 144

The measure of our service for God is not our usefulness to others. We have nothing to do with the estimate of others, nor with success in service; we have to see that we fulfil our ministry. "As Thou has sent Me into the world, even so have I also sent them into the world." PR. 108

We are here with no right to ourselves, for no spiritual blessing for ourselves; we are here for one purpose only—to be made servants of God as Jesus was. PS. 17

. . . "to serve the living God." This means a life laid down for Jesus, a life of narrowed interests, a life that deliberately allows itself to be swamped by a crowd of paltry things. It is not fanaticism, it is the stedfast, flint-like attitude of heart and mind and body for one purpose—spoilt for everything saving as we can be used to win souls for Jesus. PS. 22

What are 'dead works'? Everything done apart from God. All prayer, all preaching, all testifying, all kind, sacrificial deeds done apart from God, are dead works that clog the life. PS. 22

It is possible for practical Christian work to be active disobedience to God. We would rather work for God than sit for one moment before Him and let the Spirit riddle us through with His light. RTR. 17

It is never "Do, do" with the Lord, but "Be, be" and He will "do" *through* you. RTR. 43

If you want to be of use to God, get rightly related to Jesus Christ and He will make you of use unconsciously every minute you live. RTR. 47

Looking for opportunities to serve God is an impertinence; every time and all the time is our opportunity of serving God. RTR. 52

The idea is not that we do work for God, but that we are so loyal to Him that He can do His work through us—"I reckon on you for extreme service, with no complaining on your part and no explanation on Mine." God wants to use us as He used His own Son. RTR. 92

We are not to ask God to do what He has created us to do, any more than we are to attempt to do what He alone can do. SA. 90

It is an interesting study in psychology to watch people who are engaged in drastic social and rescue work and find out whether they are doing it for a surcease from their own troubles, to get relief from a broken heart. In a great many cases the worker wants a plaster for his own life. He takes up slum work, not because it is the great passion of his life, but because he must get something to deliver him from the gnawing pain of his own heart. The people he works amongst are often right when they say he is doing it to save his own soul. SHH. 47

Thousands of people are 'losing their life' for the sake of a cause; this is perilously wrong because it is so nearly right. Anything that rouses us to act on the line of principles instead of a relationship to a person fosters our natural independence and becomes a barrier to yielding to Jesus Christ. Have we recognized that our body is a temple of the Holy Ghost, or are we jabbering busybodies, so taken up with Christian work that we have no time for the Christ whose work it is, no time for Him in the morning, no time for Him at night, because we are so keen on doing the things that are called by His Name? SHL. 78

God never uses in His service those who are sentimentally devoted to Him; He uses only those who are holy within in heart and holy without in practice. SHL. 120

We imagine that God is going to make us walk in the light; God will not; it is we who must walk in the light. God gives us the power to do it, but we have to see that we use the power. God puts the power and the life into us and fills us with His Spirit, but we have to work it out. "Work out your own salvation," says Paul, not, 'work for your salvation,' but *'work it out';* and as we do, we realise that the noble life of a disciple is gloriously difficult and the difficulty of it rouses us up to overcome, not faint and cave in. It is always necessary to make an effort to be noble. SSM. 95

A servant is one who has given up his right to himself to the God Whom he proclaims, a witness to Jesus, i.e., a satisfaction to Jesus Christ wherever he goes. SSM. 104

My contact with the nature of God has made me realize what I can do for God. Service is the outcome of what is fitted to my nature; God's call is fitted to His nature, and I never hear His call until I have received His nature. When I have received his nature, then His nature and mine work together; the Son of God reveals Himself in me, and I, the natural man, serve the Son of God in ordinary ways, out of sheer downright devotion to Him. SSY. 12

God does not have to come and tell me what I must do for Him, He brings me into a relationship with Himself wherein I hear His call and understand what He wants me to do, and I do it out of sheer love to Him. To serve God is the deliberate love gift of a nature that has heard the call of God. SSY. 12

Be ready for the sudden surprise visits of Our Lord, and remember there is no such thing as prominent service and obscure service; it is all the same with God, and God knows better than ourselves what we are ready to do. SSY. 39

Our Lord pays not the remotest attention to natural abilities or natural virtues; He heeds only one thing—Does that man discern Who I am? does he know the meaning of My Cross? The men and women Jesus Christ is going to use in His enterprises are those in whom He has done everything. SSY. 49

Whether our work is a success or a failure has nothing to do with us. Our call is not to successful service, but to faithfulness. SSY. 123

Any work for God that has less than a passion for Jesus Christ as its motive will end in crushing heartbreak and discouragement.
SSY. 161

God grant that His choice may fall on every one of us, and that we may learn with patience and discipline how He is going to teach us to be patient, to be powerful and to be passionate in His service! Never losing heart, never being discouraged, never being excited over a big catch. Many a worker has rendered himself useless to God by his undue hilarity over a big revival for God. "Notwithstanding in this rejoice not, that the spirits are subject to you," said Jesus; "but rather rejoice, because your names are written in heaven."
WG. 85

Week 44

SIN

If we confess our sins, He is faithful and just to forgive us our sins and to cleanse us from all unrighteousness.

—1 John 1:9

God made His own Son to be sin that He might make the sinner a saint. The Bible reveals all through that Jesus Christ bore the sin of the world by *identification,* not by sympathy. He deliberately took upon Himself and bore in His own Person the whole massed sin of the human race, and by so doing He rehabilitated the human race, that is, put it back to where God designed it to be, and anyone can enter into union with God on the ground of what Our Lord did on the Cross. AUG. 71

Sin is not measured by a creed or a constitution or a society, but by a Person. AUG. 106

. . . every bit of moral wrong is counted by God. BE. 8

Sin is the outcome of a relationship set up between man and the devil whereby man becomes 'boss' over himself, his own god. BE. 52

God never lays the sin of the human race on anyone saving Himself; the revelation is not that God punished Jesus Christ for our sins, but that *"Him who knew no sin, He made to be sin on our behalf . . ."* BE. 62

Sin has to be cleansed, *sins* must be forgiven; the Redemption of Jesus Christ deals with *sin*. BE. 63

. . . in the Cross God "condemned *sin* in the flesh," not sins. Sins I look after; sin God looks after. The Redemption deals with sin. BE. 68

. . . if you are not delivered from any particular element of sin, the reason is either you don't believe God can deliver you or you don't want Him to. Immediately you want Him to deliver you, the power of God is yours and it is done, not presently, but now, and the manifestation is wonderful. Let a man give up the right to himself to Jesus Christ, and the efficacy of His Redemption works out instanter. BE. 69

Conviction of sin and being guilty of sins are not the same thing. Conviction of sin is produced by the incoming of the Holy Spirit because conscience is promptly made to look at God's demands and the whole nature cries out, in some form or other, "What must I do to be saved?" BE. 76

Knowledge of what sin is is in inverse ratio to its presence; only as sin goes do you realize what it is; when it is present you do not realize what it is because the nature of sin is that it destroys the capacity to know you sin. BE. 78

Sin is not a creation, it is a relationship set up between the devil (who is independent entirely of God) and the being God made to have communion with Himself. BE. 82

If we have light views about sin we are not students in the school of Christ. The fact of sin is the secret of Jesus Christ's Cross; its removal is the secret of His risen and ascended life. BE. 114

Sin is not wrong doing, it is wrong *being,* deliberate and emphatic independence of God. That may sound remote and far away from us, but in individual experience it is best put in the terms of 'my claim to my right to myself.' BE. 115

The characteristic of sin is to destroy the capacity to know we sin, and the Bible talks about unregenerate men as 'dead,' not dead physically, but dead towards God. BE. 116

The Bible distinctly states that sin is not the natural result of being a finite being, but a definite stepping aside from what that finite being knew to be right. BE. 116

The disposition of sin that rules our human nature is not suppressed by the Atonement, not sat on, not cabined and confined, it is removed. BE. 117

Sin is not man's problem, but God's. God has taken the problem of sin into His own hands and solved it, and the proof that He has is the Cross of Calvary. The Cross is the Cross of God. BFB. 102

There is no such thing as God overlooking sin. That is where people make a great mistake with regard to love; they say, 'God is love and of course He will forgive sin': God is holy love and He *cannot* forgive sin. Jesus Christ did not come to forgive sin; He came to save us from our sins. The salvation of Jesus Christ removes the 'sinner' out of my heart and plants in the 'saint.' That is the marvellous work of God's grace. BP. 135

The Bible says that "sin entered into the world by one man," but sin is not an act on my part at all. Sin is a disposition, and I am in no way responsible for having the disposition of sin; but I am responsible for not allowing God to deliver me from the disposition of sin when once I see that that is what Jesus Christ came to do. BP. 157

Sin is not a creation, it is a relationship. The essential nature of sin is my claim to my right to myself. BSG. 12

The New Testament says Jesus became literally identified with the sin of the human race. "Him Who knew no sin" (here language almost fails) "*He made to be sin* on our behalf" for one purpose only—"that we might become the righteousness of God in Him." BSG. 26

The essence of sin is my claim to my right to myself. BSG. 50

'No crime has ever been committed that every human being is not capable of committing.' BP. 104

What our Lord Jesus Christ wants us to present to Him is not our goodness, or our honesty, or our endeavour, but our real solid sin, that is all He can take. "For He hath made Him to be sin for us, Who knew no sin." And what does He give in exchange for our solid sin? Great solid righteousness—"that we might be made the righteousness of God in Him"; but we must relinquish all pretence of being anything, we must relinquish in every way all claim to being worthy of God's consideration. That is the meaning of conviction of sin. CD. VOL. 1, 129

We are delivered from sin that we might actually live as saints amongst men who treat us as we once treated our Heavenly Father. CD. VOL. 2, 28

Sin is a revelation fact, not a common sense fact. No natural man is ever bothered about sin; it is the saint, not the sinner, who knows what sin is. If you confound *sin* with *sins,* you belittle the Redemption, make it "much ado about nothing." It is nonsense to talk about the need of Redemption to enable a man to stop committing sins—his own will power enables him to do that, a decent education will prevent him from breaking out into sinful acts, but to deny that there is *an heredity of sin* running straight through the human race, aims a blasphemous blow at the Redemption. The only word that expresses the enormity of sin is "Calvary." CHI. 16

Sin is mutiny against God's rule; not vileness of conduct, but red-handed anarchy. CHI. 17

The essence of sin is my claim to my right to myself, it goes deeper down than all the sins that ever were committed. Sin can't be forgiven because it is not an act; you can only be forgiven for the sins you commit, not for an heredity. CHI. 18

The Cross of Christ spells hope for the most despairing sinner on the face of the earth. ". . . the Son of man hath power on earth to forgive sins." CHI. 97

God can never save human pride. Jesus Christ has no mercy whatever when it comes to conviction of sin. He has an amazing concern for the sinner, but not pity for sin. CHI. 98

To say that what God condemned in the Cross was social sins is not true; what God condemns in the Cross is *sin,* which is away further down than any moral quirks. CHI. 108

The sin that shocks God is the thing which is highly esteemed among men—self-realization, pride, my right to myself. CHI. 123

Am I becoming more and more in love with God as a holy God, or with the conception of an amiable Being who says, 'Oh well, sin doesn't matter much'? DI. 14

The guilt abroad to-day can never be dealt with by pressing a social ethic or a moral order, or by an enfolding sympathy for man, while pooh-poohing the demands of a holy God. DI. 27

Our Lord did not scathe sin; He came to save from it. DI. 63

It is not our business to convict men of sin, the Holy Ghost alone convicts of sin, our duty is to lift up the One who sets free from sin. It is not a question of something being curbed, or counteracted, or sat on, it is a radical alteration on the inside, then I have to assimilate that alteration so that it is manifested in the practical relationships of my life. DI. 64

The attitude of Jesus towards *sin* is to be our attitude towards *sins*. DI. 64

The life of the Holy Spirit in a saint is fierce and violent against any tendency to sin. DI. 64

Many a man gets to the place where he will call himself a sinner, but he does not so readily come to the place where he says, *"Against Thee, Thee only, have I sinned . . ."* DI. 65

Sin is reality; sins are actuality. DI. 65

On the threshold of the Christian life people talk a lot about sin, but there is no realization of what sin is, all that is seen is the effects of sin. DI. 65

Measure your growth in grace by your sensitiveness to sin. DI. 65

It was not social crimes, but the great primal sin of independence of God, that brought the Son of God to Calvary. DI. 66

When you come in contact with the great destructive sins in men's lives, be reverent with what you don't understand. God says, 'Leave that one to Me.' DI. 90

If you have never realized the impossibility of God dealing with sin on any other ground than that of the Redemption, you are living in a fool's paradise rationally. GW. 83

We would fly from sin in terror if we knew its nature, but it presents itself as a most desirable thing. GW. 83

It is of the mercy of God that no man is convicted of *sin* before he is born again; we are convicted of *sins* in order to be born again, then the indwelling Holy Spirit convicts us of sin. If God gave us conviction of sin apart from a knowledge of His Redemption, we would be driven insane. When conviction of what sin is in the sight of God comes home to me, language cannot support the strain of the verbal expression of its enormity; the only word that expresses it is 'Calvary.' If I see sin apart from the Cross, suicide seems the only fool's way out. GW. 84

Sin in me is a disposition of self-sufficiency which connects me with the body of sin; the connection is not in my human nature, but in my claim to my right to myself, which is the essence of sin—I'll do what I like. GW. 84

Beware of attempting to deal with sin apart from a complete reliance on the Redemption, and when you see men sinning, remember, your heart should be filled with compassion, because if you have ever had the slightest dose of conviction of sin yourself, you will know what awaits them when the recognition of sin comes home. GW. 85

The final issue in every life is—God must kill sin in me, or sin will kill God out of me. GW. 85

It is blasphemy to make little of sin. GW. 85

. . . it is perilously easy to have amazing sympathy with God's truth and remain in sin. GW. 91

Sins are wrong acts; sin is an independence that will not bow its neck to God, that defies God and all He presents, that will not go to the excellency of a broken heart. HG. 79

When Jesus Christ came near men, He convicted them of sin, but He convicted them also of this, that they could be like He was if they would only come to Him. HG. 80

We shall find over and over again that God will send us shuddering to our knees every time we realize what sin is, and instead of it increasing hardness in us towards the men and women who are living in sin, the Spirit of God will use it as a means of bringing us to the dust before Him in vicarious intercession that God will save them as He has saved us. HG. 89

The sense of sin is in inverse ratio to its presence, that is, the higher up and the deeper down we are saved, the more pangingly terrible is our conviction of sin. The holiest person is not the one who is not conscious of sin, but the one who is most conscious of what sin is. HG. 89

The one who talked most about sin was our Lord Jesus Christ. We are apt to run off with the idea that a man in order to be saved from sin must have lived a vile life himself; but the One who has an understanding of the awful horror of sin is the spotlessly holy Christ, Who "knew no sin." The lower down we get into the experience of sin, the less conviction of sin we have. When we are regenerated and lifted into the light, we begin to know what sin means. HG. 89

The cry on the cross, "My God, My God, why hast Thou forsaken Me?" is not the desolation of an isolated individual: it is the revelation of the heart of God face to face with the sin of man, and going deeper down than man's sin can ever go in unconceivable heartbreak in order that every sin-stained, hell-deserving sinner might be absolutely redeemed. HG. 98

Sin is not measured by a standard of moral rectitude and uprightness, but by my relationship to Jesus Christ. The point is, am I morally convinced that the only sin there is in the sight of the Holy Ghost, is disbelief in Jesus? HG. 108

Born from above, I realize that the life of God has entered into me. God gives me 'Himself,' "The gift *of God* is eternal life" and 'eternal life' consciously in me is to know God. The life of God cannot commit sin, and if I will obey the life of God, which has come into me by regeneration, it will manifest itself in my mortal flesh. It is only when I disobey the life of God that I commit sin; then I must get back again into the light by confession. If I walk in the light as God is in the light, sin is not. HG. 117

We don't take Jesus Christ's way, our first aim is to convict people of sin; Jesus Christ's aim was to get at them where they lived. HGM. 33

As long as Jesus Christ will remain the 'meek and mild and gentle Jesus' I will listen to Him, but immediately He sets His face against my particular sin, my un-righteousness, my self-indulgence, I am going to have no more of Him; then the nemesis comes, and I realize that I am siding with the forces which are against Jesus Christ. HGM. 40

The nature of sin is that it destroys the possibility of knowing that you sin. Sin ceases when I am in the light as God is in the light, and in no other way. HGM. 132

Sin enough and you will soon be unconscious of sin. HGM. 132

This is the principle of sin. Anything in spiritual life or in sensual life that makes us draw our life from anything less than God is of the essence of sin. IWP. 20

Talk about conviction of sin! I wonder how many of us have ever had one five minutes' conviction of sin. It is the rarest thing to know of a man or woman who has been convicted of sin. IWP. 25

Cleansing from all sin does not mean conscious deliverance from sin only, it means infinitely more than we are conscious of. The part we are conscious of is walking in the light; cleansing from all sin means something infinitely profounder, it means cleansing from all sin in the sight of God. God never bases any of His work on our consciousness. MFL. 44

Any deflection in obedience to God is a sin. MFL. 46

Sin is the disposition of my right to myself, and it is also independence of God. These two aspects of sin are strikingly brought out in the Bible. Sin has to be dealt with from the ethical and intellectual aspect as well as from the spiritual aspect. MFL. 122

The way sin works in connection with the life of the soul is in independence of God. MFL. 122

Many people are never guilty of gross sins, they are not brought up in that way, they are too refined, have too much good taste; but that does not mean that the disposition to sin is not there. The essence of sin is my claim to my right to myself. I may prefer to live morally because it is better for me: I am responsible to no one, my conscience is my god. That is the very essence of sin. MFL. 22

The true characteristic of sin is seen when we compare ourselves with Jesus Christ. We may feel quite happy and contented as long as we compare ourselves with other people, because we are all pretty much the same; but when we stand before Jesus Christ we realise what He meant when He said, "If I had not come . . . they had not had sin: . . . but now they have no cloke for their sin." MFL. 122

To be born of God means that I have the supernatural power of God to stop sinning. In the Bible it is never—Should a Christian sin? The Bible puts it emphatically—*A Christian must not sin.* The effective working of the new birth life in us is that we do not commit sin, not merely that we have the power not to sin, but that we have stopped sinning. MUH. 228

No man knows what sin is until he is born again. MUH. 361

Transgression is nearly always an unconscious act, there is no conscious determination to do wrong; sin is never an unconscious act. We blunder when we refuse to discern between these two. NKW. 28

Because a man who has lived in sin stops sinning, it is no sign that he is born from above. NKW. 59

The moral demand is for the punishment of sin. NKW. 78

Divorce stands for apostasy. We must be *divorced* from sin, not separated from sin. NKW. 104

Sin belongs to hell and the devil; I, as a child of God, belong to heaven and God, and I must have nothing to do with sin in any shape or form. NKW. 105

Remember, we cannot touch sin. NKW. 149

Sin dwells in human nature, but it has no right there, it does not belong to human nature as God created it. OBH. 111

Sin is nothing but a big bully. Sin was killed at the Cross of Christ; it has no power at all over those who are set free by the Atonement of Jesus and are prosecuting their life in Him. OBH. 113

Our Lord never taught us to deny sin: sin must be destroyed, not denied. Nothing sinful can ever be good. OBH. 115

Sin does not belong to human nature as God designed it, it is abnormal, therefore to speak of sin being 'eradicated,' rooted up, is nonsense, it never was planted in. OPG. 4

The diabolical nature of sin is that it hates God, because when I am face to face with the holiness of God I know there is no escape, consequently there is nothing the natural heart of man hates like a holy God. OPG. 8

If God overlooked one sin in me, He would cease to be God. OPG. 16

If God were to say of any sin, 'Oh well, he didn't mean it, I will let it go,' that would be a change in God's purpose. OPG. 16

If you indulge in practices which the Holy Spirit condemns, or in imaginations you have no business to indulge in, the appalling lash of ruined sanctity is that 'my sins finds *me* out.' 'If I could only fling the whole thing overboard!'—but you cannot. God has made the way of transgressors hell on earth. The first mark of degeneration is to deem a wrong state permissible, and then propose it as a condition of sanctity. OPG. 48

To experience conviction of sin is not a cause for misgiving, but an occasion for understanding the impossible thing God has done in the Redemption. OPG. 51

The Bible always speaks of sin as it appears in its final analysis. Jesus does not say, 'You must not covet because it will lead to stealing'; He says, 'You must not covet because it *is* stealing.' He does not say, 'You must not be angry with you brother because it will lead to murder' He says, 'You must not be angry with your brother it is murder.' 'Whosoever hateth his brother is a murderer.' When the climax of these things is reached we begin to see the meaning of Calvary. OPG. 70

We are easily roused over things that hurt us; we are scandalised at immorality because it upsets us. There is something infinitely more vital than the horror roused by social crimes, and that is the horror of God's Son at sin. PH. 36

External sins are to a large extent the accident of upbringing, but when the Spirit of God comes in and probes to the depths and reveals the disposition of sin, we begin to understand what salvation is. God cannot take anything from the sinner but his solid sin, otherwise salvation would have no meaning for him. PH. 54

This is the greatest revelation that ever struck the human life, viz., that God loves the sinner. God so loved the world when it was sinful that He sent His Son to die for it. Our Lord has no illusions about any of us. He sees every man and woman as the descendants of Adam who sinned, and with capacities in our hearts of which we have no idea. PH. 54

By conviction of sin a man is probed wide awake and made to realise that he needs to be regenerated; when he gets there, Jesus says—'Blessed are you.' PH. 61

If once the moral equilibrium has been upset by conviction of sin, holiness is the only result or no peace for ever. PH. 61

We say that sin is the enemy of God—sin is *our* enemy. PH. 101

The climax of sin is that it crucified Jesus Christ. PH. 188

When we begin our life we do not reconcile ourselves to the fact of sin; we take a rational view of life and say that a man by looking after his own instincts, educating himself, controlling the ape and the tiger in him, can produce that life which will slowly evolve into the life of God. But as we go on we find there is something that we have not taken into consideration, viz., sin, and it upsets all our calculations. Sin has made the basis of things not rational, but wild. PH. 188

If sin rules in me, the life of God will be killed in me; if God rules in me, sin will be killed in me. There is no possible ultimate but that. PH. 189

In our mental outlook we have to reconcile ourselves to the fact that sin is the only explanation as to why Jesus Christ came, the only explanation of the grief and the sorrow that there is in life. There may be a great deal that is pathetic in a man's condition, but there is also a lot that is bad and wrong. There is the downright spiteful thing, as wrong as wrong can be, without a strand of good in it, in you and in me and in other people by nature, and we have to reconcile ourselves to the fact that there *is* sin. That does not mean that we compromise with sin, it means that we face the fact that it is there. PH. 189

Always beware of a friendship, or of a religion, or of a personal estimate of things that does not reconcile itself to the fact of sin; that is the way all the disasters in human friendships and in human loves begin, and where the compromises start. PH. 193

Sin is not a creation; sin is the outcome of a relationship which God never ordained, a relationship set up between the man God created and the being God created who became the devil. PR. 11

God did not create sin, but He holds Himself responsible for the possibility of sin, and the proof that He does so is in the cross of our Lord Jesus Christ. PR. 11

We preach to men as if they were conscious of being dying sinners; they are not, they are having a good time, and our talk about being born again is from a domain of which they know nothing. The natural man does not want to be born again. PR. 12

By regeneration God puts in us the power not to sin. PR. 35

When we are born into the new realm the life of God is born in us, and the life of God in us cannot sin. That does not mean that we *cannot* sin; it means that if we obey the life of God in us, we *need not* sin. PR. 35

There is a difference between sin and sins; sin is a disposition, and is never spoken of as being forgiven, a disposition must be cleansed.

Sins are acts for which we are responsible. Sin is a thing we are born with, and we cannot touch it; God touches sin in redemption. PR. 35

By His bearing away the sin of the world, the way is opened up for every human being to get to God as if there had been no sin. PR. 48

The revelation in the Bible is not that Jesus Christ was punished for our *sins;* but that He took on Him the *sin* of the human race and put it away—an infinitely profounder revelation. PR. 49

Only when we are driven to extremes do we realize that the Bible is the only Book that gives us any indication of the true nature of sin, and where it came from. PS. 10

Sin is that factor in human nature which has a supernatural originator who stands next to God in power. PS. 11

To sin alone is never possible. PS. 12

Watch how our Lord faced men, He always faced this disposition of sin, He never summed men up by their external conduct. He was not driven into panics by immorality and fleshly sordidness, that sort of sin never seemed to bother Him half as much as the respectable pride of men and women who never were guilty of those things. PS. 14

It is only the right view of sin and right thinking about sin that ever will explain Jesus Christ's Life and Death and Resurrection. It is sin that He came to cope with; He did not come to cope with the poor little mistakes of men, they cope with their own mistakes; He came to give them a totally new stock of heredity, that is, He came to implant into them His own nature, so that Satan's power in the soul is absolutely destroyed, not counteracted. PS. 16

. . . salvation is as radical as sin, and if God has not radically altered your heredity, thank God you may know He can by the power of Jesus Christ's Atonement. PS. 16

To say that 'God loves the sinner, but hates his sin' sounds all right, but it is a dangerous statement, because it means that God is far too loving ever to punish the sinner. PS. 25

If I refuse to let God destroy my sin, there is only one possible result—I must be destroyed with my sin. PS. 25

The light of the Lord's presence convicts of sin. PS. 25

Jesus Christ came to save us so that there should be no 'sinner' left in us. PS. 25

Sin is never imputed unless it is conscious. PS. 25

Sin has got to be satisfied, or else strangled to death by a supernatural power. PS. 41

To walk in the light, as God is in the light, is the one condition of being kept cleansed from all sin. PS. 43

The possibility of sin and the inclination to sin are different things. Every man has the possibility of committing murder, but the inclination is not there. The inclination is as the deed, whether it is carried out or not. PS. 54

The sinless perfection heresy arises out of this confusion—it says that because the disposition of sin is removed, it is impossible to sin. The inclination to sin, thank God, is removed, but never the possibility. PS. 55

The disposition of sin is fundamental anarchy against God's rule over me, and as long as that disposition remains; temptation finds an inclination to sin in me; but when Our Lord delivers me from the disposition of sin, the hour of temptation discovers no inclination to sin, it tests the door of possibility only. PS. 55

Sin is a disposition of self-love that obeys every temptation to its own lordship. Sin is literally self-centred rule, a disposition that rules the life apart from God. PS. 56

The sense of sin is in proportion to the sense of holiness. PS. 64

If you want to know what sin is, don't ask the convicted sinner, ask the saint, the one who has been awakened to the holiness of God through the Atonement; he is the one who can begin to tell you what sin is. PS. 65

Sin in its beginning is simply being without God. PS. 71

God did not create sin; but He took the responsibility for it; and that He did so is proved in the Cross of Jesus Christ. SA. 46

Sin, according to the Bible, is something that has no right in human nature at all, it is abnormal and wrong. SA. 59

Conviction of sin makes a man's beauty "to consume away like a moth." SA. 95

There is no such thing as sin outside the Bible; sin is a revelation fact, and it is the one fact that accounts for the curious twist we find in things. We must take into account that there is a bias in human nature, viz., self-interest, self-realization; it may be refined or low, but it is there. SA. 105

Sin is a thing we are born with, and we cannot touch sin; God touches sin in Redemption. SA. 105

Sin is not an act, but an hereditary disposition. Sin must be cleansed, and the revelation of Redemption is that God through Jesus Christ has power to cleanse us from the heredity of sin. The curious thing is that we are blind to the *fact* of sin, and deal only with the effects of sin. SA. 116

Other religions deal with sins; the Bible alone deals with sin. SA. 116

The revelation is not that Jesus Christ took on Him our fleshly sins—a man stands or falls by his own silly weaknesses—but that He took on Him *the heredity of sin*. SA. 120

The revelation is not that Jesus Christ was punished for our sins, but that He was made *to be sin*. "Him who knew no sin" was made to be sin, that by His identification with it and removal of it, we might become what He was. SA. 120

God Himself became sin, and removed sin; no man can touch that. SA. 120

Sin is not a creation, sin is a relationship set up in time between the creation called man and the being who became the devil, whereby man took the rule over himself. My claim to my right to myself—that is the disposition of sin. SHH. 24

The Bible reveals that God holds a man responsible for acts of sin he commits, but not for the disposition of sin that he has inherited. God Himself has deliberately accepted the responsibility for sin, and the proof that He has done so is the Cross of Jesus Christ. SHH. 24

No good man is impeccable, that is, he never arrives at the place where it is impossible to sin. A man is able not to sin, but it never becomes impossible for him to sin. "Whosoever is born of God doth not commit sin; for his seed remaineth in him; and he cannot sin, because he is born of God." SHH. 100

The life of God is born in us, and the life of God cannot sin; that does not mean that we *cannot* sin; but that if we obey the life of God in us, we *need not* sin. SHH. 101

Nowadays we have come to the conclusion that a man must be a down-and-out sinner before he needs Jesus Christ to do anything for him; consequently we debase Jesus Christ's salvation to mean merely that He can save the vile and sensual man and lift him into a better life. We quote our Lord's statement that 'the Son of Man came to seek and to save that which was lost' and misinterpret His meaning by limiting 'the lost' to those who are lost in our eyes. SHL. 40

Cleansing from all sin by the blood of Jesus is far deeper than we can be conscious of, it is cleansing from all sin in the sight of God because the disposition of His Son is working out in every particular, not to our consciousness, but deeper than our consciousness. We are not cleansed more and more from all sin, if we walk in the light, as God is in the light, we *are* cleansed from all sin. In our consciousness it works with a keen poignant knowledge of what sin is. SHL. 50

Sin is not measured by a creed or social order: sin is measured by a Person, Jesus Christ. SHL. 59

The characteristic of sin is independence of God—'I can look after myself; I know exactly how far to go.' SHL. 64

Jesus Christ never tolerated sin for one moment, and when His nature is having its way in us the same intolerance is shown. SHL. 65

Deliverance from sin is not deliverance from conscious sin only, it is deliverance from sin in God's sight, and He can see down into a region I know nothing about. SSM. 28

Jesus Christ went through identification with sin, and put away sin on the Cross, so that every man on earth might be freed from sin by the right of His Atonement. God made His own Son to be sin that He might make the sinner a saint—*'that we might become the righteousness of God in him.'* SSY. 144

Week 45

SUFFERING

To you it has been granted on behalf of Christ, not only to believe in Him, but also to suffer for His sake.
—Philippians 1:29

When we talk about suffering we are apt to think only of bodily pain, or of suffering because we have given up something for God, which is paltry nonsense. AUG. 28

Why there should be suffering we do not know; but we have to remain loyal to the character of God as revealed by Jesus Christ in the face of it. BE. 93

There is suffering before which you cannot say a word; you cannot preach 'the gospel of temperament'; all you can do is to remain dumb and leave room for God to come in as He likes. BFB. 24

We miss the mark when we think on the aesthetic line and take Our Lord as a specimen of a highly strung, superbly fine nature, suffering from contact with coarse natures; we are talking nonsense if we put His suffering there. He never paid the remotest attention to that kind of suffering, nor is there any allusion made to it in the New Testament. His suffering is not the suffering of a man of refined sensibilities among brutes, of a holy character among unholy characters; His suffering is in a totally different domain and along a different line from anything from which we suffer, it is the suffering of a Saviour. BSG. 45

The awful problem of suffering continually crops up in the Scriptures, and in life and remains a mystery. CD. VOL. 1, 61

. . . to be able to explain suffering is the clearest indication of never having suffered. Sin, suffering, and sanctification are not problems of the mind, but facts of life—mysteries that awaken all other mysteries until the heart rests in God, and waiting patiently knows *"He doeth all things well."* CD. VOL. 1, 61

To suffer because of meekness is an exalting, refining and God-glorifying suffering. And mark this and mark it well, to suffer "as a Christian" is a shameful thing in the eyes of the societies of this world. The friends who in your hour of trial and slander, gather round to support and stand with you, are first amazed, then dazed, and then disgusted, when they find that you really do not mean to stand up for yourself, but meekly to submit. CD. VOL. 1, 68

To 'suffer as a Christian' is not to be marked peculiar as of your views, or because you will not bend to conventionality; these things are not Christian, but ordinary human traits from which all men suffer irrespective of creed or religion or no religion. To 'suffer as a Christian' is to suffer because there is an essential difference between you and the world which rouses the contempt of the world, and the disgust and hatred of the spirit that is in the world. To 'suffer as a Christian' is to have no answer when the world's satire is turned on you, as it was turned on Jesus Christ when He hung upon the cross, when they turned His words into jest and jeer; they will do the same to you. He gave no answer, neither can you. CD. VOL. 1, 69

This spring of suffering, suffering 'according to the will of God,' is a great deep. Job did not know the preface to his own story, neither does any man. Job was never told that God and the devil had made a battleground of his soul. Job's suffering was not for his own sake, not for his perfecting or purifying, that was incidental; Job suffered *"according to the will of God."* CD. VOL. 1, 73

Suffering is the heritage of the bad, of the penitent, and of the Son of God. Each one ends in the cross. The bad thief is crucified, the pentient thief is crucified, and the Son of God is crucified. By these signs we know the widespread heritage of suffering. CD. VOL. 1, 77

Suffering is grand when the heart is right with God. But for the night *"the moon and the stars, which Thou hast ordained,"* would never be seen. And so God giveth to His own *"the treasures of darkness."* CD. VOL. 1, 85

Oh, the sublimity of the sufferings of the sanctified! Suffering according to the will of God, not so much for personal perfecting as to enable God to express His ideas in the life. CD. VOL. 1, 89

To suffer from the hatred of men, to be separated from their company, to be reproached of men, to be considered as having an evil name, is not necessarily to have fellowship with His sufferings. We only have fellowship with Him if we suffer *"for the Son of man's sake."* To suffer martyrdom, to lose your life, to leave father and mother, houses and lands, is not to have fellowship with His sufferings unless it is done because of Him and for His sake. CD. VOL. 1, 92

After all that can be said, is said, the sufferings of the saint arise, not from inbred sin, but from obedience to the will of God, which can rarely be stated explicitly. CD. VOL. 2, 105

. . . the saint knows not why he suffers as he does, yet he comprehends with a knowledge that passeth knowledge that all is well. CD. VOL. 2, 105

The Bible makes little of physical suffering. The modern mind looks on suffering and pain as an unmitigated curse; the Bible puts something akin to purifying in connection with suffering, e.g., "for he that hath suffered in the flesh hath ceased from sin." CHI. 111

There is suffering that is preventable, but there is an inevitable suffering that is essentially God's will for us. GW. 129

The picture of God in the Bible is of One who suffers, and when the mask is torn off life and we all see its profound and vast misery, the suffering, sorrowing God is the only One who does not mock us. 'He was despised, and rejected of men; a man of sorrows, and acquainted with grief.' GW. 129

We do not know the preface to our own story any more than Job did; we suffer, and God alone knows why. It is beside the mark to say that it is because we deserve to suffer; Job did not deserve to suffer for he was a man 'perfect and upright. . . .' There was more in Job's suffering than was required to develop his character, and so it is with the sanctified soul. GW. 129

Suffering was inevitable to our Lord before God could make his Saviourhood a fact; He 'learned obedience by the things which He suffered.' Jesus Christ is not our Example, He is the Captain of our salvation.' His position is unique. We do not suffer in order that we may become saviours; we suffer in order to enable God to fulfil His Idea of saintship in us. GW. 130

If you are suffering, it is intensely difficult to look up. HG. 18

It is strange that God should make it that "through the shadow of an agony cometh Redemption"; strange that God's Son should be made perfect through suffering; strange that suffering should be one of the golden pathways for God's children. HG. 25

We are called to fellowship with His sufferings, and some of the greatest suffering lies in remaining powerless where He remained powerless. LG. 56

To choose to suffer means that there is something wrong; to choose God's will even if it means suffering is a very different thing. No healthy saint ever chooses suffering; he chooses God's will, as Jesus did, whether it means suffering or not. MUH. 223

A man may be perfected through suffering or be made worse through suffering, it depends on his disposition. PH. 53

We all know people who have been made much meaner and more irritable and more intolerable to live with by suffering: it is not right to say that all suffering perfects. It only perfects one type of person—the one who accepts the call of God in Christ Jesus. PH. 153

Beware of the line of thinking which has sympathy with your sufferings but has no sympathy with Jesus Christ. "Arm yourself with the mind of Christ," and the very suffering you go through will benefit others. PH. 214

The sufferings of Jesus Christ were not an accident, they are what He came for; He knew that His life was to be a ransom for many. The men who do not suffer in this world are not worth their salt. PR. 112

The finest men and women suffer, and the devil uses their sufferings to slander God. God is after one thing—bringing many sons to glory, and He does not care what it costs us, any more than He cared what it cost Him. PR. 113

God has taken the responsibility for the possibility of sin, and the proof that He did so is the Cross. He is the suffering God, not One Who reigns above in calm disdain. PR. 113

The sufferings of Job were not in order to perfect him. The explanation of Job's sufferings was that God and Satan had made a battleground of his soul, and the honour of God was at stake. SHH. 2

Very few of us know anything about suffering for Christ's sake. A man who knows nothing about Christ will suffer for conscience or conviction's sake. To suffer for Christ's sake is to suffer because of being personally related to Him. SHH. 83

Suffering, and the inevitable result of suffering, is the only way some of us can learn, and if we are shielded God will ultimately take the one who interferes by the scruff of the neck and remove him. The fingers that caress a child may also hurt its flesh; it is the power of love that makes them hurt. SHH. 96

You rarely hear a man who has been through the real agony of suffering who says he disbelieves in God; it is the one who watches others going through suffering who says he disbelieves in God. SHH. 97

When God is putting His saints through the experience of the millstones, we are apt to want to interfere. Hands off! No saint dare interfere in the discipline of the suffering of another saint. God brings these things into our lives for the production of the bread that is to feed the world. SHL. 118

To choose suffering is a disease; but to choose God's will even though it means suffering is to suffer as Jesus did—*'according to the will of God.'* SHL. 121

Week 46

TEMPTATION

Blessed is the man who endures temptation; for when he has been approved, he will receive the crown of life which the Lord has promised to those who love Him.

—James 1:12

Jesus Christ was tempted, and so shall we be tempted when we are rightly related to God. BP. 191

Temptation is no temptation at all if it is clearly to evil. BSG. 30

The temptation which beset Our Lord with such fascination and power is the very temptation which is besetting the modern Christian—'Heal bodies, cast out devils, feed the poor, and men will crown You King.' The temptation is more powerful to-day than ever it has been in the history of the Church, to put mens' needs first, not God; to spell God in the term 'humanity'; to make God an *etcetera* for blessing humanity. BSG. 31

We have to get rid of the idea that because Jesus was God He could not be tempted. Almighty God cannot be tempted, but in Jesus Christ we deal with God as man, a unique Being—God-Man. CHI. 56

God Almighty was never "tempted in all points like as we are," Jesus Christ was. God Almighty knows all that Jesus Christ knows; but, if I may say it reverently, *God in Christ* knows more, because *God in*

Christ "suffered being tempted," and therefore He is "able to succour them that are tempted." CHI. 99

When temptation comes, stand absolutely true to God no matter what it costs you, and you will find the onslaught leaves you with affinities higher and purer than ever before. CHI. 57

Our deadliest temptations are not so much those that destroy Christian belief as those that corrupt and destroy the Christian temper. DI. 5

Every temptation of Satan is the acme of human wisdom, but immediately the Spirit of God is at work in a man the hollow mockery at its heart is recognized. DI. 75

To be raised above temptation belongs to God only. DI. 75

Satan does not tempt to gross sins, the one thing he tempts to is putting myself as master instead of God. DI. 76

How are we to face the tempter? By prayer? No. With the Word of God? No. Face the tempter with Jesus Christ, and He will apply the word of God to you, and the temptation will cease. DI. 76

We are apt to imagine that our Lord was only tempted once and that then His temptations were over. His temptations went on from the first moment of His conscious life to the last, because His holiness was not the holiness of Almighty God, but the holiness of man, which can only progress by means of the things that go against it. LG. 152

Temptations in the life of faith are not accidents, each temptation is part of a plan, a step in the progress of faith. NKW. 117

Jesus Christ's temptations and ours move in different spheres until we become His brethren by being born from above. PH. 35

Temptation is a short cut to what is good, not to what is bad. PH. 35

The agony Jesus went through in the Temptation was surely because He had the vision of the long way and saw the suffering it would entail on men through all the ages if He took His Father's way.

He knew it in a way we cannot conceive. His sensitiveness is beyond anything we can imagine. PH. 99

Temptation is not sin; we are bound to meet it if we are men. Not to be tempted would be to be beneath contempt. PR. 60

Jesus Christ was not born with a heredity of sin; He was not tempted in all points as ordinary men are, but tempted like his brethren, those who have been born from above by the Spirit of God and placed in the Kingdom of God by supernatural regeneration. PR. 61

The temptations of Jesus are not those of Man as man, but the temptations of God as Man. The statement that our Lord was tempted as ordinary men are is readily accepted, but the Bible does not say He was so tempted. PR. 61

The devil does not tempt us to do wrong things; he tries to make us lose what God has put into us by regeneration, the possibility of being of value to God. When we are born from above the central citadel of the devil's attack is the same in us as it was in our Lord—viz., to do God's will in our own way. PR. 63

Temptation yielded to is lust deified. PR. 69

The practical test for us when we have been through a season of temptation is whether we have a finer and deeper affinity for the highest. PR. 70

Temptation must come, and we do not know what it is until we meet it. When we do meet it, we must not debate with God, but stand absolutely true to Him no matter what it costs us personally, and we will find that the onslaught will leave us with higher and purer affinities than before. PR. 70

God does not keep us from temptation, He succours us in the midst of it. PR. 71

Temptation is not something we may escape; it is essential to the full-orbed life of a son of God. PR. 71

We have to beware lest we think we are tempted as no one else is tempted. What we go through is the common inheritance of the race, not something no one ever went through before. It is most humiliating to be taken off our pedestal of suffering and made to realise that thousands of others are going through the same thing as we are going through. PR. 71

The tendencies that make temptation possible are inherent in man as God created him, Adam and Our Lord Jesus Christ being witnesses; and we have to bear in mind that regeneration does not remove those tendencies but rather increases them. The possibility of temptation reaches its height in Jesus Christ. PS. 47

Temptation is not sin; temptation must always be possible for our sonship to be of worth to God. It would be no credit for God to bring mechanical slaves to glory—"for it became Him . . . in bringing many *sons* unto glory"—not slaves, not useless channels, but vigorous, alert, wide-awake men and women, with all their powers and faculties devoted absolutely to God. PS. 50

Temptation trains innocence into character or else into corruption. There are some temptations, however, by which we have no business to be tempted any longer; we should be on a higher plane dealing with other temptations. We may have our morality well within our own grasp and be comparatively free from temptation, but as soon as we are regenerated by the Spirit of God we begin to understand the force of spiritual temptations of which we were unconscious before. PS. 54

Temptation yielded to is the birth of sin in the personal life and ends in death. PS. 56

The records of the temptation of Jesus are the records of how God as man is tempted, not of how man is tempted as man. PS. 57

The temptation of Jesus are not those of a man as man, but the temptation of GOD as man. Jesus Christ was not born with an heredity of sin. "Wherefore, it behoved Him in all things to be made like unto His brethren." His "brethren" are those in whom He is born. PS. 57

The devil does not need to bother about the majority of us; we have enough lust on the inside to keep us in sin, but when once a man is born from above, the temptations alter instantly, and he realizes where the temptation is aimed, viz. at the disposition. PS. 58

There is a limit to temptation. "God is faithful who will not suffer you to be tempted above that ye are able." God does not save us from temptations, but He succours us in the middle of them. PS. 59

The devil does not tempt to wrong things, he tries to make us lose what God has put into us by regeneration, viz. the possibility of being of value to God. PS. 59

Impeccable—liable not to sin. The idea that because Jesus Christ was without sin therefore He could not be tempted, has become woven into religious belief. If that were so, the record of His temptation is a mere farce. Could Jesus Christ be tempted? Undoubtedly He could, because temptation and sin are not the same thing. SSH. 100

TESTIMONY

We also believe and therefore speak.

—2 Corinthians 4:13

You cannot draw on the grace of God for testimony if these three things are not there—the word of God, the power of God, and the consciousness that you are walking in the integrity of that testimony in private, if they are there, then there is an unfaltering certainty. AUG. 127

The first motive of testimony is not for the sake of other people but for our own sake; we realize that we have no one but God to stand by us. Always give your testimony in the presence of God, and ever remember God's honour is at stake. AUG. 127

It is easier to stand true to a testimony mildewed with age, because it has a dogmatic ring about it that people agree with, than to talk from your last moment of contact with God. DI. 77

It is never our testimony that keeps our experience right: our experience makes us testify. DI. 77

To say a thing is the sure way to begin to believe it. That is why it is so necessary to testify to what Jesus Christ has done for you. DI. 77

You cannot bring a knowledge of Jesus Christ to another, you can only tell him what He is to you, but until he gets where you are he will never see what you see. DI. 78

Be prepared to be unreserved in personal testimony; but remember, personal testimony must never be lowered into personal biography. DI. 78

If my testimony makes anyone wish to emulate me, it is a mistaken testimony, it is not a witness to Jesus. DI. 78

The Holy Spirit will only witness to a testimony when Jesus Christ is exalted higher than the testimony. DI. 78

When Jesus talked to the woman of Samaria He did not use a prescribed form of address, He told her Divine truth and made her aware of her sin. When He talked to the disciples on the road to Emmaus, their hearts burned within them. The characteristic of the man of God's method is that he can speak to a sinner and win him before the sinner knows where he is; he can speak to saints and make their hearts burn. GW. 48

How few of us do speak! When we talk to a soul, we talk like a tract! GW. 48

If you have been saved from sin, say so; if you ave been sanctified by God's grace, say so. Don't substitute some other refinement in its place. By using other words you are not testifying to God, but compromising with the atmosphere of those to whom you are talking. HG. 96

The weakness of many a testimony is that it is based on what the Lord has done—'I have to testify to what God has done for me in order that other people may have the same thing done for them.' It sounds all right, but it is not the New Testament order of testimony. Jesus Christ never sent out a disciple on the ground that He had done something for him, but only because he had seen the Lord after He had done something for him. HGM. 55

People testify to conversion and to the grace of God in their lives, but plainly they do not know Him. There is no question about His having emancipated them from sin and done a mighty work in them, but the great passion of the life is not Jesus Christ. HGM. 55

As soon as we see Jesus and perceive who He is by His Spirit, He says 'Go'—'Go out into actual life and tell My brethren, not what I have done for you, but that I am risen.' HGM. 57

It is easy to preach, nothing easier, but it is another thing to confess. Confessing means to say with every bit of me that Jesus Christ has come into my flesh. HGM. 98

To say a thing is the sure way to thinking it. That is why it is so necessary to testify to what Jesus Christ has done for us. A testimony gets hold of the mind as it has hold of the heart; but the same thing is true of the opposite, if we say a wrong thing often enough we begin to think it. IWP. 30

It is impossible to go on in our life with God if the element of personal testimony is left out. NKW. 23

Whenever God reveals something which we have never seen before and which affects others, a public testimony must be made, and the peril is lest we say—'But if I stand up and give that testimony, other people will be stumbled.' Whenever we start this doubtful weighing of things we are acting not in accordance with our reliance on God, but in presumptuous confidence that God will see us through if we trust our wits: God will see us through only if we stand stedfastly true to what He has told us. NKW. 24

To say 'I have got the victory' is a selfish testimony; the testimony of the Spirit of God is that the Victor has got me. NKW. 40

In the Bible confession and testimony are put in a prominent place, and the test of a man's moral calibre is the "say so." I may try and make myself believe a hundred and one things, but they will never be mine until I "say so." PH. 209

There are some people we are always the better for meeting, they do not talk piously, but somehow they give us a feeling of emancipation, they have a larger horizon. The reason is that they have opened the door for themselves by their "say so," and now the Word of God becomes spirit and life through them to others. PH. 212

If you cannot express yourself on any subject, struggle 'till you can. You must struggle to get expression experimentally, then there will come a time when that expression will become the very wine of strengthening to someone else. Try to re-state to yourself what you implicitly feel to be God's truth, and you give God a chance to pass it on to someone else through you. RTR. 22

For one man who can introduce another to Jesus Christ by the way he lives and by the atmosphere of his life, there are a thousand who can only talk jargon about Him. Whenever you come across a man or woman who in your time of distress introduces you to Jesus Christ, you know you have struck the best friend you ever had, one who has opened up the way of life to you. SA. 41

Sometimes it is cowardly to speak, and sometimes it is cowardly to keep silence. SHH. 27

. . . we are losing sight of the real meaning of testimony; it is not for the sake of others, but for our own sake. It makes us know we have no one to rely on but God. SHL. 15

Our Lord never tells us to confess anything but Himself, "Whosoever shall confess *ME* before men . . ." SSM. 83

If a thing has its root in the heart of God, it will want to be public, to get out, it must do things in the external and the open, and Jesus not only encouraged this publicity. He insisted upon it. SSM. 102

It is God's law that men cannot hide what they really are. If they are His disciples it will be publicly portrayed. SSM. 102

The word 'confess' means that every particle of our nature says the same thing, not our mouth only, but the very make up of our flesh and blood, confesses that Jesus Christ has come in the flesh. SSY. 72

To be a witness means to live a life of unsullied, uncompromising, and unbribed devotion to Jesus. A true witness is one who lets his light shine in works that exhibit the disposition of Jesus. Our Lord makes the one who is a witness His own possession; He becomes responsible for him. SSY. 171

Week 48

THOUGHT

Casting down arguments and every high thing that exalts itself against the knowledge of God, bringing every thought into captivity to the obedience of Christ.

—2 Corinthians 10:5

The intellect works with the greatest intensity when it works continuously; the more you do, the more you can do. We must work hard to keep in trim for God. Clean off the rust and keep bright by use. AUG. 37

The doctrines of the New Testament as applied to personal life are moral doctrines, that is, they are understood by a pure heart, not by the intellect. AUG. 45

'Think proper thoughts.' *Live proper lives!* and you will think proper thoughts. AUG. 59

Continual renewal of mind is the only healthy state for a Christian. Beware of the ban of finality about your present views. BE. 40

You can never become a Christian by thinking, you can only become a Christian by receiving something from God; but you must think after you are a Christian. BE. 50

Jesus Christ lived in the moral domain and, in a sense, the intellect is of no use there. Intellect is not a guide, but an instrument. BFB. 35

If we can know God by means of our intellect, then Jesus Christ's claim to reveal God is a farce, and the Redemption nonsense. BFB. 96

In the Bible the heart, and not the brain, is revealed to be the centre of thinking. BP. 97

Mere intellectuality leads to bloodlessness and passionlessness, to stoicism and unreality. The more merely intellectual a person becomes the more hopelessly useless he is, until he degenerates into a mere criticizing faculty, passing the strangest and wildest verdicts on life, on the Bible, and on our Lord. BP. 103

It is not sufficient to experience the reality of the Spirit of God within us and His wonderful work; we have to bring our brains into line with our experience so that we can think and understand along Christian lines. It is because so few do think along Christian lines that it is easy for wrong teaching and wrong thinking to come in, especially in connection with the Spirit. BP. 209

We understand the things of the world by our natural intelligence, and we understand the things of God by "the spirit which is of God." BP. 212

When the Holy Spirit has transformed our practical life, He begins to stir up our minds, and the point is, will we bring our minds into harmony with the new way of living? Jesus Christ laid down a remarkable principle for practical living and for practical thinking, that is, He taught His disciples how to think by 'correspondences.' "I am the true Vine." Is the natural vine false? No, the natural vine is the shadow of the real. "My Father giveth you the true Bread from heaven." Is the bread we eat false? No, it is the shadow of the real bread. "I am the Door," and so on. BP. 229

"I am the Way," not only the way to be saved and sanctified and to live as a Christian, but the way to think as a Christian. BP. 231

. . . when Jesus was led away to be crucified, they "come unto a place called Golgotha, that is to say, a place of a skull," and that is where Jesus Christ is always crucified; that is where He is put to shame to-day, viz., in the heads of men who won't bring their thinking into line with the Spirit of God. BP. 232

We have not only to be good lovers of God, but good thinkers, and it is only along this line that we can "try the spirits whether they are of God." BP. 234

The Spirit of Jesus is given to us in new birth, but we have not the mind of Christ until we form it. How our minds express themselves depends entirely on the way we use our brains. BSG. 20

To bring every thought into captivity is the last thing we do, and it is not done easily; in the beginning we have to do violence to our old ways of thinking just as at sanctification we had to do violence to our old ways of living. Intellect in a saint is the last thing to become identified with Jesus Christ. BSG. 67

We are called upon not only to be right in heart, but to be right in thinking. When we have become personally related to Jesus Christ we have to do the thing that is in our power to do, viz. think aright. BSG. 69

The Christian method of thinking puts the intellect second, not first; the modern view puts intellect on the throne. God does not sum up a man's worth by his thinking, but by the way he expresses his thinking in actual life, that is, by his character. It is possible for there to be a tremendous divorce between a man's thinking and his practical life; the only thing that tells in the sight of God is a man's character. Beware of putting principles first instead of a Person. Jesus Christ puts personal relationship first—'Be rightly related to Me, then work out your thinking.' BSG. 71

It is because we have failed to realize that God requires intellectual vigour on the part of a saint that the devil gets his hold on the stagnant mental life of so many. To be transformed by the renewing of our mind means the courageous lifting of all our problems, individual, family, social and civic, into the spiritual domain, and habitually working out a life of practical holiness there. It is not an easy task, but a gloriously difficult one, requiring the mightiest effort of our human nature, a task which lifts us into thinking God's thoughts after Him. CHI. 83

A Christian accepts all he knows about God on the authority of Jesus Christ; he can find out nothing about God by his own unaided intellect. DI. 12

The mind that is not produced by obedience to the Holy Spirit in the final issue hates God. DI. 23

The discipline of our mind is the one domain God has put in our keeping. It is impossible to be of any use to God if we are lazy. God won't cure laziness, we have to cure it. DI. 67

Your mind can never be under your control unless you bring it there; there is no gift for control. You may pray till Doomsday but your brain will never concentrate if you don't make it concentrate. DI. 67

Don't insult God by telling Him He forgot to give you any brains when you were born. We all have brains, what we need is *work*. DI. 68

Irritation may be simply the result of not using your brain. Remember, the brain gets exhausted when it is not doing anything. DI. 69

Make your mind sure of what our Lord taught, and then insist and re-insist on it to the best of your ability. DI. 71

Think of the labour and patience of men in the domain of science and then think of our lack of patience in endeavouring to appreciate the Atonement, and you see the need there is for us to be conscientious in our thinking, basing everything on the reality of the Atonement. We prefer to be average Christians, we don't mind it having broken God's heart to save us, but we do object to having a sleepless night while we learn to say 'Thank you' to God so that the angels can hear us. We need to be staggered out of our shocking indolence. DI. 79

Obedience is the basis of Christian thinking. Never be surprised if there are whole areas of thinking that are not clear, they never will be until you obey. DI. 80

Intellectual obstinacy produces the sealed mind—"Jesus said unto them, If ye were blind, ye would have no sin: but now ye say, We see: your sin remaineth." DI. 81

With regard to other men's minds, take all you can get, whether those minds are in flesh-and-blood editions or in books, but remember, the best you get from another mind is not that mind's verdict, but its standpoint. Note the writers who provoke you to do your best mentally. DI. 81

Never cease to think until you think things home and they become character. DI. 81

Our thinking is often allowed to be anti-Christian while our feelings are Christian. The way I think will colour my attitude toward my fellow-men. DI. 81

Keep the powers of your mind going full pace, always maintaining the secret life right with God. DI. 82

If you have ever done any thinking you don't feel very complacent after it, you get your first touch of pessimism; if you don't, you have never thought clearly and truly. DI. 82

The first thing that goes when you begin to think is your theology. If you stick too long to a theological point of view you become stagnant, without vitality. DI. 82

We command what we can explain, and if we bring our explanation into the spiritual domain we are in danger of explaining Jesus away—"and every spirit which annulleth Jesus is not of God." We have to be intelligently more than intelligent, intellectually more than intellectual, that is, we have to use all our wits in order not to worship our wits but be humble enough to worship God. DI. 83

We know that we are not perfect yet in outer manifestation, but in thinking we have to remember what we received Jesus for, to be absolute Lord, absolute Saviour. GW. 13

My reason and my intellect are the finest instruments I have, but they are not 'me,' I am much more than my intellect and my reason. If I am going to get at Reality I must have my conscience at work as well as my intellect and reason, otherwise I will ignore the fact of sin, ignore all the moral perplexities, ignore the fact that God became Incarnate. Intellect is meant to be the handmaid of God, not the dictator of God. GW. 16

We are saved in only one way, by the supernatural efficacy of the Redemption; but to be saved and never *think* about it is a crime. 'My people doth not consider,' says God; they won't think. GW. 16

We have to work out, not our redemption, but our human appreciation of our redemption. We owe it to God that we refuse to have rusty brains. GW. 17

People won't go through the labour of thinking, consequently snares get hold of them, and remember, thinking is a tremendous labour. We have to labour to 'bring every thought into captivity to the obedience of Christ'. GW. 104

Whenever the Holy Spirit gets us into a corner, He never convinces our intellect; He is busy with the will which expresses itself in our intellect. HG. 107

Intellect is never first in spiritual life. We are not born again by thinking about it, we are born again by the power of God. HGM. 28

Definitions can only be given of things that are perfectly understood and are inferior to the mind that defines them. It is absurd to try and put God into a definition; if I can define God I am greater than God. Intellectual definition is of no use whatever in the spiritual life. HGM. 143

A child does not work from a conscious ambition, it obeys the law of the life that is in him without thinking. When we are born again and rightly related to God we will live the right kind of life without thinking. IWP. 21

It is because people will not take the labour to think that the snare gets hold of them, and remember, thinking is a tremendous labour. IWP. 74

An intellectualist never pushes an issue of will. Our Lord uses the word 'believe' in a moral sense, not in an intellectual sense. 'Commit yourself to Me.' We are to believe in a Person, not to believe for something. LG. 119

The great lack to-day is of people who will *think* along Christian lines; we know a great deal about salvation but we do not go on to explore the 'unsearchable riches of Christ'. We do not know much about giving up the right to ourselves to Jesus Christ, or about the intense patience of 'hanging in' in perfect certainty that what Jesus says is true. LG. 133

When we become spiritual we have to exercise the power of thinking to a greater degree than ever before. MFL. 18

We starve our mind as Christians by not thinking. MFL. 18

The old idea that we cannot help evil thoughts has become so ingrained in our minds that most of us accept it as a fact. But if it is true, then Paul is talking nonsense when he tells us to choose our thinking, to think only on those things that are true, and honourable, and just, and pure. MFL. 35

. . . we can and we must choose our thinking, and the whole discipline of our mental life is to form the habit of right thinking. It is not done by praying, it is done only by strenuous determination, and it is never easy to begin with. MFL. 36

We are so extraordinarily fussy that we won't give ourselves one minute before God to think, and unless we do we shall never form the habit of abiding. We must get alone in secret and think, screw our minds down and not allow them to wool-gather. Difficult? Of course it is difficult to begin with, but if we persevere we shall soon take in all the straying parts of our mental life, and in a crisis we shall be able to draw on the fact that we are one with Jesus in God's sight. MFL. 38

We begin by thinking we know all about ourselves, but when a man gets a dose of 'the plague of his own heart,' it upsets all his thinking. MFL. 43

Never pray about evil thoughts, it will fix them in the mind. 'Quit'—that is the only thing to do with anything that is wrong; to ruthlessly grip it on the threshold of your mind and allow it no more way. MFL. 49

If you have received the Holy Spirit, you will find that you have the power to bring "every thought into captivity to the obedience of Christ." MFL. 49

Never submit to the tyrannous idea that you cannot look after your mind; you can. If a man lets his garden alone it very soon ceases to be a garden; and if a saint lets his mind alone it will soon become a rubbish heap for Satan to make use of. MFL. 49

We are meant to use our brains to express our thought in words, and then to behave according to the way we have thought. A man's spirit only expresses itself as soul by means of words; the brain does not deal with pure thought. No thought is ours until it can be expressed in words. Immediately a thought is expressed in words, it returns to the brain as an idea upon which we can work. MFL. 51

The only mind that understands the things of God is the child mind; our Lord continually mentioned this simplicity . . . It is the simplicity of God, not of an imbecile, a fundamental simplicity of relationship. MFL. 66

Thinking is the habit of expressing what moves our spirit. In order to think we must concentrate. Thinking is a purely physical process. No one can tell us how to begin to think, all they can do is to tell us what happens when we do think. In the grey matter of the brain are multitudes of blood-vessels, distributed equally all over the brain, and when we think, the blood gathers to the one part of the brain we are using. This is called concentration. Dissipated thinking means that the blood goes back to the other parts of the brain and wakens up associated ideas. When we focus our will around certain thoughts, the blood converges to that particular part of the brain, and if we can hold our wills fixed there for five minutes, we have done a tremendous thing, we have begun to form the habit of mental concentration. The majority of us allow our brains to wool-gather, we never concentrate on any particular line. Concentration is physical, not spiritual. The brain must be brought into order by concentration, then when the Spirit of God brings a spontaneous illumination of a particular theme instantly the brain is at the disposal of God. If we have not learned to concentrate, the brain cannot focus itself anywhere, it fusses all round and wool-gathers. No one is responsible for that but ourselves. MFL. 79

When people say, 'I cannot think, I have not the gift,' they mean that they have never used their brains. We all have bodies and brains. When we use our brains in concentration in a way we have never done before, we will have growing pains; a headache after thinking is a sign we have brains. MFL. 81

Our minds are apt to be all abroad, like an octopus with its tentacles out to catch everything that comes along—newspaper garbage, spiritualistic garbage, advertisement garbage, we let them all come and make a dumping ground of our heads, and then sigh and mourn and say we cannot think right thoughts. MFL. 86

Beware of saying you cannot help your thoughts; you can; you have all the almighty power of God to help you. We have to learn to bring every thought into captivity to the obedience of Christ, and it takes time. We want to reach it in a moment like a rocket, but it can only be done by a gradual moral discipline, and we do not like discipline, we want to do it all at once. MFL. 86

The danger in spiritual matters is that we do not *think* godliness; we let ideas and conceptions of godliness lift us up at times, but we do not form the habit of godly thinking. Thinking godliness cannot be done in spurts, it is a steady habitual trend. MFL. 93

We cannot form the mind of Christ once for always; we have to form it *always;* that is, all the time and in everything. MFL. 102

. . . the mind of Christ is supernatural, His mind is not a human mind at all. MFL. 102

God will not make me think like Jesus, I have to do it myself; I have to bring every thought into captivity to the obedience of Christ. "Abide in Me"—in intellectual matters, in money matters, in every one of the matters that make human life what it is. It is not a handbox life. MUH. 166

Beware of saying, 'Oh well, it doesn't matter much what I think about in secret'; it does, for the opportunity will come when what you think about in secret will find expression and spurt out in an act. OPG. 70

We starve our minds as Christians by not thinking, and we cannot think as Christians until we are born from above. So many of us have a good spiritual experience, but we have never thought things out on Christian lines. It is just as true that a man may *live* a Christian life without thinking as that a man may *think* a Christian life without living it. We have to learn to combine the two, and to do this we must build up our minds on these great truths. PR. 116

Intellectual curiosity will not take us one inch inside moral problems, but immediately we obey, in the tiniest matter, instantly we see. PH. 220

If a man lets his garden alone, it pretty soon ceases to be a garden; and if a saint lets his mind alone, it will soon become a garbage patch for Satan's scarecrows. PS. 31

As long as the devil can keep us terrified of thinking, he will always limit the work of God in our souls. RTR. 33

Intellect has never changed a man as yet; it may have made him look different, but it will not have altered him. If intellect is the way to get to God, what about the men who have no intellect? There would be whole streaks of man's life and experience to blot out. Or if I can get at God by a fine sense of beauty only what about the men who have no sense of beauty? Some men have a magnificent heredity, while others are practically damned into existence. Rationalism is not the basis; my reason and my intellect are instruments, but there is something deeper about every human life than can be fathomed by intellect. SA. 26

As long as we are intellectualists and forget that we are men, our intellect tells us that God and man ought to be one, that there should be no gap between. Exactly so! But they are *not* one, and there *is* a gap, and a tragedy. SA. 40

All our darkness comes because we will try to get into the thing head first. We must be born into the kingdom of God, Jesus says, before we can begin to think about it. SA. 112

We do not think on the basis of Christianity at all. We are taught to think like pagans for six days a week and to reverse the order for one day, consequently in critical moments we think as pagans and our religion is left in the limbo of the inarticulate. Our thinking is based not on Hebrew Wisdom and confidence in God, but on the Wisdom of the Greeks which is removed from practical life, and on that basis we persuade ourselves that if a man knows a thing is wrong he will not do it. That is not true. The plague with me, apart from the grace of God, is that I know what is right, but I'm hanged if I'll do it! What I want to know is, can anyone tell me of a power that will alter my "want to"? SHH. 106

The test Jesus gives is not the truth of our manner but the temper of our mind. Many of us are wonderfully truthful in manner but our temper of mind is rotten in God's sight. The thing Jesus alters is the temper of mind. SSM. 31

Notion your mind with the idea that God is there. If once the mind is notioned on that line, when we are in difficulties it is as easy as breathing to remember, 'Why, my Father knows all about it!' SSM. 84

A wrong temper of mind is the most blameworthy thing there is. It is not only what we say but what we think that tells. SSY. 46

One way in which Satan comes as an angel of light to Christians today is by telling them there is no need to use their minds. We *must* use our minds; we must keep the full power of our intellect ablaze for God on any subject that awakens us in our study of His word, always keeping the secret of the life hid with Christ in God. Think of the sweat and labour and agony of nerve that a scientific student will go through in order to attain his end; then think of the slipshod, lazy way we go into work for God. SSY. 148

Week 49

TRUTH

You shall know the truth, and the truth shall make you free.

—John 8:32

Jesus Christ talked rugged unmitigated truth, He was never ambiguous, and He says it is better to be maimed than damned. BE. 49

The Bible does not reveal all truth, we have to find out scientific truth and common-sense truth for ourselves, but knowledge of the Truth, our Lord Himself, is only possible through the reception of the Holy Spirit. BE. 123

Truth is moral, not intellectual. We perceive Truth by doing the right thing, not by thinking it out. 'If any man will do His will, he shall know of the doctrine . . .' BFB. 102

The one great Truth to keep steadfastly before us is the Lord Jesus Christ; He is the Truth. Only the whole truth is The Truth, any part of the truth may become an error. If you have a ray of light on The Truth never call it the whole truth; follow it up and it will lead you to the central Truth, the Lord Jesus Christ. BSG. 69

Would that men who name the Name of Christ realised that He *is* the Truth, not the proclaimer of it; that He *is* the Gospel, not the preacher of the Gospel; that He *is* the Way of the Fatherhood of God. CD. VOL. 1, 138

We do not create truth, we receive it. CHI. 30

Truth is not in a particular statement; Truth is a Person, "I am the Truth." CHI. 46

If a man is talking the truth of God those who listen will meet it again whether they like it or not; if he is not talking God's truth they won't come across it any more. CHI. 48

Every partial truth has so much error in it that you can dispute it, but you can't dispute 'truth as it is in Jesus'. DI. 3

You can't unveil Truth when you like; when the unveiling comes, beware. That moment marks your going back or your going on. DI. 3

Truth is of the implicit order, you can't define Truth, and yet every man is so constituted that at times his longing for Truth is insatiable. It is not sufficient to remain with a longing for Truth, because there is something at the basis of things which drives a man to the Truth if he is honest. DI. 3

The test of God's truth is that it fits you exactly; if it does not, question whether it is His truth. DI. 7

No man is ever the same after listening to the truth, he may say he pays no attention to it, he may appear to forget all about it, but at any moment the truth may spring up into his consciousness and destroy all his peace of mind. DI. 44

Jesus Christ is the Truth, an Incarnate Ideal; to be 'in Christ' means that through regeneration and sanctification that Ideal can become a reality, so that in my mortal flesh there is manifested that which is easily discerned to be 'the life also of Jesus.' We are to be incorporated into the truth. GW. 34

'The Truth' is our Lord Himself; 'the whole truth' is the inspired Scripture interpreting the truth to us; and 'nothing but the truth' is the Holy Spirit, 'the Spirit of truth,' efficaciously regenerating and sanctifying us, and guiding us into 'all the truth.' GW. 35

With God a thing is never too good to be true; it is too good not to be true. HG. 34

It is perilous to listen to the truth of God unless I open my will to it. HG. 102

The right attitude to the truth is, 'Lord, Thou knowest'; otherwise we shall find to our cost that what Jesus said about the human heart is true. HGM. 40

The Truth is our Lord Himself, consequently any part of the truth may be a lie unless it leads to a relation to *the* Truth. Salvation, sanctification, the Second Coming are all parts of the Truth, but none is the Truth; and they are only parts of the Truth as they are absorbed by the Truth, our Lord Himself. IWP. 10

We are not told to expound the way of salvation, or to teach sanctification, but to lift up Jesus, i.e. to proclaim the truth. IWP. 10

"But ye have an unction from the Holy One, and ye know all things," and, "the same anointing teacheth you of all things." The meaning of that is very practical and sane—Test all you hear, all you read, by this inner anointing, by the indwelling Spirit; He will test all the truth of God. IYA. 79

If one moment, we have discerned the truth, we can never be the same again; we may ignore it, or forget it, but it will not forget us. Truth once discerned goes down into the subconscious mind, but it will jump up in a most awkward way when we least expect it. MFL. 20

The things of truth are things which are in keeping with the Person of Truth, the Lord Jesus Christ: *"I am the Truth."* Truth therefore means not only accuracy, but accuracy about something that corresponds with God. MFL. 85

The only way in which a truth can become of vital interest to me is when I am brought into the place where that truth is needed. MFL. 98

Spiritual truth is learned by atmosphere, not by intellectual reasoning. God's Spirit alters the atmosphere of our way of looking at things, and things begin to be possible which never were possible before. MUH. 286

You can never be the same after the unveiling of a truth. MUH. 364

Reality is not found in logic; Reality is a Person. *'I am the Truth.'* NKW. 36

It takes a long while for us to begin to see that Jesus Christ is The Truth. Truths exist that have no meaning for us until we get into the domain of their power. PH. 102

Jesus does not take men and say—'This is the truth and if you don't believe it you will be damned.' He simply shows us the truth—"I am the Truth," and leaves us alone. PH. 102

It is a great emancipation in a man's life when he learns that spiritual and moral truths can only be gained by obedience, never by intellectual curiosity. All God's revelations are sealed, and they will never be opened by philosophy, or by thinking; whereas the tiniest fragment of obedience will bring a man right through into the secret of God's attitude to things. PH. 219

If we refuse any one way of getting at the truth because we do not like that way, we are dishonest. PR. 21

Truth is not discerned intellectually, it is discerned spiritually. PR. 116

Beware of paddling in the ocean of God's truth, when you should be out in it, swimming. RTR. 42

If you only take your own ideas, you will never know the truth. The whole truth is the only truth, and the whole truth is Jesus Christ—"I am the Truth". Any bit of truth is an error if taken alone. RTR. 87

We benefit most by things over which we cannot be articulate, and if the truths we read or hear are the truths of God, they will crop up again. SHH. 66

Beware of turning your back on what you know is true because you do not want it to be real. SHL. 60

There is no one in the world more easy to get to than God. Only one thing prevents us from getting there, and that is the refusal to tell ourselves the truth. SHL. 76

We are never the same after listening to the truth; we may forget it, but we will meet it again. SHL. 114

Let people do what they like with your truth, but never explain it. Jesus never explained anything; we are always explaining, and we get into tangles by not leaving things alone. SSM. 40

A man may say wonderfully truthful things, but his thinking is what tells. It is possible to say truthful things in a truthful manner and to tell a lie in thinking. SSM. 42

There are some truths that God will not make simple. The only thing God makes plain in the Bible is the way of salvation and sanctification, after that our understanding depends entirely on our walking in the light. SSM. 82

The central truth is not Salvation, nor Sanctification, nor the Second Coming; the central truth is nothing less than Jesus Christ Himself. "I, if I be lifted up from the earth, will draw all men unto Me." Error always comes in when we take something Jesus Christ does and preach it as the truth. It is part of the truth, but if we take it to be the whole truth we become advocates of an idea instead of a Person, the Lord Himself. SSM. 83

Week 50

WILL

For it is God who works in you both to will and to do for His good pleasure.

—Philippians 2:13

We have no choice about being born into the world, but to be born again, if we will but come to Jesus and receive His Spirit, is within our own power. This is true all along in the Christian life, you can be renewed in the spirit of your mind when you choose, you can revive your mind on any line you like by sheer force of will. BE. 40

A human soul can withstand the devil successfully, and it can also withstand God successfully. This self-living power is the essence of the human spirit, which is as immortal as God's Spirit and as indestructible; whether the human spirit be good or bad, it is as immortal as God. This power of the soul enables it to put itself on a par with God; this is the very essence of Satan. BP. 58

When the Spirit of God comes into a man, He brings His own generating will power and causes him to will with God, and we have the amazing revelation that the saint's free choices are the predeterminations of God. That is a most wonderful thing in Christian psychology, viz., that a saint chooses exactly what God predetermined he should choose. If you have never received the Spirit of God this will be one of the things which is 'foolishness' to you; but if you have received the Spirit and are obeying Him, you find He brings your spirit into complete harmony with God and the sound of your goings and the sound of God's goings are one and the same. BP. 215

The first fundamental characteristic of the mighty nature of God is will; consequently when God's Spirit comes into our spirit, we can will to do what God wants us to do. "For it is God which worketh in you both to will and to do of His good pleasure." BP. 216

Will is not a faculty. We talk of a person having a weak will, or a strong will; that is misleading. 'Will' means the whole nature active, and when we are energized by the Spirit of God, we are enabled to do what we could not do before; that is, we are able to obey God. BP. 217

You will find the supreme crisis in your life is 'will-issues' all the time. *Will* I relinquish? *Will* I abandon? It is not that God won't make us fit, it is that He cannot. CD. VOL. 1, 135

God cannot make us fit to meet Him in the air unless we are willing to let Him. He cannot make us fit as the dwellings of His Son unless we are willing, because He wants sons and daughters. If you are up against a crisis, go through with it, relinquish all, and let Him make you fit for all He requires of you in this day. CD. VOL. 1, 135

Remember, you must urge the will to an issue; you must come to the point where you *will* to believe the Redeemer, and deliberately wash your hands of the consequences. CHI. 29

Let me stake my all, blindly, as far as feelings are concerned, on the Reality of the Redemption, and before long that Reality will begin to tell in my actual life, which will be the evidence that the transaction has taken place. But there must be the deliberate surrender of will, not a surrender to the persuasive power of a personality, but a deliberate launching forth on God and what He says. CHI. 29

The great impelling power of the Holy Spirit is seen in its most fundamental working whenever an issue of will is pushed. It is pleasanter to listen to poetical discourses, more agreeable to have your affinities appealed to, but it is not good enough, it leaves you exactly as you were. The Gospel appeal comes with a stinging grip—'Will you?' or 'Won't you?' 'I will accept,' or, 'I'll put it off,'—both are decisions, remember. DI. 25

It is never our wicked heart that is the difficulty, but our obstinate will. DI. 31

"If any man would come after Me, let him deny himself," i.e., 'deny his right to himself'. Jesus never swept men off their feet in ecstasy, He always talked on the line that left a man's will in the ascendant until he saw where he was going. It is impossible for a man to give up his right to himself without knowing he is doing it. DI. 34

Is Jesus Christ absolutely necessary to me? Have I ever shifted the basis of my reasoning on to Incarnate Reason? ever shifted my will on to His will? my right to myself on to His right to me? DI. 35

The man who has achieved a moral victory by the sheer force of his will is less likely to want to become a Christian than the man who has come to the moral frontier of his own need. GW. 132

Our Lord's attitude to the human will is not that frequently presented to-day; He never says that a man must make vows and decisions. 'Decisions for Christ' fail, not because men are not in earnest, but because the bedrock of Christianity is left out. The bedrock of Christianity is not strength of will, but the realization of my inability to decide: if I am ever going to be what Jesus Christ wants me to be, He must come in and do it, I am an abject pauper morally and spiritually. Fundamental free well is never possible, if it were our vowing would be omnipotent, we could do as we liked. GW. 141

There is no limit to what God can make us are we but willing. His great love is ever overshadowing us and He waits to visit us with His saving life. GW. 146

We are at liberty to stop short at any point, and our Lord will never cast it up at us; but think what we shall feel like when we seeHim if all the 'thank you' we gave Him for His unspeakable salvation was an obstinate determination to serve Him in our own way, not His. HG. 55

Be yourself exactly before God, and present your problems, the things you know you have come to your wits' end about. Ask what you *will*, and Jesus Christ says your prayers will be answered. We can always tell whether our will is in what we ask by the way we live when we are not praying. IYA. 13

Beware of praising Jesus Christ whilst all the time you cunningly refuse to let the Spirit of God work His salvation efficaciously in your life. Remember, the battle is in the will; whenever we say 'I can't', or whenever we are indifferent, it means 'I won't'. It is better to let Jesus Christ uncover the obstinacy. If there is one point where we say 'I won't' then we shall never know His salvation. LG. 143

Will is the essential element in God's creation of a man. I cannot *give up* my will: I must exercise it. MFL. 9

Will is the very essence of personality, and in the Bible will is always associated with intelligence and knowledge and desire. The will of a saint is not to be spent in dissipation in spiritual luxuries, but in concentration upon God. MFL. 31

Will is the whole man active. I cannot *give up* my will, I must exercise it. I must *will* to obey, and I must *will* to receive God's Spirit. When God gives a vision of truth it is never a question of what He will do, but of what we will do. MUH. 190

The complete life is the life of a child. When I am consciously conscious, there is something wrong. It is the sick man who knows what health is. The child of God is not conscious of the will of God because he *is* the will of God. When there has been the slightest deviation from the will of God, we begin to ask—What is Thy will? MUH. 233

Surrender is not the surrender of the external life, but of the will; when that is done, all is done. There are very few crises in life; the great crisis is the surrender of the will. God never crushes a man's will into surrender, He never beseeches him, He waits until the man yields up his will to Him. MUH. 257

The moments when I truly live are the moments when I act with my whole will. MUH. 309

God's command is—Take *now*, not presently. It is extraordinary how we debate! We know a thing is right, but we try to find excuses for not doing it at once. To climb to the height God shows can never be done presently, it must be done now. The sacrifice is gone through in will before it is performed actually. MUH. 316

When God draws me, the issue of my will comes in at once—will I react on the revelation which God gives—will I come to Him? Discussion on spiritual matters is an impertinence. Never discuss with anyone when God speaks. Belief is not an intellectual act; belief is a moral act whereby I deliberately commit myself. Will I dump myself down absolutely on God and transact on what He says? If I will, I shall find I am based on Reality that is as sure as God's throne. MUH. 357

We cannot remain boss by the sheer power of will; sooner or later our wills must yield allegiance to some force greater than their own, either God or the devil. NKW. 52

God allows ample room for man and the devil to do their worst; He allows the combination of other wills to work out to the last lap of exhaustion so that that way need never be tried again, and men will have to confess, either reluctantly or willingly, that God's purpose was right after all. NKW. 56

We are potentially sons and daughters of God through God's claim upon us in Christ, but we are only sons and daughters of God *in reality* through our will. OBH. 27

When we are rightly related to God we have uncovered to us for the first time the power of our own wills. Our wills are infirm through sin, but when we are sanctified there is revealed to us the pure pristine will-power with which God created us, and which the Holy Ghost calls into action. Then we have to submit our will to Jesus as He submitted His will to His Father. OBH. 81

We are to have only one aim in life, and that is that the Son of God may be manifested; then all dictation to God will vanish. Our Lord never dictated to His Father, and we are not to dictate to God; we are to submit our wills to Him so that He works through us what He wants. OBH. 83

Will is the essential element in the creation of man; sin is a perverse disposition that has entered into man. The profound thing in man is his will, not sin. OBH. 129

All the forces of nature and of grace are at the back of the man who does God's will because in obedience we let God have His amazing way with us. OBH. 130

Doing God's will is never hard. The only thing that is hard is *not* doing His will. OBH. 130

If I am a child of God, I realize not only that God is the source of my will, but that God is *in* me to will. I do not bring an opposed will to God's will, God's will *is* my will, and my natural choices are along the line of His will. Then I begin to understand that God engineers circumstances for me to do His will in them, not for me to lie down under them and give way to self-pity. OBH. 130

Will is 'me' active, not one bit of me but the whole of me. Self-will is best described as the whole of myself active around my own point of view. PH. 158

If I am going to maintain the honour of a saint, I have deliberately to go to the death of my self-will. PH. 161

Within certain limits we have the power to choose, for instance, a man has the power to refuse to be born again, but no man has absolute free will. There comes a time when the human will must yield allegiance to a force greater than itself. PR. 89

Our Lord's first obedience was not to the needs of men, not to the consideration of where He was most useful, but to the will of His Father, and the first need of our life is not to be useful to God, but to do God's will. PR. 108

We are slandering God if we sympathise with the wilfulness of a person and think how difficult God makes it for him. It is never hard to get to God unless our wilfulness makes it hard. PR. 113

When we say "Thy will be done," do we say it with a sigh? If so, we have never realized that the character of God is holy love; nothing can ever happen outside His purposeful will. RTR. 37

Jesus Christ gives the vision of God, God's order; but He also gives us God's permissive will. God's order, according to Jesus Christ, is no sin, no sickness no limitation, no evil, and no wrong: His permissive will allows these things, and I have to get at God's order through His permissive will by an effort of my own. SA. 89

There is a philosophy which says that if a man wills it, he need never die; but he cannot will it! There is a limit to will; no man can will pure will. SHH. 38

Will is not a thing I possess; will is the whole man active. SHH. 89

Whenever our spiritual life is unsatisfactory it is because we have said to God—"I won't." SHH. 92

Every man has power to go to hell because by nature man's will is towards self-realisation. SHH. 118

Will is the whole man active; there are terrific forces in the will. SSM. 85

Our Lord's first obedience was not to the needs of men, not to the consideration of where He would be most useful, but to the will of His Father. 'Lo, I am come to do thy will, O God.' SSY. 95

Week 51

WORDS

Preach the word! Be ready in season and out of season. Convince, rebuke, exhort, with all longsuffering and teaching.

—2 Timothy 4:2

The Holy Spirit will bring us to the practical test, it is not that I *say* I am righteous, but that I prove I am in my deeds. BE. 22

The greatest insult you can offer God is pious talk unless it is backed up by holy actions. BE. 35

The only way the words of God can be understood is by contact with the Word of God. The connection between our Lord Himself, who is the Word, and His spoken words is so close that to divorce them is fatal. "The words that I speak unto you, they are spirit, and they are life." BE. 122

The power of the spoken word accounts for the prominent place given in the Bible to prophesying and preaching. BFB. 69

The Bible says that words are born in the heart, not in the head. BP. 125

. . . the mainspring of the heart of Jesus Christ was the mainspring of the heart of God the Father, consequently the words Jesus Christ spoke were the exact expression of God's thought. In our Lord the tongue was in its right place; He never spoke from His head, but always from His heart. BP. 126

The words of the Bible express the inner soul; the words we use today are nearly all technical, borrowed from somewhere else, and our most modern words do not express the spirit at all, but cunningly cloak it over and give no expression. BP. 246

The only way we can understand the Bible is by personal contact with the Living Word, then the Holy Spirit expounds the literal words to us along the line of personal experience. "The words I speak unto you, they are spirit and they are life." BSG. 63

The stupendous profundities of God's will, surging with unfathomable mysteries, come down to the shores of our common life, not in emotions and fires, nor in aspirations and vows, and agonies and visions, but in a way so simple that the wayfaring men, yea fools, cannot make a mistake, viz., in words. CD. VOL. 1, 16

Words are full of revelation when we do not simply recall or memorize them but receive them. Receive these words from Jesus—'Father,' 'heaven, 'Hallowed be Thy Name,' 'kingdom,' 'will,' there is all the vocabulary of the Deity and Dominion and Disposition of Almighty God in relation to men in these words. Or take the words—'bread,' 'forgiveness,' 'debts,' 'temptation,' 'deliverance,' 'evil,' in these words the primary psychological colours which portray the perplexing puzzles and problems of personal life are all spelled out before our Father.

Or, lastly, look at such words as 'power,' 'glory,' for ever, 'Amen,'—in them there sounds the transcendant triumphant truth that all is well, that God reigns and rules and rejoices, and His joy is our strength. CD. VOL. 2, 26

The revelation of God's will has been brought down to us in words. GW. 70

Jesus was killed for His words, He would not have been crucified if He had kept quiet. HG. 79

Our Lord crowned the words that the powers of this world detest—'servant,' 'obedience,' 'humility,' 'service.' MFL. 105

Jesus Christ says a great deal that we listen to, but do not hear; when we do hear, His words are amazingly hard. MUH. 230

Our Lord never pleaded, He never cajoled, He never entrapped; He simply spoke the sternest words mortal ears ever listened to, and then left it alone. MUH. 230

God never fits His word to suit me; He fits me to suit His word. NKW. 118

To take God at His word may mean expecting God to come up to my standard; whereas true faith does not so much take God at His word as take the word of God as it is, in the face of all difficulties, and act upon it, with no attempt to explain or expound it. NKW. 120

If we are Christians that is where the word of God is—in our hearts. OBH. 68

The word is "not in heaven . . . neither is it beyond the sea . . . but the word is very nigh unto thee, in thy mouth, and in thy heart, that thou mayest do it." OBH. 68

The Spirit of God has the habit of taking the words of Jesus out of their scriptural setting and putting them into the setting of our personal lives. OBH. 121

The fanatic hears only the word of God that comes through the Bible. The word of God comes through the history of the world, through the Christian Church, and through Nature. We have to learn to live by every word of God, and it takes time. If we try to listen to all the words of God at once, we become surfeited. PH. 35

The Bible never glorifies our natural conception of things; it does not use the words 'rest' and 'joy' and 'peace' as we use them, and our common-sense interpretation of words must be keyed up to the way God uses them, otherwise we lose the 'humour' of God. PH. 39

Morally and spiritually we live, as it were, in sections, and the door from one section to another is by means of words, and until we say the right word the door will not open. PH. 209

The door into a moral or spiritual emancipation which you wish to enter is a word. Immediately you are prepared to abandon your reserve and say the word, the door opens and in rushes the Godward side of things and you are lifted on to another platform immediately. "Speech maketh a full man." PH. 210

When we take Jesus Christ's words about His Cross, the least thing we can do is to endeavour to get at His mind behind His words. Jesus says things from a different point of view from ours, and unless we receive His Spirit, we do not even begin to see what He is driving at. PH. 218

No one is ever the same after listening to the word of God, you cannot be; you may imagine you have paid no attention to it, and yet months after maybe a crisis arises and suddenly the word of God comes and grips you by the throat, so to speak, and awakens all the terrors of hell in your life, and you say, 'Wherever did that word come from?' Years ago, months ago, weeks ago, it sank straight into our unconscious mind, God knew it was there though you did not, and it did its damaging work, and now it has suddenly come to light. PS. 26

God says that His word shall not return unto Him void—the abiding success of the word of God! PS. 26

I like to listen to this talk about Jesus Christ, but don't put your finger on the thing that upsets my mind. Why should I bother with a standard of things that upset me? SA. 95

Sow the Word of God, and everyone who listens will get to God. If you sow vows, resolutions, aspirations, emotions, you will reap nothing but exhaustion' '. . . and ye shall sow your seed in vain, for your enemies shall eat it'; but sow the Word of God, and as sure as God is God, it will bring forth fruit. SHL. 114

"Depart from Me," the most appallingly isolating and condemning words that could be said to a human soul. SSM. 106

'Build up your character bit by bit by attention to My words,' says Jesus, then when the supreme crisis comes, you will stand like a rock. SSM. 109

Our Lord says that His word was not His own, but His Father's. Jesus never spoke from His right to Himself. 'The words that I say unto you, I speak not from myself.' Jesus Christ is the Word of God in His own Person; He spoke the words of God with a human tongue, and He has given to His disciples the words the Father gave to Him. The disciple has not only to speak the words of God with his tongue, but to bear the evidence of being a word of the Son, as Jesus was the Word of God. SSY. 96

The administering of the word is not ministering it where we think it is needed; the word has to be sown in living touch with the Lord of the harvest, sown in touch with Him in solitude and prayer, and He will bring the folks round—black and white, educated and uneducated, rich and poor. They are all there, 'white already to harvest,' but most of us are so keen on our own notions that we do not recognize that they are ripe for reaping. If we are in touch with Jesus Christ, He says all the time—This is the moment; this one here, that one there, is ready to be reaped. We say—'Oh, but I want to go and get scores of heathen saved, I do not want to be the means of reaping my brother'; but your brother happens to be the one who is white to harvest. The commission is to teach, to disciple—that is, to administer the word. SSY. 139

WORLD

Do not love the world or the things in the world. If anyone loves the world, the love of the Father is not in him.

— 1 John 2:15

"My Kingdom is not of this world," said Jesus, and yet we are more inclined to take our orders from the world than from Jesus Christ. AUG. 17

"Seek ye first the kingdom of God"—and apply it to modern life and you will find its statements are either those of a madman or of God Incarnate. AUG. 63

To follow Jesus Christ to-day is to follow a madman according to the ideals of present-day civilization. AUG. 63

When the world comes before us with its fascination and its power, it finds us dead to it, if we have agreed with God on His judgement about sin and the world. AUG. 102

What is the world? The set of people with the ambitions, religious or otherwise, that are not identified with the Lord Jesus Christ. AUG. 102

The world is the system of things which man has erected on God's earth. BE. 24

Never have the idea that the worldling is unhappy; he is perfectly happy, as thoroughly happy as a Christian. BE. 32

The people who are unhappy are the worldlings or the Christians if they are not at one with the principle which unites them. BE. 32

If a worldling is not a worldling at heart, he is miserable; and if a Christian is not a Christian at heart he carries his Christianity like a headache instead of something worth having, and not being able to get rid of his head, he cannot get rid of his headache. BE. 32

To be 'of' the world means to belong to the set that organizes its religion, its business, its social life and pleasures without any concern as to how it affects Jesus Christ, as to whether He lived or died matters nothing at all. BE. 34

It is easy to denounce wrong in the world outside me—anyone without a spark of the grace of God can do that; easy to denounce the sins of others while all the time I may be allowing all sorts of worldly things in my own religious life. BE. 34

When Our Lord said "Be of good cheer; I have overcome *the world,*" He obviously did not mean the world in the material physical sense, the rocks and trees, the seasons, and the beautiful order of Nature, the sea and sky; it was not these He overcame, but the world in its ordered system of religion and morality, with all its civilizations and progress, which system reveals in the final analysis that is organized absolutely apart from any consideration of God. A clean cut from everything that savours of the world in this sense is essential for the Christian. BE. 34

The counsel of the Spirit of God to the saints is that they must allow nothing worldly in themselves while living among the worldly in the world. Those who live otherworldly in this world are the men and women who have been regenerated and who dare to live their life according to the principles of Jesus. BE. 35

The hatred of the world is its intense objection to the principles exhibited by the saint, and frequently it is the best specimens of the worldly spirit who positively hate and detest the otherworldly spirit of the saint. It is not that they hate you personally, they may be very kind to you, but they hate what you represent of Jesus Christ. BE. 36

When you meet the hatred of the whole world-system unspiritual people around you will laugh to scorn the idea that you have a struggle on hand, but you realize that you are wrestling not against flesh and blood, but against the spiritual hosts of wickedness in the heavenly places. BE. 36

Look at the world through either a microscope or a telescope and you will be dwarfed into terror by the infinitely minute or the infinitely great; both are appalling. BFB. 38

No man is capable of solving the riddle of the universe because the universe is mad, and the only thing that will put it right is not man's reason, but the sagacity of God which is manifested in the Redemption of Jesus Christ. BFB. 38

The world as God originally designed it, was the best of all possible worlds, but it has now become the worst of all possible worlds; in fact, the Bible reveals that it could not be any worse than it is. Individual men who take the wrong line get worse, but the world itself cannot get worse. BFB. 40

The Cross of Calvary and the Redemption have to do with the sins of the world. If God began to punish the nations for their sins there would be no nation left on the face of the earth. BFB. 81

The order and beauty of this world were created by God for man. BP. 5

There ought to be in us a holy scorn whenever it comes to being dictated to by the spirit of the age in which we live. The age in which we live is governed by the prince of this world who hates Jesus Christ. His great doctrine is self-realization. BP. 39

One of the most misleading statements is that worldlings have not a happy time; they have a thoroughly happy time. The point is that their happiness is on the wrong level, and when they come across Jesus Christ, Who is the enemy of all that happiness, they experience annoyance. BP. 79

Both Jesus Christ and Paul were unquestionably mad, according to the standard of the wisdom of this world; they were related to affairs differently from the majority of other men, consequently, for the sake of self-preservation, they must be got rid of. Our Lord was crucified, and Paul was beheaded. When we are imbued with Jesus Christ's Spirit and are related to life as He was, we shall find that we are considered just as mad according to the standard of this world. BP. 160

. . . in all probability there was a former order of things, which was ruined by disobedience, thereby producing the chaos out of which God reconstructed the order of things which we know, and which we so differently interpret. BP. 227

One thing we are realising to-day is that to the majority of us civilised life is an elaborate way of doing without God. We have not been living a life hid with Christ in God, we have been living in the abundance of the things which we possess. CD. VOL. 1, 131

The world means what it says, but it cannot impart. Our Lord imparts what He says, He does not give like the world does. CD. VOL. 1, 152

The world pays no attention to those who tell them how God convicted of sin and how He delivered them; the warnings of God are of no use to sinners until they are convicted of sin and the warnings become applicable to them. CHI. 67

God so loved the world that He hates the wrong in it. CHI. 69

As men and women we have to live in this world, in its misery and sinfulness, and we must do the same if we are disciples. CHI. 127

Have I ever had a glimpse of this—that God would not be altered if all our civilized life went to pieces? DI. 15

God has no respect for our civilizations because He did not found them. While civilization is not God's, it is His providential protection for men, generally restraining the bad, and affording His children the means of developing their life in Him. DI. 15

In a time of calamity God appears to pay scant courtesy to all our art and culture, He sweeps the whole thing aside till civilization rages at Him. It is 'the babe' and 'the fool' who get through in the day of God's visitation. DI. 15

Beware of the temptation to compromise with the world, to put their interests, their needs, first—'They have kindly become interested in our Christian work, given so much time to it, now let us winsomely draw them in'—they will winsomely draw you away from God. DI. 85

The whole teaching of Jesus is opposed to the idea of civilization, viz., possessing things for myself—'This is mine.' GW. 28

The constructed world of man is not the created world of God. GW. 44

The popular evangelical idea that we are to be against the world in the sense of a pitched battle with it, is simply an expression of the spirit of the world dressed up in a religious guise. Our Lord was not against the world in that sense; He submitted to its providential order of tyranny, but there was no compromise in His spirit, and the model of the Christian's spirit is Christ Himself. GW. 56

It is by our spiritual choices that we maintain a right relation to the world. When a man ceases conflicting the world by spiritual choices, he succumbs to it and becomes part of the world that needs saving instead of being a saviour in the world. GW. 56

Civilization was started by a murderer, and the whole of our civilized life is based on competition. GW. 136

The kingdoms of this world are founded on strong men, consequently they go. Jesus Christ founds His kingdom on the weakest link, a Baby. God made His own Son a Babe. We must base our thinking on the rugged facts of life according to God's Book, and not according to the finesse of modern civilization. Let us not be so careful as to how we offend or please human ears, but let us never offend God's ears. HG. 41

If we try and live the life Jesus Christ lived, modern civilization will fling us out like waste material; we are no good, we do not add anything to the hard cash of the times we live in, and the sooner we are flung out the better. HG. 72

Jesus knew He was here for His Father's purpose and He never allowed the cares of civilization to bother Him. He did nothing to add to the wealth of the civilization in which He lived, He earned nothing, modern civilization would not have tolerated Him for two minutes. HG. 72

. . . civilizations are despatched at a minute's notice, armies come together and annihilate one another and God seems to pay no attention. His attitude is one which makes us blaspheme and say that He does not care an atom for human beings. Jesus Christ says He does, He says He is a Father, and that He, Jesus, is exactly like His Father. The point is that Jesus saw life from God's standpoint, we don't. We won't accept the responsibility of life as God gives it to us, we only accept responsibility as we wish to take it, and the responsibility we wish to take is to save our own skins, make comfortable positions for ourselves and those we are related to, exert ourselves a little to keep ourselves clean and vigorous and upright; but when it comes to following out what Jesus says, His sayings are nothing but jargon. We name the Name of Christ but we are not based on His one issue of life, and Jesus says, "What shall it profit a man, if he shall gain the whole world,"—and he can easily do it—"and lose his own soul?" HG. 72

God keeps open house for the universe. HGM. 29

. . . if civilized life is right and the best we can know, Christianity is a profound mistake; but if you turn back to the Bible you find that its diagnosis of civilization is not that it is the best we know, it is on an entirely wrong basis. Civilized life is based on the *reason* at the heart of things; Jesus Christ's teaching is based on the *tragedy* at the heart of things, and consequently the position of true spiritual life is that of the forlorn hope. HGM. 69

When civilized life goes into the crucible, as it is doing just now, men lose their wits, Jesus said they would; but to His disciples He said, "When ye hear of wars and rumours of wars: *see that ye be not troubled*." HGM. 84

Every forgiven soul will love the world so much that he hates to death the sin that is damning men; to love the world in any other sense is to be "an enemy of God": to love the world as God loves it is to spend and be spent that men might be saved from their sins. HGM. 118

The sign for the world without God is a circle, complete in and for itself; the sign for the Christian is the Cross. The Christian knows by bitter yet blessed conviction of sin that no man is sufficient for himself, and he thereby enters into identification with the Cross of Calvary, and he longs and prays and works to see the sinful, self-centred world broken up and made the occasion for the mighty Cross to have its way whereby men may come to God and God come down to men. HGM. 118

Jesus Christ does not make monks and nuns, He makes men and women fit for the world as it is. IYA. 56

The worldling is annoyed at the worker because the worker is always dealing with a crisis that he does not see and does not want to see. No matter what he touches on, the worker always comes back to the claim of God, and the worldling gets annoyed at this. The man of the world analyses the easy parts of life and tells you that these are all quite obvious, all the practical outcomes of life are within his reach; but when the worker begins to touch on God's message he says, 'That is nonsense, you are up in the clouds and unpractical'. That is why the worker's voice is always an annoyance to the worldling. LG. 93

The world is glad of an excuse not to listen to the Gospel message, and the inconsistencies of Christians is made the excuse. LG. 94

There are no nations in Jesus Christ's outlook, but *the world.* MUH. 290

Instead of being pilgrims and strangers on the earth, we become citizens of this order of things and entrench ourselves here, and the statements of Jesus have no meaning. NKW. 135

The genius of the Spirit of God is to make us pilgrims, consequently there is the continual un-at-home-ness in this world. NKW. 135

Jesus warns the disciple never to be afraid of the contempt of the world when he possesses spiritual discernment. Those who are in the heavenly places see God's counsels in what to the wisdom of the world is arrogant stupidity. OBH. 36

The first civilization was founded by a murderer, and the whole basis of civilized life is a vast, complicated, more or less gilded-over system of murder. We find it more conducive to human welfare not to murder men outright, we do it by a system of competition. It is ingrained in our thinking that competition and rivalry are essential to the carrying on of civilized life; that is why Jesus Christ's statements seem wild and ridiculous. They are the statements either of a madman or of God Incarnate. OPG. 13

When the Spirit of God comes into a man, He gives him a worldwide outlook. God has no favourites. PH. 81

The conditions of our civilized life to-day ought to be realised more keenly by the Christian than by the natural man, but we must see that the worship of God is put on the throne and not our human wits. PR. 65

Immediately Jesus Christ comes in, He produces havoc, because the whole world system is arrayed against His Redemption. It was the world system of His day, and particularly the religious system, that killed the Son of God. PR. 95

The world is that system of things which organises its life without any thought of Jesus Christ. PR. 105

There is a rivalry between men, and we have made it a good thing; we have made ambition and competition the very essence of civilised life. No wonder there is no room for Jesus Christ, and no room for the Bible. We are all so scientifically orthodox nowadays, so materialistic and certain that rationalism is the basis of things, that we make the Bible out to be the most revolutionary, unorthodox and heretical of books. SHH. 45

The curious things about civilisation is that it tends to take men away from the soil, and makes them develop an artificial existence away from the elemental. Civilisation has become an elaborate way of doing without God, and when civilised life is hit a smashing blow by any order of tyranny, most of us have not a leg to stand on. SHH. 62

The manipulation of civilised life has not resulted in the development of the tillage of the land, but in the building up of treasure, and it is not only the miser who grabs. SHH. 63

The wisdom of God is arrant stupidity to the wisdom of the world, until all of a sudden God makes the wisdom of the world foolish. SHH. 83

The line where the world ends and Christianity begins alters in every generation. What was worldliness in Paul's day is not worldliness in our day; the line is altering all the time. To-day the world has taken on so many things out of the Church, and the Church has taken on so many things out of the world, that it is difficult to know where you are. SHL. 17

The powers that press from the natural world have one tendency, and one only, to deaden all communication with God. SHL. 25

Those who deal with the great secrets of the universe imply that our planet is such a tiny spot in the tremendous universe that it is a piece of stupid conceit on our part to think that God watches over us. And to make our planet the centre where God performed the marvellous drama of His own history of the Incarnation and Atonement is absurd, they say. But watch a simple-minded person, one who is right with God and is not terrified by the reasonings of men, as he looks at the stars and exclaims, 'when I consider Thy heavens, the work of Thy fingers, the moon and the stars, which Thou hast ordained; what is man, that Thou are mindful of him?' It is said not in despair, but in adoring wonder. SHL. 34

Look at the world either through a telescope or a microscope and you will be dwarfed into terror by the infinitely great or the infinitely little. Naturalists tell us that there are no two blades of grass alike, and close inspection of a bee's wing under a microscope reveals how marvellously it is made. What do I read in the Bible? I read that the God of heaven counts the hairs of our heads. Jesus says so. I read that the mighty God watches the sparrows so intimately that not one of them falls on the ground without His notice. I read that the God who holds the seas in the hollow of His hand and guides the stars in their courses, clothes the grass of the field. Through the love of God in Christ Jesus we are brought into a wonderful intimacy with the infinitely great and the infinitely little. SHL. 35

Prosperous worldliness is unspiritual and those who do not pray and who are not at all holy get on well. SHL. 93

The saint has to remain loyal to God in the midst of the machinery of successful civilization, in the midst of worldly prosperity, and in the face of crushing defeat. SHL. 96

. . . there is a division as high as heaven and as deep as hell between the Christian and the world. "Whosoever therefore will be a friend of the world is the enemy of God." SSM. 64

The birds of civilization come and lodge in the branches of the spiritual tree and men say 'Now this is what is to be!' and they have not seen God's purpose at all. If we do not see God's purpose we shall continually be misled by externals. SSY. 80

The introduction of civilization, without the emphasis on living the life hid with Christ in God, tends to increase the power of evil because it covers it with a veil of refinement. SSY. 121